A MOST NOBLE ENTERPRISE

The Story of Kent State University, 1910–2010

WILLIAM H. HILDEBRAND

THE KENT STATE UNIVERSITY PRESS

Kent, Ohio

Frontis: A student descends the stairs facing the east entrance of Franklin Hall.

Library of Congress Catalog Card Number 2009008302
ISBN 978-1-60635-030-0
Manufactured in China

Except as noted below, the photographs in *A Most Noble Enterprise* are courtesy of Kent State University's Department of Communications and Marketing and its photographers past and present: Robert Christy, Jeffrey Glidden, Gary Harwood, Douglas Moore, and Donald Shook; and the University Photographs Collection, Kent State University Libraries, Special Collections and Archives, including *A Book of Memories*, edited by William H. Hildebrand, Dean H. Keller, and Anita D. Herington (Kent State University Press, 1992), *The Chestnut Burr*, and *Years of Youth*, by Philip Shriver (Kent State University Press, 1960).

Page 71, Prentice Memorial Gateway photo by Daniel Doherty, *Daily Kent Stater;* page 274, Oscar Ritchie Hall interior photo by Steven Elbert of Moody Nolan; page 274, Halloween celebrants, photo by David A. Ranucci, *Daily Kent Stater;* page 312, Kent State Folk Festival photo by Leslie Cusano, courtesy WKSU.

LIBRARY OF CONGRESS CATALOGING-IN-PUBLICATION DATA
Hildebrand, William H.
A most noble enterprise : the story of Kent State University, 1910–2010 / written by William H. Hildebrand.
p. cm.
Includes bibliographical references and index.
ISBN 978-1-60635-030-0 (hardcover : alk. paper) ∞
1. Kent State University—History. I. Title.
LD4191.O72H55 2009
378.771'37—dc22   2009008302

British Library Cataloging-in-Publication data are available.

13 12 11 10 09   5 4 3 2 1

To

ANN MEINZEN HILDEBRAND

cor cordium

HAIL TO THEE, OUR ALMA MATER

From the beauty land Ohio comes a universal praise,
   'Tis the song of Alma Mater that her sons and daughters raise,
'Tis a Hail to Kent forever, on the Cuyahoga shore,
   Now we join the loving thousands as they sing it o'er and o'er.

      Hail to thee, our Alma Mater
      O, how beautiful thou art,
      High enthroned upon the hilltop,
      Reigning over every heart.

From the hilltop Alma Mater gazing on her portals wide,
   Sees the coming generations as they throng to seek her side,
Seek her side to win her blessing, throng her gates to bear her name,
   Leave her gates to sing her praises, go afar to spread her fame.

      Hail to thee, our Alma Mater
      O, how young and strong thou art,
      Planning for the glorious future,
      Firm enthroned in every heart.

CONTENTS

PREFACE

This book tells the story of Kent State University's first hundred years. It is a story replete with hairbreadth escapes and pratfalls, with moments of low comedy, high drama, and real tragedy. It features a cast of complex, talented, dedicated, and imperfect individuals. It is, in short, a story about very human beings engaged in what Henry Steele Commager called that "most noble enterprise, the advancement of learning"[1] as carried out for the past hundred years at Kent State University. And it is, I believe, a story both instructive and inspiring.

As this book was about to go to press, and nearly thirty-eight years after the event, visitors to the Ohio Newspaper Association's Web site ranked "the deadly shooting of students at Kent State University during a Vietnam War protest" the top news event in Ohio in the past seventy-five years.[2] The tragic events of May 4, 1970, and its tumultuous aftermath, are the hinge of the Kent State story. They extorted an unbearable price from the victims and their families, and they thrust Kent State into the center of a grave national crisis. For an entire decade the campus was a battleground across which the contending forces of the cultural, social, political, and generational revolution marched and countermarched.

Those thirteen seconds of gunfire on May 4 and the concatenation of explosive protests and demonstrations they set in train severely tested and tempered Kent's character like a refiner's fire. And in the process they strengthened its capacity not only to endure but to prevail. Yet, as this chronicle of its crinkum-crankum history will show,

Kent State had been forced to struggle for survival against formidable external opposition and fierce internal disputes from the beginning.

A few words about the book, about what it is and what it is not, are in order. In recounting Kent's first half-century, I have stood on the broad shoulders of Phillip R. Shriver, author of the superb *The Years of Youth: Kent State University, 1910–1960*. Though grounded in my own research, my account of Kent's first fifty years is inevitably a retelling of Shriver's history, which provided the working scenario from which all future versions will take their departure. There are two consequential differences, however, between *The Years of Youth* and this book.

First, by interpreting Shriver's story in light of the school's second fifty years, *A Most Noble Enterprise* is able to reveal several recurrent themes and patterns, conflicts and resolutions, tendencies and traits of the sort that constitute the distinctive characteristics of any institution—or, for that matter, organism—and that become apparent only when viewed through the clarifying lens of a functional historical perspective. That, I take it, is what is meant when one hears it said that each generation must interpret its nation's history in terms of its own experience of the world.

When I set out to research Kent's early history, for example, I had no inkling that the Board of Trustees would figure so prominently in the story. A moment's reflection might have told me otherwise, but like most people I gave as little thought to the trustees as I did to the ghostly beings on Mount Olympus. Nor did I expect that President Brage Golding would turn out to be one of the conspicuous heroes of my story. I had known all the other presidents between George Bowman and Carol Cartwright, to varying degrees, at firsthand, but my relations with Golding had been largely ceremonial. As a result, my half-baked opinion of him as having been little more than a highly efficient academic engineer was based largely on his aloof personality and my snap impressions—an opinion that slowly succumbed to the salutary evidence of his voluminous papers in the University Archives and to the testimony of respected colleagues who worked closely with him.

My book differs from Shriver's comprehensive institutional history in another respect. I have chosen instead to write a work of popular history for several reasons. For one, it welcomes narrative writing of the sort I wanted to do, a story about people and their doings rather than one that also includes a full treatment of curricular, administrative, departmental, and plant development; there is some of that here, but not, I hope, enough to get in the way of the story. For another, I wanted to tell the story in my own voice and to use a wider range of rhetorical tones and fictional devices than is permissible in academic history. Thus, the reader can expect to find occasional switches into vernacular English, to indicate shifts in points of view intended to convey the feeling or attitude of or about an individual under discussion.

For yet another reason, I wanted to be free of the requirement for that tone of meditative neutrality that often characterizes traditional academic history. I knew that it would be impossible for me to write coolly about the place where I'd been educated and for thirty-six years was privileged to teach so many fine young people and work with so many generous and talented colleagues. Kent State University is an exasperating yet wonderful institution, with its wrong-headedness and near-sightedness, its follies and fads, its occasionally rude and ungrateful but mostly good-hearted and honest nature. It is, in fact, far different from the ideal university of my vain imaginings when I came as a freshman in 1948—and, when weighed in the scales of seasoned reflection, far, far better.

Of the many people who contributed to this book perhaps none is more representative of Kent State than my longtime friend and collaborator, alumnus Dean Keller, Emeritus Professor of Libraries and Media Services. Dean's mother and aunt matriculated at Kent State in 1924, when Kent's founder, John McGilvrey, was president. They came from their home near Elyria, Ohio, traveling by trolley, like so many other Kent students in those days. Here Dean found his wife, Patricia Scheid of Willard, as I found mine, Ann Meinzen of Canton. The children—and one grandchild—from those two marriages were educated here as well. All are deeply rooted in and indebted to Kent State University.

One

WISHES AND FISHES

{1910–1915}

Every great and enduring cultural institution has an origin story that tells about its beginning, about how it came to be. Kent State University is no exception. Such stories usually have features found in creation myths and high romances—resourceful characters, dramatic events, dovetailing coincidences, sudden reversals of fortune, moments of comedy and farce, and sometimes fabulous creatures. Kent's story has all these elements—if you count the lowly bluegill. For according to local tradition, the school owes its very existence to the bluegill—or, more precisely, to a catch of magical bluegill consumed by some visiting dignitaries at a Twin Lakes farm in September of 1910.

That was when the state commissioners investigating sites for the first normal school to be built in northeastern Ohio stepped off an eastbound train at the Erie Depot. They expected to be met by a group of Kent officials like the ones that had welcomed them with hearty smiles and vigorous handshakes at previous stops along their inspection route. But there was no welcoming committee anywhere in sight at the Kent depot.

The absence of the welcoming committee is remarkable because the future of the town hung in the balance. If the commissioners could be persuaded that Kent, of all the forty communities in the competition, was the best site, then the small railroad town of 4,500 inhabitants on the banks of the Cuyahoga River would prosper and become, in time, a humming center of commerce and culture. If they failed, Kent would probably idle away like all those down-at-mouth settlements along America's forlorn back roads and river fronts. But the issue was in doubt that late September morning as the commissioners stood casting puzzled looks around the fast-emptying Erie station for the Kent officials who were scheduled to show them the site where Kent hoped to plant the normal school.

The town's future had looked gloomy all year. The population had shrunk by fifty-three since the 1900 census, while Ravenna, its friendly rival, five miles to the east, had added 1,307 residents, which gave its boosters the right to crow that their town was no mere village but a full-blown city as well as the county seat. In fact, though much of the country was riding a wave of prosperity, Kent's economy, which had been limping along for years, was still staggering from a major industrial disaster that had struck late in 1909. Early on Friday morning, December 10, 1909, a fire had broken out in the dolly shop of the Seneca Chain Company and, whipped by surging winds, spread so fast that nothing was left but a heap of smoldering timbers and ashes. Overnight, the entire workforce of one of the town's biggest employers was out of work: 259 men and boys (this was before the passage of child labor laws) had no means of supporting themselves and their families.

The effects of the fire spread throughout the village and surrounding area, registering in nearly every cash drawer, pocketbook, and wallet. Alarmed, Kent's leaders began casting about for ways not only to lure new businesses to town but to find a new source of vitality for their reeling community. Otherwise, the residents whose jobs had gone up in the smoke of the Seneca plant would go elsewhere for work, an exodus that would irreversibly damage the town.

Bleak as the future looked to many that holiday season, Kent had many resources to call on, among them a cadre of talented young professional and business men with pluck, optimism, and the American can-do spirit. One of the first to spring into action was Martin L. Davey, son of the John Davey who had founded the Davey Tree Expert Company thirty years earlier and was widely known as "the father of tree surgery." At twenty-five, Martin was already general manager of the company and a person of influence in the community. Bristling with energy, ideas, and ambition, Davey had the unforced amiability and air of purposefulness that often mark a life of distinction. On January 14, 1910, he invited Kent's civic leaders to a meeting in the village council room and proposed that they form a Board of Trade (later the Chamber of Commerce). The town, he told them, needed a group devoted to encouraging and promoting its economic and civic life.

Ten days later at the Statehouse in Columbus, Rep. John Hamilton Lowry, from the rural northwestern part of the state, submitted House Bill Number 44 (the Lowry Bill) calling for a commission to establish two new normal schools—one in the northeast, another in the northwest—to satisfy the growing demand for professionally trained public school teachers in the fastest-growing half of the state. The Lowry Bill might have gone unnoticed in Kent if it had not caught the eye of John G. Paxton, editor of the *Kent Courier*. Betting against the odds that the bill would not be enacted, Paxton started a newspaper campaign to galvanize village leaders to apply for the new normal school.

The Lowry Bill was the latest in a long string of attempts to secure public support for staffing public schools with professional teachers. In the decades after the Civil War, the industrial revolution and urbanization transformed northeastern Ohio so rapidly that by 1900 hundreds of new factories and industries were drawing masses of immigrants from other states and nations, all hungry for work and education. Yet between 1902, when Ohio (OU) and Miami universities were granted normal schools, and 1910, the legislature chartered only one new normal, at Ohio State University (OSU), also in the southern part of the state. During that same span it rejected twenty-one separate bills calling for a normal school in the burgeoning northeastern sector, where industrialization and urbanization were forcing the legislature to provide more quality high schools and to improve the elementary systems.

The prevailing educational model of the time was the normal school developed in Germany and later adopted widely across the United States—everywhere except in Ohio and four other backward states and territories. Because Ohio refused to provide normal school training for its public schools, every year a quarter of its elementary teachers were new, untried, and untrained. For decades the issue of public support for teacher training schools had been a political tug-of-war. On one side was a coalition advocating state support of teacher training as a way of ensuring a steady flow of qualified teachers. On the other side was a muscular alliance of die-hard defenders of the state's private colleges who argued, in effect, that it was educationally and fiscally preferable for the state to staff its schools with liberal arts graduates who financed their own educations. This faction was supported by two other powerful groups: ideologues, with their principled opposition to any attempt by the government to take their hard-earned money to fund other people's education in public schools, and sectionalists, who wanted to keep the majority of state funds for state-supported institutions located in Ohio's southern half, the home of OU, Miami, and OSU.

Yet the principle of public support for education had circulated through Ohio's veins since its birth, pumped directly from its nurturing documents. The Land Ordinance of 1785 dedicated a section of each township to the support of public schools; and the Northwest Ordinance of 1787, America's first bill of rights, stipulated that knowledge, religion, and morality "being necessary to good government and the happiness of mankind, Schools and the means of education shall forever be encouraged."[1] In fact, the state's first colleges—Ohio University (1804) and Miami University (1809)—had been partly state supported from the beginning. But whenever the matter came before the legislature, the nexus of pro-private/anti-public school and sectionalist forces had flexed too much political muscle for normal school advocates to overcome.

The Lowry Bill, however, had one great advantage over its predecessors: it was handcrafted by a coalition of public education advocacy organizations representing teachers, superintendents, and state granges and chaired by Superintendent Edwin F. Moulton of Warren. And working behind the scenes was the canny new state commissioner of common schools, John W. Zeller, who organized the coalition and masterminded its tactics. Zeller believed that a major educational crisis was looming for the state and that bold steps were needed to head it off. The demographics of his 1909 annual report to the governor showed that state schools would need 5,000 new teachers in 1910 and in every year thereafter for the foreseeable future. Many of those new teachers would be asked to teach subjects not taught in Ohio's private colleges, such as manual training and agriculture. Zeller's solution was for the state to put normal schools in the fastest-growing section, the northeast. Convinced that earlier normal bills had failed because they had lacked the support of the state's agricultural interests, he persuaded the coalition to draft a bill that required any new normals to train teachers for Ohio's rural schools. To present the bill, the coalition chose the ideal advocate, onetime teacher and farmer John L. Lowry, who during three terms in the Ohio House representing

Henry County in northwestern Ohio had a hand in sponsoring so many education bills that he became known as "the father of school legislation."[2]

On January 28, three days before the Lowry Bill went to committee for consideration, *Kent Courier* editor Paxton started thumping his editorial drum: There was no time for shilly-shallying. Ravenna was likely to go after the normal school, and Hudson was already drafting its application. Hudson had a mouth-watering offer to sweeten its proposal. On a gentle rise on the northern shoulder of the village stood a ready-made campus with a number of handsome red-brick buildings that had been languishing for teachers and students since Western Reserve Academy had moved seven years before.

Meanwhile, the Kent Board of Trade held its first official meeting on February 15 and chose John Wells, superintendent of the Williams Brothers' Flour Mill, as president; hardware-store owner John G. Getz as vice president; and William W. Reed, village postmaster and descendant of Kent pioneers, as secretary. The board offered a $5 gold piece for the snappiest slogan for the village. In April the gold piece was awarded to Kent resident Ralph Heighton for his entry: "Kent, Home of Hump and Hustle!"

A few weeks after the board meeting, fortune favored Kent. The Erie Railroad optioned thirty-three acres adjacent to its Kent holdings and planned to build $150,000 worth of new shops, which meant new jobs. About that time the town's most venerable citizen, William S. Kent, stepped in. Kent was the grandson of Zenas Kent, pioneer industrialist, and son of railroad builder Marvin Kent. President of the town bank, owner of the town newspaper, and national leader of the Republican Party, Marvin Kent was a man to reckon with. He decided that the Seneca Chain Company should be rebuilt to provide jobs for the 259 workers and their families left derelict by the fire. To spearhead a drive to sell $50,000 worth of Seneca stock, he picked businessman Elmer E. France. And just a short month later France stood before an overflow crowd in the Opera House on Depeyster Street and announced, amid deafening cheers, that the stock sale had been oversubscribed. More jobs were on the way!

Meanwhile, editor Paxton beat his drum faster and louder. In the February 25 *Courier,* the day the Lowry Bill came out of committee, the newspaperman challenged Kent's Board of Trade to show some of that vaunted "hump and hustle": "If Kent wants a state normal school there's no use being bashful about it. Let's go after it."

The Lowry Bill sailed through the House on April 28 and the Senate on April 29. Representatives from OU's and Miami's districts voted for the bill, but two of three representatives from OSU voted against it—a harbinger of future trouble. Governor Judson Harmon signed it into law on May 19 and appointed a site selection committee of five men—two professors, a retired banker, a newspaperman, and a retired businessman—tasking them to report their recommendations to him by December 1, 1910. To ensure impartiality in a matter sure to stir intense rivalries among competing communities across the state's northern sector, Harmon chose men from the southern half of the state.

The commission, under the lash of a brutally short deadline, agreed on a number of criteria. The weightiest specified that to be selected, the two communities must be centrally located in their districts and have adequate railroad facilities and infrastructure (light, gas, water, sewer, roads, etc.) available to the school; at least 250 children for the eight-grade training school; a good public health system; and, perhaps most important, a large parcel of suitable land available for the campus.

Word of the bill's passage spurred the Kent Board of Trade into a gallop. It selected three of its most capable members to lead its campaign: Elmer E. France; Duncan B. Wolcott, prosecuting attorney and scion of a distinguished Kent family; and David Ladd Rockwell, whose bold hand would scribble many colorful lines in Kent's history.

The thirty-two-year-old Rockwell was owner and director of several local businesses (including the Seneca Chain Company) and an authentic political prodigy. In 1910, when he was just twenty-two, he had been elected Kent's mayor, winning brief newspaper fame as the youngest mayor in the country, and he served as secretary to the Ohio delegation at the national Democratic convention, where he was spotlighted as the youngest delegate present. In 1908, after successful terms as mayor and probate judge, Rockwell ran for the lieutenant governorship—high office for a man of thirty to reach for, but one that must have seemed within easy grasp, given his reputation as a political wunderkind. But Rockwell lost—a bitter blow and an embarrassing surprise, given Judson Harmon's easy gubernatorial victory. Thereafter, Rockwell seems to have devoted his political energies largely to party matters rather than to elective office. He changed residence to Ravenna but kept his hand in his Kent businesses and village affairs, especially the normal school campaign. And to that cause he brought invaluable personal and political attributes. Vigorous, knowledgeable, polished, Rockwell was an impressive public figure with the natural politician's gift for intimacy and power brokering.

Kent's application, drafted by Wolcott, was a straightforward presentation of the village's eminent suitability for the normal school, accenting its central location in the district; its major railroad lines (Erie and B&O) and interurban connection; its attractive setting on the banks of the Cuyahoga River and its necklace of neighboring fresh water lakes; its pure drinking water; its moral health as evidenced by eight churches; its modern infrastructure; its paved, tree-lined streets; its proximity to the Silver Lake chautauqua and the popular summer resort at Brady Lake; its schools and large supply of school-aged children; its wide range of businesses. But the crown jewel of the application, the attraction that was expected to outshine Hudson's ready-made campus, was the 52.89-acre tract of land comprising the Kent farm on East Main Street, which William S. Kent was offering as the school site.

The town had good reason for investing its hopes in the Kent property. Although low, marshy land with a small farm bordered the south side of East Main, a steeply rising hill covered by a woods of elm, birch, maple, and chestnut trees embraced it on three sides. Its summit afforded a stirring panoramic view of the Cuyahoga River as it flowed through the village below and snaked among the flanks and folds of its beautiful valley: an Arcadian tapestry of farms and forests pleasing the eye in every direction.

By August 8 the commission, after peremptorily rejecting a number of applicants for failing to meet certain requirements, announced hearings in Columbus at which each of the remaining communities, including Kent, had forty minutes in which to make its case. On September 8 the Kent delegation made its presentation, emphasizing the town's centrality, railroads, lakes, and its ideal tract of land. As they were filing out of the chamber, Hudson's delegation filed in. The timing was awkward, and symbolic of the intense competition.

That rivalry soon flared up in the public press, and Rockwell was the flashpoint. While the other Kent delegates headed home, he stayed in Columbus on business. When L. H. Chapin, chair of the Hudson delegation and editor of the village paper, heard that Rockwell had been at large in the statehouse, his darkest suspicions were confirmed. Chapin mounted his editorial chair and accused Kent of "crooked political" skullduggery.[3] In William S. Kent of the Republican and David Ladd

Rockwell of the Democratic parties, Kent had two potent advocates, and Chapin was only stating what others were thinking. After the names of the fourteen communities still in the running became known—Kent, Ravenna, and Hudson among them—rumors spread that the state was sure to spend as much as a million dollars on the normal school. Because of the intensifying rivalries, the site commissioners asked to be permitted to slip in and out of the competing towns without fuss—no ceremonies, no brass bands, no parades, no formal luncheons—for they had a busy schedule.

But, as the commissioners stood in the nearly deserted Erie station in Kent on that cold, wet day in September 1910, they were nonplused. For the first time a community had actually taken them at their word—too much so, perhaps. Where were the Kent officials who were supposed to show them the town? How were they supposed to find their own unaided way to the proposed site of the normal school?

The Kent officials were a mile away. They had decided at the last minute to ignore the commissioners' request for no fanfare and give them instead a hump-and-hustle Kent welcome. Assuming the commissioners would motor to Kent from Wadsworth, site of the previous day's visit, the Kent men had risen early and headed to the eastern outskirts of town, where they were stationed along the roads leading into Kent, peering expectantly at every approaching motorcar that bumped toward them down the rutted, muddy roads. How were they to know, these citizens of a railroad town, that the commissioners would decide to come by train?

One can only speculate what Kent's fate would have been if Board of Trade member and postmaster Walter Reed had not come to the station to collect the incoming mail and noticed a group of official-looking strangers shifting from one foot to the other while casting perplexed glances around the station. When he asked if he could help, they identified themselves and informed him, pointedly, that they were due in Ravenna in exactly one hour—it was almost 11:00 A.M.—for their next visitation. After Reed sent a posse to round up the Board of Trade representatives, he commandeered motorcars to transport the commissioners to the site and borrowed rain gear and boots for them to wear when they got there.

It was a day when dawn never happened. Kent had awakened to a world swathed in the thick folds of a heavy gray fog, pierced by a slow chilly drizzle. The fog was so low lying and dense that the commissioners could glean only vague impressions of the village as they were trundled hastily about the town. Nothing was going as planned. Everybody in town had worked so hard to put the best possible face on their community—repairing and repainting fences, cutting yards and weeding empty lots, clearing alleys of trash, washing storefront windows, sweeping up delivery-horse droppings. Now all that seemed wasted effort.

And worse was to come. As the party was forcing its way through thorny tangles of brambles up the steep flank of the hill, the Kent men trumpeted the beautiful view the commissioners would see from the summit. But when they got there, nothing could be seen through the shroud of mist and fog.

Noticing the commissioners' impatience and discomfort, one of the Kent men seized the moment and saved the day. A hot meal, he told them, was already waiting for them at Frank Merrill's place, where they could get warm and dry. When the commissioners demurred, the Kent men "persuaded them, much against their will," to eat a lunch prepared for them at a place "on the Ravenna Road"—thus demonstrating the little known geometric principle that the fastest way to a normal school is not a straight line but a fish fry.[4]

What the Kent men told the commissioners was true, mostly; but it was untrue enough to be completely misleading. There were two roads to Ravenna from the west: one was Main Street, just down the hill from where they were standing; the other was Ravenna Road, which angled eastward from Hudson past the Merrill farm toward Ravenna. It took twice as long to go via the Merrill farm on Ravenna Road as it did to go via Main Street. It is important to freeze-frame this moment, because ill-natured skeptics have claimed that the Kentites won the normal school by duplicity. True, the meal awaiting them at the Merrill farm featured fresh-caught, crisp-fried bluegill along with fried chicken and savory side dishes, a welcome repast on a wet, chilly day. And it's also true that they repaired to the porch overlooking the glassy lake for postprandial cigars with glasses of cider (whether sweet or hard is unknown), where the conversation turned to Kent as the ideal site for the new normal school.

So when the motorcars escorting the commissioners from Kent pulled into Ravenna four hours too late for the luncheon that had been ready since noon, the suspiciously jolly camaraderie between the Kent men and the commissioners told the impatient Ravennans that, by swiping their luncheon time, Kent had probably swiped their chances of getting the normal school. Ravenna had gambled on an impressive luncheon to put the commissioners into a proper frame of mind to listen to Ravenna's pitch for its site, but Kent had trumped them. Of course, the commissioners bear some culpability; they must have assumed that their noon appointment in Ravenna would involve some sort of meal, yet they had accepted Kent's invitation, perhaps in compensation for the dismal weather that had spoiled the view from the summit. Besides, the commissioners did spend the night in Ravenna, and its good citizens surely took full advantage of that opportunity to press their case. Still, that bluegill luncheon rankled and made Ravenna's prospects problematic.

Optimism and competitiveness being America's distinctive virtues, all the communities visited by the commissioners expressed confidence that they would be chosen for the normal school. Hudson's newspaper claimed that the village was far in front of the pack. And Kent's hopes floated kite high on October 19 when Governor Harmon's reelection campaign against Warren Gamaliel Harding brought him to town. With Martin Davey at the wheel, Harmon and Rockwell drove up Summit Street to enjoy the view in all its autumnal glory. He was impressed, he told a large crowd of supporters that evening in the Opera House. And, in historian Phillip Shriver's words, he "brought the partisan crowd to its feet by stating that he could not think of a better site for the normal school."[5]

Amid a swirl of rumors, the commissioners steadfastly refused to disclose anything about their deliberations and procedures, wanting to avoid the fuss and furor that bedeviled their previous visits. This became apparent on Friday, November 11, when the citizens of Wadsworth realized that the five commissioners had arrived unannounced to tour the town and take another look at the farm proposed as their school site.

They came with the same suddenness of surprise to Kent the next day to get a clear view of the Kent tract. Presumably the descriptions of Summit Hill that had accompanied their bluegill feast had tickled their curiosity. They motored up cold, snow-glazed Summit Street to the top of the south side of the hill, and there—in the vivid clarity of the early winter light, the trees bare branched to the open sky, the graceful contours of the land clearly etched by the angled sunlight, their senses sharpened by the cold air—they beheld the breathtaking beauty of the scene below, the valley and the town and the river running through.

On November 19 the site commission called the delegations from communities still in the competition to Columbus for a final round of secret hearings. Each delegation was asked to present a formal commitment by its board of education to the new normal school's board of trustees (to be named later) to designate a district encompassing at least 250 pupils for the training school. At the hearing the Kent delegates agreed to three additional requirements: first, to enlarge the Kent tract by purchasing several small adjacent farm properties suitable to the agricultural curriculum of the normal school, thus making a campus of 85 acres; second, to offer the enlarged site to the state free of cost and legal entanglements; and third, to pave East Main Street on the north side of the property.

At this critical moment William S. Kent informed the site commission that he would donate his land to the state for the use of the normal school. Kent's offer relieved the village of most of its share of the cost for the normal school. When word leaked out, state newspapers hailed Kent as a true philanthropist, and rumors flew that Kent was now odds-on favorite to win the northeast normal school. That night an exuberant crowd of citizens clustered outside the *Courier* offices went wild with delight when reports came that Kent had won. Solid proof came the next day in the *Cleveland Plain Dealer*, which reported that the northwestern normal school would be in Bowling Green and the northeastern one in Kent. Of particular significance in the *Plain Dealer* article is a statement attributed to the commissioners that Kent fit their normal school profile perfectly and that the site was "by far the most beautiful of all" they had seen.

Charming as the bluegill story is, and as neatly as it satisfies a good story's requirements of symmetry and symbol, it is not the reason the commission chose Kent for the northeastern normal school. Nor is William S. Kent's generosity. The best evidence points to the Kent farm itself as having made the decisive impression: its proximity to the village, its spaciousness, its rich forest of virgin timber, its free-flowing spring, and, preeminently, its sheer natural beauty. This puts to rest the notion that Kent won the normal school competition through duplicity or through Rockwell's wire pulling. The Board of Trade did mislead the commissioners to the Merrill farm, where they abandoned all sense of time while indulging in gustatory delights. The commissioners were not politicians susceptible to Rockwell's politicking, however, and there is no reason to doubt their integrity. Although what they heard at the bluegill feast may have persuaded them to give Kent a second look, it was the magnificent land itself that won the normal school.

And the happy citizens of Kent knew this full well. That afternoon, Sunday, November 20, five days before the national day of Thanksgiving, several hundred Kentites spontaneously trekked through the heavy snow up to the top of what they already were calling "Normal Hill" to survey the land where the school would stand and to contemplate the magnificent view of the future unfolding for their village.

Kent villagers soon discovered it was far easier—and pleasanter—to stand on snowy Normal Hill that bright afternoon and picture the landscape transformed into a lively campus peopled with scores of eager students bustling in and out of handsome ivy-bearded buildings than it would be to realize that dream. They soon learned that the legislature was far less willing to finance the school than to decree it. Financing it meant allocating money that was tenaciously fought over by hundreds of competing government agencies, institutions, and power blocks, money raised by taxes levied on property and businesses. Our nation began with a fight over taxes, someone has observed, and has been fighting over them ever since. And none of our institutions has felt the sharp teeth of this axiom more acutely than state-supported institutions of higher learning. In 1911, Kent, along with its sister normal, Bowling Green, was on the front line in the fight.

For one thing, not everyone rejoiced in Kent's good fortune. Some, like the Hudson paper, groused that it was political pull, not fortune, that got Kent the normal school. Wadsworth's *Banner Press* named Rockwell as the string puller, while the representative of Fremont threatened legislative action to reverse the commission's decisions.[6] In time wounded feelings lost their smart, of course, but by then real politics had raised its unlovely green head in the form of money. In its efforts to persuade the legislature to pay for the school, Kent would suffer much more from politics than it was alleged to have benefited.

Early in 1911, despite informal assurances that each new normal would get as much as a million dollars, the House approved a bill to give Kent and Bowling Green each $50,000 to start construction. Kent's leaders blanched at the paltry sum but then comforted themselves with the hope that it was just a down payment on more to come. But a month later the Senate approved an amended version that counted the $50,000 previously allocated for Kent and Bowling Green as part of a "total" amount, not to exceed $250,000—an amount breathtakingly incommensurate to the cost of the undertaking. More worrisome was the ambiguous wording of the bill, which seemed to say that neither normal would ever be permitted to grow. House supporters of the new schools, deciding to take what they could get now and fight for more later, accepted the revision, and on March 21, 1911, the amended bill was passed. To veteran observers of the Ohio political scene, the penny-pinching bill bore the fingerprints of the usual gang of taxophobes, sectionalists, and supporters of established colleges.

Worse news came at the end of May when the Senate's final appropriation gave each new normal just $100,000 in addition to the $50,000 awarded earlier. Despite the uncertainty cast by the legislature's stinginess, the Kent Board of Trade continued to lobby for the school, writing letters, passing resolutions, and applying pressure wherever and whenever it could. Meanwhile, the axis of responsibility for making the school a reality shifted to those entrusted by law with starting the school and overseeing its affairs: the five members of the Board of Trustees appointed by the governor on May 17. The trustees' concept of the normal school's mission and their choice of its first president would have historic consequences.

Three of the five trustees were seasoned public school men with extensive experiences as superintendents: John A. McDowell of Ashland, Frank A. Merrill of Kent, and Edwin F. Moulton of Warren. The others were Mansfield lawyer John P. Seward and Hudson farmer Peter W. Doyle. In addition to having professional expertise and reputations for sound judgment, these men were chosen to assuage hurt feelings still lingering among the losing communities. At two organizational meetings, the trustees elected Moulton president, Seward vice president, and McDowell secretary and authorized a crew from the Davey Tree Company, supervised by Merrill, to start clearing the tangled underbrush from the flanks and crest of the site.

Agreeing that they wanted the "best normal school in the land," the trustees began looking for what they called a "big man" to build it, someone with successful experience as teacher and administrator in both public and normal school education, a man who was "in the prime of life," an individual of "rare moral and intellectual attainment."[7] On July 17 the trustees unanimously voted to offer the job to professor John Edward McGilvrey, head of the department of education and supervisor of the training school at Western Illinois State Normal at Macomb. His credentials matched those set by the board. He had degrees from Indiana State Normal School at Terre Haute and Indiana University and had been a high school teacher, principal, and superintendent. His contract stipulated that for the first year he would continue full-time at Macomb while serving as Kent's part-time president for consultation during the planning stage, visiting Kent when needed. He was forty-five, and he and his wife, Mary Holly, had two children.

Though he was of average height, contemporary photographs show a man of arresting presence and force, intensely aware and alert, with an abundance of vital energy, a man who seemed to lean into the next moment, even when in repose. As often happens when wishes come true, in McGilvrey the trustees got all they wanted and far more than they expected.

At that same July 17 meeting they named the state normal school in honor of William S. Kent, on whose land it would arise, making Kent the only state institution of higher education to carry the name of an individual. They also chose the man who would help decide how that land would be used, architect George F. Hammond. He, in consultation with McGilvrey, drew up a master plan for the school's development and designed its first classroom building (Merrill Hall) and first dormitory for women (Lowry Hall), both of which were somehow to be constructed and furnished out of the $150,000 allocation. Both structures would be of Ohio light-yellow brick and have two stories plus basements. The classroom building, initially called the administration building, would have thirty rooms for classes, a training school, laboratories, a library, and offices, with the top floor doubling as auditorium and chapel. The dormitory would feature three-room suites (two bedrooms and a study), with four women per suite, as well as a kitchen and dining space capable of serving as many as 250. Both structures would be located on the northeast rise of Normal Hill.

While the land was being cleared and graded for construction, which began in March, the sitting president of Western Illinois State Normal died suddenly, and McGilvrey was picked to succeed him, at a salary far larger than the one contracted with Kent. McGilvrey promptly sent his resignation to Kent's trustees, who sent it back in the next mail, along with a new one that jumped his salary from the contracted $3,000 to $3,750 a year. The trustees had seen enough of the man to know they couldn't afford to let him get away.

On June 18, 1912, McGilvrey came to Kent for the cornerstone laying of the administration/classroom building, to be named for trustee Merrill of bluegill luncheon fame. The village celebrated with much pomp and circumstance and old-fashioned, small-town American hoopla.

Businesses closed at 10:00 A.M., bright bunting streamed from street signs and telephone poles, and a brass band led a parade of motorcars and bicycles and pedestrians to the campus. There, standing on a makeshift platform holding a score of officials and dignitaries, with the cornerstone of Merrill Hall waiting near at hand for the dedication ceremony, trustee president Moulton introduced McGilvrey as the man "with the ability to make this school the finest in the world."

The town then had its first opportunity to take McGilvrey's measure, insofar as it was reflected in his philosophy of education, which for him was a philosophy of teaching. Taking as springboard for his remarks the German proverb "Whatever you would have appear in a nation's life you must put into its schools," McGilvrey gave it a twist: whatever "knowledge, ideals, moral strength, or courage" a nation wished its schools to impart to its youth to prepare them for life's responsibilities must be presented "to the impressionable life of the child through the life of the teacher." The teacher's life is the medium and the message: in the act of teaching a subject, whether history or geography or arithmetic, the teacher necessarily is validating and enriching it by expressing it through his or her whole experience of life. Brushing aside the familiar caviling about born and made teachers, he said that while it's certainly true that a teacher must be born, "it is just as evident that he must be made." As it is essential to understand the basic laws of nature in order to progress in the increasingly complex industrial world, it is just as essential for the teacher who wishes to instill useful knowledge and values in students to understand the laws governing the child's mind, the growth and development of its character, laws as "definite as those in physics and chemistry." Then, clinching his analogy, he said that the future teacher studying in a normal school must be taught "in the most effectual way of reaching the untaught mind at its various points of contact with the social order—if she is to reach that mind with any degree of precision and skill."

When a soft rain began falling as he spoke, McGilvrey called it the school's "baptism." At the rhetorical peak of his address, he spoke spiritedly of teaching as a high calling. The normal school ideal, he said, is to foster the "professional spirit," which he likened to a restorative spring of "influence and power far beyond the limits of mere knowledge: the sense of consecrated devotion to one's work," a stay against the "deadening effect of routine" that causes so much waste in education.[8]

McGilvrey's first challenge was to get the normal school up and running—but how was he to do that when there was no place for students to live and no classrooms to teach them in? By the end of October 1912, both Merrill Hall and what would later be named Lowry Hall had roofs but nearly all the finishing work remained, making their interiors unfit for use. Nevertheless, Kent State Normal School had already been holding classes for three weeks.

Sometime the previous summer McGilvrey had realized that neither Merrill nor Lowry would be ready by fall. The school was already greatly underfunded, and he dare not let another academic year slide by without making some attempt to carry out Kent's mission of training teachers. Further delay would jeopardize any chance of getting adequate funds from the legislature. If teachers were needed, he reasoned—and Kent was founded to train teachers—then that was what Kent would do, and as fast and efficiently as possible. If the students couldn't come to the school, the school would go to them.

The extension concept originated at the University of Chicago at the end of the nineteenth century, and McGilvrey had pioneered it at Western Illinois. Enacting it at Kent was another matter, however, because he had no teachers to take the school to the students and no funds for hiring any. So he decided to get help from the state emergency fund. He persuaded the trustees to appeal for $7,000, and, to nearly everyone's surprise, he got the money.

McGilvrey designed the extension program to help elementary teachers satisfy state normal certification requirements by taking evening classes offered near their homes during the school year before coming to Kent for summer classes. They could earn credits toward a provisional four-year state certificate that would become permanent after two years of successful teaching and the passing of the state board examination.[9] He used the emergency funds to hire four professors, who arrived in Kent on October 1. They were the school's original faculty: May H. Prentice (training school director), Helen M. Atkinson (registrar, presidential assistant), John T. Johnson (biology, agriculture)—all from Western Illinois—George E. Marker (head, education). Almost before they could catch their breath, the faculty found themselves dashing out to twenty different centers McGilvrey had set up over the cardinal points of the district: south to Canal Dover, west to Ashland, north to Ashtabula, east to East Liverpool. They taught twenty-nine different courses in such subjects as the history of education, principles of teaching, school administration, psychology, and agriculture.

McGilvrey had announced that Kent was sending the school to the teachers, and in a few weeks 849 working teachers were enrolled as students in its extension classes. Demand swiftly outpaced his ability to satisfy it, so in mid-February 1913 he added another teacher, biologist Lewis S. Hopkins, and planted five more extension centers. Barely five months after it started, the program had 1,045 registered students.

Given the exigencies of the situation, McGilvrey expected his faculty to be bold and flexible. He encouraged them to improvise, to draw on their experience and general knowledge—to learn on the job. Professor Johnson later recalled how one day in 1913 McGilvrey came to him and said, "'Johnson, over there in Ravenna they have no teacher of psychology.' 'But I am teaching agriculture,' I replied. McGilvrey said, 'You go over and teach that class.'"[10] An experienced teacher himself, McGilvrey knew that the best way to learn a subject is to have to teach it.

Word of Kent's fast-growing extension program spread. Most people applauded it, especially teachers and superintendents who thought it would improve the quality of education in public schools. But the educational leaders in Columbus were skeptical. What others saw as ingenious they saw as unorthodox and unprofessional. William Oxley Thompson, president of Ohio State University, perceived in McGilvrey's soaring enrollment a serious threat to the status quo, which had long favored his institution. If McGilvrey's methods worked, Kent would soon be demanding a larger piece of the money pie.

While launching his extension initiative with one hand, McGilvrey was preparing to open on-campus classes with the other. In the October catalog, the *Quarterly*, he detailed a two-year program for elementary teachers requiring thirty credits: six in educational theory, three in observation of teaching, twelve in "matter and method" in the various grades, and nine in such fields as agriculture, biology, English literature and grammar, civics, physical training, physiology, chemistry or physics, and Ohio history and geography. All this was informative and innocuous, exactly what an educator like William Oxley Thompson would expect to see while thumbing through a normal school course catalog. But not so one particular paragraph that jumped out at him, the paragraph in which McGilvrey alluded to plans for offering a four-year course leading to a bachelor of pedagogy degree for high school teachers and administrators. A statement of such brash ambition from an unproven newcomer still in the diaper stage of a two-year diploma-granting school, not a single one of whose buildings was yet finished, hit Thompson like a safe dropped from a skyscraper. McGilvrey was all but declaring his intention of making Kent a four-year college, a move bound to reduce OSU's share of state appropriations. Moving quickly, Thompson summoned all five presidents to a conference in Columbus, where he warned McGilvrey to abide by the limits of Kent's normal school mission: Kent was to remain a two-year school for training elementary teachers, and any idea of expanding it into a college must be abandoned.

But McGilvrey was not one to dance to any man's tune. He returned to Kent and on January 13 issued a new catalog announcing May 19, 1913, as the starting date of classes on Kent's campus and coolly reiterating his plan to offer a four-year course leading to a bachelor of education degree (B.Ed), if justified by demand. He added a new detail: starting with the 1913 summer session, Kent would offer "graduate" (that is, junior- and senior-level) courses in various aspects of education for students who had finished a two-year course or its equivalent, each class having a ten-student minimum.

As senior president in Ohio's higher education system, Thompson had long been accustomed to speaking ex cathedra on matters educational; his word had the moral force of law—at least in his own mind. But he sorely misjudged McGilvrey, in whose veins ran the blood of his Scots forebears, whose passionate commitment to the life of the mind was inseparable from their fierce individualism and steel-necked pride. And McGilvrey, for his part, failed to gauge accurately Thompson's conceit and pugnacity, not to mention the vast resources at his command.

It wasn't pride or vainglory or bullheadedness that drove McGilvrey to lock horns with Thompson. Rather, it was his longheadedness, for he had a gift, rare in any sphere of life, for apprehending the future taking shape beneath the shifting surface of current events. Long before he came to Kent, he sensed that the normal school movement had already crested, that the next wave in education would favor institutions capable of training high school as well as elementary teachers, and that high school teachers, already in growing demand, would need liberal arts coursework in addition to training in pedagogy and education.

The stages of his plan, which Thompson could read between the lines of the catalog, called for the two-year normal education curriculum to evolve into a four-year college, with a liberal arts component that in turn would develop into a degree-granting liberal arts college.

A key component in the success of his plan would be a strong alumni association to organize normal school graduates into advocates for their school. This is why McGilvrey had planned an alumni association well before he had any students on campus, before any buildings were finished, before he had a faculty, even before he came to Kent.

By spring 1913 the legislature was so taken with McGilvrey's imaginative use of the $150,000 appropriation of 1911 that it jettisoned the $250,000 limit and voted funds for everything he and the trustees had requested in 1913–14: an agricultural and training school (Kent Hall); a building to house an auditorium, library, gymnasium, and offices; a power house; an expansion of Lowry Hall; and money for staffing and maintenance. The staffing money brought eleven new faculty members who would be followed by many more as enrollments grew and new buildings rose.

Meanwhile, Bowling Green, moving at a more sedate gait, projected that it would not open until its buildings were ready in 1915. McGilvrey, however, was much too "dynamic, restless, impatient with tradition" to put off doing what he earnestly believed must be done.[11] Always responsive to student needs, he dovetailed his academic-year extension classes with the Kent campus summer sessions. Classes starting at Kent on May 19 were keyed to teachers of rural schools, which closed on May 17, thus enabling them to complete a third of an academic year's work toward their diplomas before their fall term began. A shorter summer term began on June 16 to suit the schedules of urban teachers. He aimed to ensure a continuously flowing course of study for the teachers whose career dreams he was dedicated to helping fulfill.

By the end of that November, with extension enrollment still booming and interest in on-campus classes rising, it became clear that Lowry Hall would not hold all the students expected for the May 1913 summer term. When a canvass showed too few rooms for rent—292 in Kent, 78 in Cuyahoga Falls, and 61 in Ravenna—he cast his net to rural communities and found many willing cottage owners at Brady, Silver, and Twin lakes. And those cottages he advertised to stunning effect. Catalogs and brochures with photographs of cottages dreaming beside blue waters beckoned teachers to "spend summer at the lakes." And it was cheap. Groups of students could rent a furnished cottage for $10 a week and ride the trolley to campus for a nickel.

Cost was always one of McGilvrey's chief concerns. Knowing that most people in the country could not afford higher education and that his particular students usually had to pinch pennies, he got the trustees to set fees for dormitory rooms and meals at $4 a week per student and to pass a resolution that Kent students would not be charged fees or tuition, a move that irked his fellow presidential colleagues. This meant that a student could take the twelve-week term for as little as $60, including tuition, room and board, laundry, classroom supplies, and books. As he wrote in the April 1913 catalog, "No obstacle of any kind will be placed in the way of students or teachers seeking to prepare themselves for better public service." Though he could not realize his dream of providing a completely free public education, which he believed was implicit in the American Dream, he strove to make a Kent education available to as many as possible.

The first summer term began on a dissonant note, and in a minor key. Forty-seven students showed up, fewer than hoped for, and President McGilvrey was not there to welcome them. He was one of the many victims of what until then was the greatest flood in Ohio's history. On Monday, March 31, 1913, after days of drenching rains, the Cuyahoga River surged over its banks into downtown Kent. It rose rapidly for the next two days, bursting the reservoir, pushing aside train tracks, soaking stores and shops, and spilling sewage far and wide. Typhoid prowled behind, infecting men, women, and children. McGilvrey, already sapped by months of overwork, was hit hard. He was bedfast, too sick for visitors or school business of any kind, from early April until July 9, when he returned to a place he hardly recognized and where he was hardly known except by name.

With McGilvrey out of commission, Dean of Faculty John T. Johnson had to step in. Luckily, Johnson was blessed with a sense of humor, because problems big and small assaulted him at every turn. There were no tools for manual training or domestic science classes. The new teachers did not know one another or anything about the campus or the town. There were not enough students for some classes and too many for others. Beds and blankets did not arrive on time. One angry delegation of women students complained that the pies were cut into too many pieces; another that chirping birds kept them awake.

Johnson was constantly peppered by questions from teachers and students: Where can we eat? Or rent rooms? Or get books? By the way, where is room 210? He had to borrow silverware and dishes from a local church and then find someone to wash them. When it rained the walkways became mud chutes, so he had a carpenter make boardwalks from furniture crates shipped from Mansfield and, to his amusement, students and faculty found themselves treading on duck-boards stamped "State Reformatory." And told at the last minute that a flag must be flown on opening session, he and custodian Alexander Whyte had to borrow one and run it up the pole.[12]

The opening of the second term on June 16 was much more orderly. The enrollment spiked to 290 students, the great majority from northeastern Ohio, with only one from out of state. Trolleys and trains brought them to Kent, and Board of Trade members motored them to campus. Many lived in lakeside cottages or in rented rooms in Kent, Ravenna, and Cuyahoga Falls. A handful roomed at the newly built Normal Inn across from campus on East Main Street.

That summer jack-of-all-trades Alex Whyte laid out some tennis courts and a baseball diamond, on which he fielded a pickup team from the handful of male students and local high school boys. McGilvrey and Dean Johnson spread the grass seed around the first building, set out flowering shrubs, and planted each sprig of ivy that in time graced every building on Hilltop Drive for generations. Students trolleyed to local lakes for swimming or to Silver Lake for evening chautauqua lectures. Step singing became one of Kent's earliest traditions that summer; in the long, soft twilight students sat on the front steps of Merrill or Lowry and harmonized songs of the day.

Years later Professor Marker vividly recalled the savage state of the campus and the undeveloped condition of the east side of Kent village at that time. As Merrill and Lowry were being built, a housing boom had started in the western and northern areas along the borders of what one day would be the cultivated campus. But East Main, from the corner of Main and Water, up Main Street hill, and all the way to Ravenna, was graded with gravel but still unpaved, and after big rains horse-drawn grocery wagons sank to their axles in viscous mud.

Most of the campus was covered by a dense forest of trees with scrums of brush so thick and high that one could stand by Merrill Hall and still not see Main Street fifty or so yards below. As yet, no paved walkways or driveways stitched the campus together, few outdoor lights redeemed the night, and streams ran down the flanks of Normal Hill.[13] The Lowry women entertained themselves with blood-chilling fantasies about the dismal swamp puddled with quicksand that covered the area between the future sites of White and Rockwell halls. The campus was, in all senses, a place fraught with adventure.

All this suited McGilvrey's pathfinder spirit, and he made the adventure of a great challenge the theme of a talk he gave on July 9 after recovering from typhoid. Touched by their standing ovation, he told the students and faculty crowded into the Merrill Hall assembly room that nothing in life could match the "exhilaration and freedom" that come with the glad acceptance of a splendid challenge. He closed by daring them to join him in the great adventure of making Kent State Normal the Massachusetts Institute of Technology among teachers' colleges.[14] The coin of McGilvrey's dreams was always gold dubloons, never small change.

During the school's first full academic year, 1913–14, he introduced several unorthodox and controversial practices. Instead of following most other schools into the semester calendar, he chose the quarter plan because it offered more flexibility in scheduling and enabled students to do a quarter of a year's work in a single summer. To encourage beginning students, he experimented with a pass (white slip) and fail (blue slip) system. But these breaks with tradition, coupled with his advocacy of free education, hardened opposition to him in Columbus.

That first year was stacked high with troubles of another sort. Nasty storms turned the fall term into one long drench of chill rains that made Normal Hill a mudslide. An outbreak of cabin fever was followed by homesickness. To keep the 138 women and six men from going home, McGilvrey and the faculty staged "Stunt Nights" in which faculty and students performed skits; faculty wives sponsored on-campus dances; McGilvrey held frequent assemblies to encourage a sense of camaraderie; and the women students burned off excess energy in athletic contests. Dates with Davey "tree-skinners" (apprentice tree surgeons) provided occasions for romance. And there were always performances by the Normal Glee Club as well as movies and vaudeville at the Opera House on Water Street.

The Lowry women took to calling their dorm "Walden Hall" in honor of McGilvrey's hero Thoreau's famous experiment of living in the woods. On December 16 they formed Kent's first student organization, the Walden Dramatic Club, devoted largely to dramatic readings and social activities. To celebrate the autumnal music of prickly burrs plopping down from the chestnut trees outside their windows, they called the first campus yearbook *The Chestnut Burr*. And it may have been this winter when some snow-inspired students first slid down the north side of Normal Hill.

Spirits rebounded with the first spring zephyrs. When extension enrollment reached 1,600, McGilvrey decided to throw a party. He invited all students, along with school superintendents from northeastern Ohio, to Kent for Extension Day (later changed to Campus Day), and on Saturday, May 16, 1914, some 3,000 people, including 1,000 extension and 144 on-campus students and numerous guests, crowded the campus for a festival of maypole dancing, choral singing, speeches, food, campus tours, and a banquet for the superintendents.

While McGilvrey had hoped that Extension Day would lure large numbers of extension students to Kent for the first term, only eighty-seven showed up. So he was wholly unprepared for the wave of students, mostly urban teachers, who flooded the campus for the second summer term. He had expected 600, but the actual number—1,378—exceeded even those of his wilder dreams. He had vigorously promoted the school through bulletins, brochures, posters, and circulars mailed far and wide. He also had help from a new shotgun school law aimed at raising standards that required anyone seeking a life teaching certificate to have at least a one-year course or equivalent in summer study in a recognized training institution or a year's study at an arts college with a training component. Since observation was the petri dish of normal school training, summer students had to swelter outside overcrowded Merrill Hall and peer through ground-floor windows, watching and learning as a master teacher instructed elementary students.

The enrollment spike, welcome though it was, caused logistical headaches: Merrill Hall's thirty classrooms could not accommodate all the students, so McGilvrey persuaded the trustees to build a huge pavilion, called the Tabernacle, with wooden supports, a roof, canvas drop-curtain sides, and wooden benches. Holding up to 1,000 it served as an assembly room for the entire study body as well as a lecture hall for classes of 250. Sprawling at the foot of the steps leading down from the present Cartwright Hall, the Tabernacle was notoriously hot and noisy but was more comfortable and quieter than the four circus tents he later set up on top of the hill when the Tabernacle proved too small. These "Hot-houses" boiled in the summer sun and rattled in the rain.

In addition to the students quartered in Lowry, some 300 lived in lakeside cottages or found rooms to rent in Kent and nearby towns. The trustees purchased a red Stanley Steamer, called the "Normal Bus," to cart students from trolley and train stops up the newly laid red-brick roadway curving from Main Street up past Lowry and Merrill to the Administration Building, which was slowly rising on the crown of the hill. But construction of this and other new buildings proceeded in fits and starts, according to the financing whims of the legislature and the volatility of prices for materials and labor.

Still, it was an exhilarating time for campus and town. At a "Get Acquainted Night" on June 25, 1914, some 1,400 people gathered on campus before parading downtown, singing and cheering. They clustered around a platform that had been erected at the corner of Main and Water and heard Mayor Martin L. Davey welcome them to Kent. When McGilvrey was called onto the platform, he was greeted so lustily that he was visibly moved. There was a familial quality to town-gown relations in those halcyon days, when Kent State Normal School was embraced as a community endeavor of high promise. McGilvrey had the gift of making education scintillate with possibilities.

That summer is memorable for one of his longest-lasting initiatives to bind town and gown together. McGilvrey believed in education's responsibility not only to increase knowledge and skills but also to expand the horizons of a student's mind and sensibilities through new cultural experiences. To that end, he scheduled a series of chautauqua-like programs (free for students but paid for by guests via admission fees) that quickly became popular community events. One summer night the famous contralto Madame DeSylva sang; on another Edmund Vance Cook, poet-philosopher, lectured and read some of his poems; on yet another the Ben Greet Players, the country's leading traveling Shakespearean company, performed under the stars.

That July 1914, as Kent was preparing to graduate its first class, Governor James M. Cox came up from Columbus to congratulate the school on "its auspicious beginning." Speaking to some 3,000 students, faculty, and parents packed into the Tabernacle and spilling onto the surrounding lawn, Cox called Kent a "great institution," one that "school people" regard as "a model, an example, as an inspiration to the other institutions in Ohio."[15] Music it was to Kent's ears, but the governor's words, widely reported, stirred further resentment in Columbus.

The Kent story had been steadily attracting the attention of a variety of educational institutions and officials. Letters came from such venerable universities as Harvard, Chicago, and even OSU asking how summer school enrollments had risen so swiftly. And looking for ways to balloon their summer enrollments, the presidents of Hiram, Bowling Green, Miami, and Northern Illinois, among others, came to consult with McGilvrey.

The secret of the school's large summer school enrollments was, of course, its dynamic extension program, which brought working teachers to campus in the summer to complete their certificate requirements. A comparison of the forty-seven students who registered in the first summer term in 1913 with the 3,814 in 1924 indicates why McGilvrey could confidently inform the trustees that Kent's summer school was larger than that of any other teaching training school in the nation and that Kent was, as *The College Blue Book* of 1923 reported, America's "fastest growing college." The summer figures show that Kent's students were mostly working teachers seeking credits to qualify them for life certificates.

Though on-campus academic year enrollments were far less robust during the same period, for a time McGilvrey was able to use the summer enrollments to leverage building funds from the legislature, further straining relations with the educational establishment. Four buildings—Merrill, Lowry, and Science (Kent) halls and the Administration Building—were erected between 1913 and 1914. But during the next decade, partly because of dislocations caused by World War I, only a woman's dormitory, Moulton Hall, and the power and heating plant were added. Requests for a physical education building, a training school building, a presidential residence, and dormitory additions all went unfunded. Finally, in 1923, work began on a women's gymnasium (Wills Gym) behind the Administration Building on Blackbird Lake, long a beloved skating pond.

McGilvrey's vision of Kent as a university unfolded gradually and under the duress of the harsh realities that shape public education in a state deeply conflicted about public education. He began and, to a degree, remained a teacher-training man bent on keeping Kent essentially a training institution, as stipulated by the legislature. But, as the 1912 catalog disclosed, he knew that to compete successfully for state support, Kent must quickly evolve into a four-year training institution for high school teachers and administrators as well as for elementary teachers. Three years later, on June 5, 1915, seven weeks before he awarded ten students bachelor in education degrees, at McGilvrey's request the board changed the school's name to Kent State Normal College.

Sometime after a Boston landscape architect finished a topographical survey of the campus in 1915, McGilvrey drew up a fifty-year plan that articulated his mature vision of Kent State University. Projecting a student body of 10,000, he envisioned a campus with six colleges (education, liberal arts, social science and public service, engineering, business administration, law); an observatory; and separate buildings for seven departments (English, history, mathematics, biology, home economics, fine arts, and geography and geology); two dormitory quadrangles, one for women and one for men; a student union building; and, off campus, a training school, a field house, and a stadium. All would be centered around a "working library." Presumably he had already fixed his sights on a university as his ultimate goal when he persuaded the trustees to change Kent from a normal training school to a teacher's college. The next step toward his still-evolving vision was a liberal arts college, which he knew would involve a major struggle.

Two

THE STORMY PETREL

{1915–1926}

Between 1915 and 1920 McGilvrey became a lobbying gadfly in Columbus, button-holing legislators in the corridors of power and, armed with graphs and charts, testifying forcefully before committees. His was on a risky mission: to change the state's funding policy from one that gave the largest portion to OSU, OU, and Miami, in descending order, and a much smaller share to Bowling Green and even less to Kent. His appeal, delivered with increasing bite and pungency before each session, was for basic fairness: Was it right that Kent, which served the most populous and prosperous northeastern sector of the state—the "Ruhr of America," he called it—the region that generated almost half the state's tax revenues, should be given far less money to educate its students than the three favored southern schools?

For him, comparisons were illuminating, not odious. To make his point, he wielded raw facts like bludgeons. One of his circulars blared that taxpayers in Kent's northeastern district annually contributed to the instruction of a teacher-student "in the Fourth Quarter at Ohio State, $11.73; at Miami, $5.34; at Bowling Green, $4.40; AND AT KENT STATE TOWARD THE EDUCATION OF A TEACHER OF THEIR OWN CHILDREN, $1.88."[1] Instead of this unfair system, he argued for a per capita fee structure that would award the same amount of state support to each student, no matter the school. His tenacity, his feistiness, and his nettlesome proposal roused the drowsing dragons of sectionalism and other entrenched interests—southern legislators hated being portrayed as self-serving and unfair—and Thompson became their tribune.

McGilvrey's instincts and philosophy were egalitarian and democratic, while Thompson assumed that hierarchies were part of the natural order—such hierarchies as his own position as suzerain of state educators and his institution's ascendance, as reflected in its title: *The Ohio State University*. For Thompson, the definite article declared the plain fact that OSU was the *only* state university in Ohio and, as such, should enjoy preeminence in all matters, especially in state funding.

Meanwhile, McGilvrey was in trouble on his own campus. His relations with the board were severely strained during a "faculty rebellion" that started in 1918 when a department head was not awarded a special raise and his disgruntlement infected four other heads. Together with a former trustee unhappy over not being reappointed, they formed a cabal to oust McGilvrey, charging him with mishandling funds, inefficiency, and theft of state property. Campus and town were roiled by allegations, investigations, and libel suits for two years.[2] Although an audit by a state examiner cleared McGilvrey of the misappropriation and theft charges,[3] the poisonous contention eventually forced the legislature to intercede.

When state House and Senate investigating committees disagreed about McGilvrey's culpability, however, Kent's trustees voted 4 to 1 in his favor on June 24, 1921, and the governor ratified their decision. McGilvrey kept his job, and the troublesome faculty members either resigned or retired. But the controversy left a legacy of ill will that cost McGilvrey dearly. Shriver speculates that it was the board president, David C. Wills, who swayed the trustees in McGilvrey's favor, but Dean Raymond Manchester, addressing the Portage County Historical Society in 1954, recalled the role played by William Steward Kent, the grand old benefactor of the city and the college and a champion of McGilvrey. Kent "sat outside where the hearings were being held," Manchester recalled, "and watched who went in; he would look at those who passed and say nothing. That was his way of defending McGilvrey. Not many would be bold enough to go in and talk against McGilvrey."[4]

Internal dissension ripped other state campuses as well during this period, and interuniversity relations became increasingly cutthroat. Conferences of the college presidents must have had the sulfurous air of a gathering of Mafia dons. The cause was not far to seek: the funding formula spawned jealousy and made lobbying for funds more hotly competitive than some varsity football games.

One consequence of the squabbling was the legislature's 1921 decision to establish a state director of education (changed later to superintendent of public instruction) who would also be ex officio member of all boards of trustees. The man named to the post was Vernon M. Riegel, who, declaring he intended to raise standards, issued a directive strictly limiting the credit hours to be earned through extension study and requiring extension teachers to be regular faculty members. The target of the directive was McGilvrey, in particular his custom of staffing some extension classes with local superintendents and principals.

Undeterred, however, McGilvrey gave a new twist to extension study in 1922 when he introduced credit-bearing correspondence courses for working teachers who lived too far from extension centers but needed coursework in special subjects, for which there was small demand or few classes, to satisfy diploma or degree requirements. The program, though popular, was beset from the start with serious problems: lack of library resources and of teacher-student contact. To Riegel, an orthodox educator, long-distance learning was flawed in principle because it relied on self-study and thus lacked quality controls.

McGilvrey must have known that such a program would antagonize Riegel. But, convinced that it served the needs of a segment of teachers, he stood by it, shrugging off counsels of conciliation and compromise with what he called "goose-stepping" traditionalists who wanted to substitute standards and measurements for teaching.[5] He believed that the desire to learn, not testing and measuring, should be the measure of education and that it was his mission to make education available to as many students as possible. The correspondence courses became the basis of Kent's Department of Home Study and, though controversial, hung on until 1949.

In 1924 McGilvrey made an inspired move. He hired Dr. A. O. DeWeese, head of medicine and physical education at the University of Louisville, to start a new department of physical and health education and athletic coaching. The state legislature had passed a law mandating health and physical education programs in public schools to ensure that future national emergencies would find young men in proper physical condition, unlike so many drafted for World War I, and requiring teacher training colleges to offer physical education programs. A national expert in the field, DeWeese developed a multifaceted program featuring classes in anatomy, bacteriology, hygiene, physiology, school health administration, and zoology, along with various games and sports. In just a few years Kent's program earned a national reputation as a pioneer in its field and had more health and physical education majors than any school in the state.

Thanks to the success of this program, coupled with equally robust enrollments in Professor Clinton S. Van Deusen's manual training program, between 1925 and 1926 the number of male students on campus was five times larger than it was between 1919 and 1920. The sudden influx of men changed many aspects of campus life, none more than social relations. Effects of the nation's first sexual revolution began registering after the end of World War I. Zoe Bayliss, successor to Kent's first dean of women, Louise W. Mears, came to Kent in 1919 intending to instill propriety and decorum in the women who would teach America's children, but she soon found she was swimming upstream. Women started wearing their skirts shorter and shorter and bobbing their hair, painting their faces, smoking cigarettes, and riding, unescorted, in motorcars driven by men. And codes of conduct proscribing such behavior, no matter how detailed, proved ineffective. Frustrated, Bayliss resigned in 1922, decrying the revolution in "manners and morals" known as the Jazz Age. The syncopated rhythms of jazz and ragtime music expressed the tempo of the era. Across the country, on and off college campuses, young people danced the Varsity Drag and Collegiate Shag as America danced into a new world.

It was not only the chemistry of social relations that changed as the male population increased. It brought about an equally dramatic chemical reaction in sports, which had been slow in coming to Kent largely because of the scarcity of men, though McGilvrey's opposition to intercollegiate athletics didn't help either. Varsity sports began with the basketball team in 1914 but went nowhere else. Then education head Paul C. Chandler started the football program in 1920, by which time football was the sport most identified with college life. Handicapped by a paucity of male students, Kent's teams compiled a dismaying record of 0 for 39 until November 1925, when the school finally had an equal number of male and female students and Kent beat West Liberty College, West Virginia, 7–6 under new coach Earle E. Wagoner. Despite that victory, over the next eight years the team continued to lose many more games than it won on Rockwell Field, located behind the Heating Plant. Trustee David Ladd Rockwell could not have enjoyed seeing his school humiliated so regularly on the field that bore his name.

But sports competitions were child's play compared to academic rivalries. Periodically throughout the early twenties, Riegel and McGilvrey snarled and snapped at each other over standards. In time Riegel realized that trying to keep an eye on the moving target named McGilvrey was causing his moods to swing wildly between low anxiety and high dudgeon, so he assigned his assistant, T. Howard Winters, to watchdog McGilvrey. A nervous, niggling man, Winters soon found much to bark about. Now, if all this reads like a script ghostwritten by William Oxley Thompson, it probably was: Winters had been an education professor at OSU under Thompson as well as a scholarly collaborator with Riegel, and his view of educational matters chimed perfectly with those of both men.

McGilvrey had more on his mind than Winters and Riegel—to wit, a new college. His initiatives to add a liberal arts college—a key component of his master plan—led to several major skirmishes with Thompson during the early twenties. About 1920 the Kent Chamber of Commerce decided that a liberal arts college would enhance the school's prestige, swell its enrollment, and expand the town's economy. With help from the Kent State Alumni Association, the Kent Chamber rounded up support from dozens of other area chambers. (The Alumni Association's involvement indicates that McGilvrey stage-managed the whole production from the wings.) Two bills proposing to give Kent State a liberal arts college were introduced in the legislature, the first in 1921 and a second in 1923. Both were rejected, however, because of opposition from OSU's Thompson, who also triumphed in 1925 when McGilvrey and the trustees, hoping to catch their rival nodding, tried—and failed—to make a discreet, unpublicized appeal to the legislature. Nevertheless, as he told the *Kentonian* in July 1924, McGilvrey remained confident that Kent would soon have a liberal arts college and graduate courses leading to the master's degree and, eventually, even the doctorate.

Thompson by this time recognized that McGilvrey had acquired a reputation as one of the country's most creative and successful educational leaders whose innovative methods were widely copied.[6] This made him a formidable opponent, even for the likes of Thompson. If McGilvrey had been willing to preside over a teacher training college, Thompson would have grudgingly tolerated him and his footling school, but it became increasingly clear that McGilvrey's lobbying for an equitable per-student funding formula would ultimately succeed. And, with Kent now pressing for a liberal arts college, Thompson realized that McGilvrey would never willingly abandon the campaign on which Kent's future would depend.

Thompson called the five college presidents to Columbus in July 1922 to discuss uniform quality standards. Subsequent events show that he and Riegel were working hand in glove to mount a two-pronged attack against what they viewed as the chink in McGilvrey's armor: the lower standards inevitably resulting from his newfangled educational ideas. After the meeting, Thompson appointed an accrediting subcommittee (minus McGilvrey) to inspect every state college—except Kent State.

In due time, he summoned the five presidents to Columbus to hear the committee's report. McGilvrey's darkest suspicions were confirmed when he heard the subcommittee report that it had awarded Bowling Green a 50 percent accreditation score but a zero rating to Kent. He bolted to his feet and roundly denounced the proceedings. When Thompson answered back, they fell to berating each other, filling the air with ears and hair, and the others pitched in.

This was the opening shot of what McGilvrey called "the Credit War" between Kent and OSU that actually broke out in 1923 when Thompson decreed that OSU would no longer accept any transfer credits from Kent. This threatened to destroy Kent's reputation as an educational institution. Soon other schools, in and out of the state, followed OSU's lead like lemmings, raising fears among Kent students and alums that their degrees would become worthless pieces of paper.

It wasn't long before superintendents of large area school systems like Youngstown balked at hiring Kent graduates; others notified Kent's trustees that their systems would no longer hire teachers with Kent degrees.[7] Students, alumni, townspeople, and friends of the school—all were embarrassed and distraught by the sickening turn of events. None more so than the trustees. Yet McGilvrey maintained that Kent's educational standards and performance were high and that it did not need OSU's approval.

The next year Riegel tightened the screws on standards for provisional teaching certificates. To new tests recently mandated by the legislature, he added extra exams for prospective teachers with fewer than two years of normal school training. Kent's students would be most affected by the policy, as he and McGilvrey knew. McGilvrey also sensed that the requirement would not be applied fairly. And he objected in principle to the extra examinations, as he told Riegel in a stinging letter, denouncing them as yet another step toward substituting the mechanism of testing for the organic process of teaching. If this trend continued, Kent would "become largely an examining rather than a teaching institution." And when McGilvrey discovered that many OSU students were indeed being exempted from the exams, he accused Riegel of "evasion of the law" and "unjust discrimination."[8]

Meanwhile, newspapers played the Credit War as an academic soap opera with daily installments. The bickering upset the trustees and convinced some that McGilvrey was more trouble than he was worth—too progressive, too uncompromising, too controversial. The political reality, some board members decided, was that Kent would have no peace or prosperity until it had appeased the state's educational establishment in the persons of Riegel and Thompson.

McGilvrey also agitated the trustees at this time with another bold innovation: an extension of his cultural enrichment program. Beginning in 1922 he led a series of educational tours to various sites of cultural and historical interest, each featuring faculty lectures and bearing credits in either history or geography. The first, involving 120 students, graduates, and friends, was a tour of the Washington, D.C., area. Its success justified another, a widely advertised summer 1923 tour of the eastern seaboard, which was hugely successful and profitable. Two tours were offered in 1924, and interest ran so high that three new trips were set for 1925 (Montreal, Yellowstone, and Washington, D.C.), and the 1925 brochures announced plans for a tour of Europe in 1926.

Much more than pleasure trips, the tours were part of a four-year program planned to culminate in 1926 with the establishment of a groundbreaking foreign exchange program in which Kent students would study abroad and foreign students would come to Kent. In fact, McGilvrey subscribed to many of the ideas associated with progressive education. He believed in experiential learning, and his European exchange program was rooted in his conviction that the whole being must be educated through an expansion and refinement of the sensorium as well as of the sensibility. And what could provide a more life-enhancing, life-enriching educational experience than study in a major European institution?

If McGilvrey had enjoyed the same harmonious relationship with the current board as had defined his relations with the trustees during his first decade as president, this new program would have won Kent State great distinction and acclaim. But relations with the current trustees had become severely shredded by the Credit War, and the summer tours had, to the jaundiced eye, the flaw of seeming to smudge the fine line between education and pleasure. Besides, they were far too popular for the trustees to ignore the bleats and barks of Riegel and his watch-dog Winters that they were entertainment tricked up as education.

McGilvrey had taken the trustees at their word in 1910 and devoted his considerable intellectual and creative powers to making Kent the nation's best normal school. By temperament impulsive and careless of protocol and good form, he forgot that trustees come and go and that they come in all varieties of commitment, judgment, imagination, understanding, patience, and selflessness. And that they are susceptible to the same proprietary sense that sometimes befalls presidents, faculty, students, and alums. But trustees are legally entrusted with responsibility for the institution. And, for individuals with robust egos, individuals accustomed to having their way in the great world, it is a temptingly small step from legal responsibility to an inappropriate sense of ownership.

Such was the case with David Ladd Rockwell and trustee businessmen William A. Cluff and William A. Coursen, who, after an indeterminate point, could no longer see that McGilvrey was still energetically and single-mindedly pursuing his original mandate. To them, he was an obstacle to the school's growth and a sharpening pain in their necks. His unilateral managing of the tours—and their success—was especially galling. And his advertising campaigns made them an easy target for educators from the castor oil school of education-as-bitter-medicine, who said he was cheapening education.

Rockwell, who joined the board in 1919 along with Wills (the board president), had voted to keep McGilvrey after the faculty rebellion and so was thought to be his supporter, until it turned out he was not. He had bounced resiliently back from his defeat for the state attorney general's office and climbed quickly up to the highest circles of the national Democratic Party. His name and face became familiar to newspaper readers during the 1920 convention in San Francisco, where he floor managed Governor James Cox's successful bid for the party's presidential nomination. Four years later he was again in the news as national manager of William Gibbs McAdoo's run for the party's presidential nomination at the tumultuous convention in New York City. So when he joined the board, Rockwell became its most prominent and influential member—a power broker and a trusted adviser to the nation's movers and shakers. His early labors on behalf of the normal school, however, seem to have licensed a feeling that Kent was his school, as surely McGilvrey felt it was his. And like

McGilvrey, Rockwell was a proud, headstrong man with a muscular sense of himself and of his place in the scheme of things. A clash between two such forceful men was inevitable.

Under Wills's leadership, the trustees enjoyed a long season of amicable relations, one free of climbing ambition and personal rancor. Yet, as subsequent events revealed, Rockwell's attitude toward McGilvrey was devolving insensibly from one of general approval downward through frustration at McGilvrey's unwillingness to exercise more tact in pushing his funding formula in Columbus and exasperation over the man's truculent independence to, at last, downright anger over his unilateral decision making, his unwillingness to heed sage counsel, and his blind opposition to intercollegiate sports, particularly football. At some point, Rockwell, Cluff, and Coursen formed the flying wedge of trustees determined to knock McGilvrey down.

On November 19, 1925, a long-hoped-for letter came to McGilvrey informing him that Kent's name had been placed on the coveted "approved list" of schools whose alumni were qualified for graduate study at Columbia University. This action by Columbia, the leader of graduate education, vindicated McGilvrey in his struggles with Riegel by certifying, in effect, that Kent's standards equaled the highest in the field. Four days later McGilvrey sent the trustees a letter with the glad news. He reminded them of the stellar performances of many Kent graduates in Columbia's graduate school, which, he underscored, trained the faculties of most of the nation's teacher-training schools. Kent's inclusion on the "approved list," he wrote, established Kent State's "status in its own field by authority unquestioned."[9] He enclosed the Columbia letter for the trustees' perusal. He followed this in early December with another letter notifying board secretary Cluff of his imminent departure for Europe on business and then left for his trip on December 12.

Six weeks later, on Monday, January 25, 1926, McGilvrey was "walking on air," he said, when he strode down the gangway of the liner *Samaria,* which had just docked in New York's harbor. His four-year plan for an exchange program with Cambridge University had been clinched. He had negotiated an agreement calling for some 200 Kent students to spend the summer studying at Cambridge University while an unspecified number of Cambridge students would study American educational methods at Kent. He was sure this would "put Kent on the map."[10] Then he saw William Van Horn, the school's treasurer, waiting for him at the foot of the gangway, and Van Horn told him that the trustees had fired both of them ten days earlier.

McGilvrey returned to Kent on January 27 disheartened and defeated. Friends welcomed him when he detrained at Ravenna and drove him to Kent. Hundreds of students and townspeople lined Main Street, cheering as his motorcar passed slowly by the campus and trailing behind him to his home. There he thanked them for their kind support and asked them to refrain from any demonstrations. He would not fight the trustees' action.

Much remains unknown about this critical period in Kent's story, but one thing is virtually certain—that McGilvrey did not know that the trustees had met in conditions of unusual secrecy at the Hollenden Hotel in Cleveland just three weeks after their public meeting in June 1925. Present at that secret meeting were board president Wills, vice president Rockwell, secretary Cluff, and Coursen; the absent fifth trustee, W. Kee Maxwell, was consulted by phone. No record of the meeting exists, but there are revealing clues to what transpired in the trustees' minutes of January 16, 1926, the meeting at which they fired McGilvrey. And those clues, illuminated by inference and speculation, enable us to understand, if not see, what took place at the secret meeting.

The main business appears to have been hammering out an agreement, or "understanding," that during the upcoming fiscal year 1925–26, "ALL" college employees would work on a "month-to-month basis at current salaries set by the 'president' until"—and these are the key words—"such time as the Trustees would see fit to take such action in correcting the unsatisfactory conditions which apparently existed."[11] The carefully nuanced wording indicates that the "understanding" followed a tense, perhaps heated, discussion at the end of which the majority failed to convince at least one trustee that McGilvrey warranted firing. Though Cluff would claim later that they agreed to discharge McGilvrey at this meeting, what they actually worked out was a conditional "understanding" that they would discharge him if the alleged "unsatisfactory conditions" proved to be true. This means that at least one trustee was not persuaded that "unsatisfactory conditions" did in fact exist at Kent. Board president Wills, McGilvrey's friend and the most influential trustee, was most likely the one who denied the majority its will. And it would have been foolhardy for the majority to oust McGilvrey without Wills's support. The blowback would have been overpowering.

After arriving at this "understanding," the trustees held no public meetings for the next six months, violating a statutory requirement of four public meetings a year. They were obviously waiting for the "time" when they would "see fit" to act. And the internal logic of the chronology of events indicates that the time they were waiting for would come when McGilvrey was far from Kent and when they had a plausible excuse for firing him.

Consider the key moments in the chronology of the six months following the secret meeting. On October 22, 1925, Wills died, following a lingering illness. While his passing removed McGilvrey's staunchest supporter, the anti-McGilvrey trustees still lacked a plausible reason for ditching the school's much-loved and widely respected founder. During examination week, on December 12, 1925, McGilvrey informed Cluff of his imminent departure for England, and two days later his ship left New York. The fall term ended on Friday, December 18, and the Christmas holiday began, emptying the campus. The new quarter began on January 5, 1926, and on that day T. Howard Winters, state teacher training superintendent, began investigating the school, in all likelihood at the behest of his boss, Superintendent of Public Instruction Vernon Riegel, and at the request of the trustees.

With McGilvrey safely abroad, it was the best possible time to observe the disarray of a new term and the worst possible time for assessing the normal state of campus affairs. For Winters's purposes, of course, it was the ideal time to dig up evidence of "unacceptable conditions." During the next three days, he busied himself—visiting classes; quizzing students, teachers, staff members, and maintenance personnel; poring over class rosters, grade books, and school records; scrutinizing behavior and dress; and taking meticulous notes. On January 8, 1926, he finished his investigation and began drafting his report. Six days later he gave the report to the trustees, which they accepted at their public meeting on January 16, 1926.

The report, though addressed to McGilvrey but obviously written for Superintendent Riegel and the trustees, was a catchall of complaints and quibbles ranging from teachers not knowing how to take attendance or not caring about their students or not knowing their names or doing too much talking and not enough listening or not giving enough failing grades to classes being taught by unqualified staff, noisy construction interfering with learning, poor equipment in the training room, and Latin (a keystone of liberal arts education) offered as an alternative to manual training or home economics—all leading to the conclusion that such conditions were traceable to McGilvrey spending his energies on summer tours rather than on the school's primary mission. The report ended with the recommendation that Kent be struck from the list of approved teacher-training schools until "such time as executive problems are attacked vigorously and are in process of solution."[12]

This was what the trustees had been waiting for. Winters's report gave them a plausible reason for removing McGilvrey, it shifted the responsibility off their backs onto Riegel's, and it contradicted the letter from Columbia. It is one of the bitterest ironies of the machinations leading to McGilvrey's humiliation that the very individuals who should have rejoiced over Columbia's affirmation of the quality of education provided by the school entrusted to them were the very ones who most resented it. When they finally felt strong enough to formally acknowledge receipt of the letter, they feigned that it was too ambiguous for them to understand and forwarded it to Riegel for his interpretation, of which no record exists.[13]

On January 16, 1926, the trustees held their first public meeting in six months. All members were present—Rockwell, Coursen, and Cluff. (The governor had yet to replace either Wills or Maxwell, who had recently resigned.) The first order of business was to elect themselves president, vice president, and secretary, respectively. The second was to enact a script carefully drafted during executive sessions held on January 14–15, 1926.

According to the minutes, Rockwell "recited" (presumably from memory) the "understanding" reached at their secret meeting of July 29, 1925, and secretary Cluff then moved McGilvrey's dismissal on the grounds that his unauthorized absence from campus and his failure to inform the board of his departure constituted "an unpardonable affront and violation of all customs, ethics and responsibilities with respect to his duties as an employee and agent of this board of Trustees in the state of Ohio." The motion carried unanimously.

Then they voted to fire business manager William Van Horn and the matron of Moulton Hall and, without explanation, established the crackbrained, unenforceable policy of firing any school employee "who may be subject to the least criticism by the general public, departments or officers of the State of Ohio, or members of the Board of Trustees, or the faculty of the school, or students thereof." After forswearing any part in the exchange program with Cambridge University, they concluded the meeting by formally appointing T. Howard Winters acting president, which put Kent State College completely into the waiting hands of the state superintendent of public instruction, Vernon M. Riegel.

Although the trustees did not spotlight Winters's report in framing the dismissal charge, it gave them the hook on which they hung McGilvrey: the January 26 minutes attribute his major offense—the unauthorized absence from campus—to the summer tours, especially the European tour planned for 1926. They focused on the "affront" to the board of his going abroad without board permission rather than claiming that the tours had negatively affected the educational quality of the institution. They probably wanted to avoid the quality standards issue because of the letter from Columbia, which spooked any such claim.

When reported on January 16, 1926, McGilvrey's dismissal brought a storm of outraged protests, especially over the reason the board gave for taking such radical action. How could a board that had been absent for six months summarily fire someone for being absent for six weeks? Three days after his appointment as acting president, on January 19, 1926, Winters faced the faculty and student body in the chapel-cum-assembly room on the top floor of Merrill Hall. The shock waves from the news of the firing were still rocking campus and town when word of the assembly went out, and within hours a near-hysterical mood seems to have developed. Scary rumors spread that students were plotting to greet Winters with rotten eggs, and professors spent their early-morning class sessions calming seething passions and urging responsible behavior.

Winters was led into the high-voltage assembly by an improbable praetorian guard of male professors who flanked him while he spoke, poised to repel assaults on his person. After Professor H. D. Byrne had calmed the audience a bit by reminding everyone that Winters had not fired McGilvrey, Winters took the lectern. His aim seems to have been to establish a disciplined order appropriate to effective teaching and learning, but where tact and diplomacy were called for, he was insensitive and pugnacious. Instead of telling the students he understood their concerns and assuring them he had their welfare at heart, he told them, in essence, to forget all about a liberal arts college because Kent was going to remain a normal school for good. Considering his maladroitness, it's surprising no rotten eggs were directed his way, though loud hisses were.[14]

The next day's *Kent Tribune* reported that Winters's remarks confirmed widespread suspicions that it was William Oxley Thompson who had engineered McGilvrey's removal. (Not to steal any of Thompson's thunder, but the immediate agent of McGilvrey's downfall was Winters's exacting and inflexible puppet-master, Vernon M. Riegel. And in the tumultuous days ahead, Riegel would crack the standards whip over Winters's head with the same single-minded zeal he had devoted to McGilvrey.) The alumni outcry accusing the trustees of various outrages and calling for their dismissal grew so loud in subsequent days that it finally reached the ear of Governor Donahey in Columbus, who came to Kent to investigate.

On February 15, after hearing the trustees' defense, the governor asked if any witnesses wished to testify against them. When no one spoke up, Rockwell, heretofore one of the accused, appointed himself prosecutor and turned the hearing into "a grand and glittering" travesty, according to the *Akron Beacon Journal* of February 16, 1926. The governor then dismissed all complaints against the trustees, though he did fault them for not holding a public meeting for half a year prior to discharging McGilvrey. Cluff explained that, after deciding to remove McGilvrey at their July 1925 meeting, the trustees hadn't wanted to meet with him until they were "ready to notify Mr. McGilvrey of their stand." Then Rockwell said McGilvrey had become too controversial. Having "justly earned the title of the 'Stormy Petrel of Ohio Education,'" Rockwell said, McGilvrey had to go "for the good of the institution."[15]

The spirit of hail-fellow camaraderie that presided over the conclusion of the hearing continued through the ensuing private dinner at the Franklin Hotel, on the corner of Main and Depeyster, and spread wide its healing wings over the campus that night, as the governor and Rockwell, new president of the trustees, outdid each other in assuring a crowd of students and faculty that Kent State College was standing tiptoe on the threshold of a new era of peace, harmony, and infinite expansion.

Three

TURBULENCE AND FRUSTRATION

{ 1926–1936 }

But formidable obstacles barred access to that happy vision. For one, Riegel was determined to remake Kent in his own image. On his orders, Acting President Winters proposed a host of major reforms that, in addition to adding faculty, would have emphasized manual training, physical education, and home economics at the expense of agriculture, art, music, and commerce. They would have made testing, rather than learning, the aim of teaching and paid for it by hiking student registration fees to $10 per quarter.

While Winters's abrupt personality irritated some faculty, it repelled students who were used to McGilvrey's warmth and informality. Restive students found a voice for their discontent when a new campus newspaper appeared on February 25, 1926. Student-run and student-financed, the *Searchlight* filled the news void that had existed ever since the *Kentonian* had morphed into a literary magazine. The *Searchlight*'s debut issue declared that for too long students had been kept ignorant of matters vitally important to them and that because all students had the right of free expression on any "matter which pertains to college life," their voice would speak boldly through its columns.

For the next five months the *Searchlight* provided a mix of mundane items (the cost of women's "shingle bob" haircuts and parking regulations on Front Campus and freshman hazing) and sharp attacks on administration policies. At first the administration tried wishing the paper away, but it dropped all pretense of unconcern when the paper assailed the rigid grading formula Riegel was trying to foist on the faculty: 7 percent As; 24 percent Bs; 35 percent Cs; 24 percent Ds; 7 percent Fs. Winters's disclaimer that the grading scale would not apply in all instances did not quell student objections.

When a report by the registrar showed that the faculty was winking at his grading scale, Riegel came huffing and puffing to campus. In a series of closed-door meetings with small groups, he "tongue-lashed" faculty for intransigence and insubordination, trying to bully them into accepting his plan.[1] When the grading scale was formally unveiled on May 15, 1926, *Searchlight*'s editors called it mindless, counterproductive and predicted no one would accept it. Then the May 22 issue shocked the campus with an account of how the editor and associate editor had been cross-questioned by "state officials" about the paper's stance on the grading formula. But, still not browbeaten, in their next issue on July 1 the editors flanked the paper's masthead with defiant mottoes: "For Kent State *University*" and "Fearless Debate on All Topics."

Stronger stuff came in the July 15 issue when the editors scorched both Riegel and Winters, declaring that the school must abandon "mechanical" theories of education and return to its "old ideal." These touchstones of the McGilvrey era enraged Riegel. With C. L. Ulery, his new assistant, in tow, Riegel bucketed up to campus where he grilled the paper's editors behind closed doors for two hours. But the paper's next issue on July 22 boldly reaffirmed its pledge to continue sailing under the banner of free and fearless discussion of all matters affecting the school. Whereupon, Riegel, baying "insubordination," summarily suspended *Searchlight* editor Walter Jantz.

Jantz was gone, but the way and the why of his removal put the school back in the headlines. Area newspapers titillated readers with rehashes of Kent's history of scandals, power struggles, and investigations, all now topped by the alarming gorgon of state censorship. No sooner had Kent's registrar pooh-poohed the censorship charge than Riegel shut down the *Searchlight* and replaced it on July 28, 1926, with a new campus newspaper, the *Kent Stater,* funded by student fees and dedicated to publishing "clean and accurate news free from scandal and sensation."

By this time Winters's nerves were shot. His physician, diagnosing him as verging on a breakdown, prescribed prolonged rest. Prepared for every eventuality, Riegel replaced him with his new assistant, Ulery. Thus the school found itself in the embarrassing position of having two temporary acting presidents because one was temporarily unable to act. Small wonder that many observers and friends of the school fretted that too many hands were tussling for the tiller while the school was drifting. Newspaper editorials demanded that the trustees find a permanent president to steer the ship before it foundered.

The board promptly demonstrated that it was the principal obstacle in the school's struggle to enter the post-McGilvrey world of peace and harmony envisioned by Rockwell and Donahey. With McGilvrey gone, Rockwell and Cluff, sturdy allies despite belonging to rival political parties, ruled the board like medieval barons, until they fell out over their most urgent task.

It began over the selection of a permanent president. A panel of two eminent college presidents, with Riegel as adviser, selected three finalists from 100 applicants—David Allen Anderson, head of education and psychology at Penn State; Charles Skinner, professor of education at New York University; and T. Howard Winters, recovered acting president. After the board had met with Anderson and Skinner, Rockwell pushed hard for Anderson, who was chosen in July 1926 and given a hefty salary. But Cluff voted for Winters, with whom he had worked closely on school business matters. History is mute about what caused the split between the board's two strong men, but it would not offend common sense to point to the aphrodisiacal effect of power on unbridled egos. This was certainly true of Rockwell who gave Anderson a package of perks that proved to be an exploding cigar.[2]

At the next meeting, Cluff struck back. He conducted an inquisition into the board's awarding of contracts, focusing on the expenses run up in remodeling part of Moulton Hall as temporary quarters for Anderson and his wife. His barbed questioning led to a shouting match in which he and Rockwell exchanged personal insults. After the meeting, Cluff shot down to Columbus where he filed a formal complaint with the state auditor, who dispatched his assistant, Charles Miller, to Kent to examine the school's business accounts. It was when Miller released his report that the cigar exploded in Rockwell's face. Miller confirmed all of Cluff's charges: the board had illegally awarded contracts—$5,000 for coal as well as $4,000 for furnishings in Anderson's suite—and illegally paid $100 for one of Anderson's hotel bills, $350 for his reception, and $400 for his old car.[3]

Shaken, Rockwell immediately wired his friend Governor Donahey to come up and defuse the explosive situation. Held behind closed doors, with the press locked out of adjoining rooms, the governor's hearing reminded the *Akron Beacon Journal* reporter of a Star Chamber proceeding, except for two borrowed spittoons stationed either side of the tobacco-chewing governor.[4] That is the sum total of all the public ever learned of what transpired in that room.

When the door of the hearing room finally swung open, Rockwell and Cluff stepped out, fast friends once more, and the governor informed reporters that every issue in Miller's report had been satisfactorily explained. And, he assured them, Miller would file a "supplemental statement" to that effect. But Miller, interviewed in Columbus the next day, announced that, since his original report was accurate, he would not alter it in any respect.[5] Though the trustees were not rebuked or disciplined for breaking the law, the board's moral authority was severely damaged by the affair. And the secrecy of the hearing confirmed the students' feeling that they were ignorant pawns in a power struggle among adults who were only nominally concerned with their welfare.

As for the board's choice to succeed McGilvrey, the only surviving photograph of the fifty-two-year-old Anderson reveals an owlish-looking man with a round head and face, small features, and half-shut eyes behind wire-framed spectacles. His credentials were sound: a long teaching career at all levels; a reputable book on Norway's school system; and, most potently, a scholarly port and mien. During his brief time as Kent's president, he introduced significant curricular reforms, conformed standards with state guidelines, added several talented faculty with doctorates, and thrust scholarship into the limelight. All this fit his resume. The problem was his personality, his temperament, his disposition. He was cold and suspicious, and so petty and vengeful that he made many faculty and even some students pine for the Winters of their discontent.

Anderson's reign of terror began with a faculty member's attempt to curry favor with Anderson by dispelling the cloud left hanging over Anderson's head by the governor's investigation of the board dispute. A professor circulated a petition declaring faculty support of Anderson, but two department heads, who had been candidates for the presidency, publicly accused some petition circulators of trying to bully them by warning that they would be "given one more opportunity later" if they refused to sign the petition. And after rejecting several other solicitations, they were indeed dismissed—"not-re-employed," Anderson said. The trustees denied them an opportunity to plead their case.[6]

So, his axe still smoking, Anderson, with one fell chop, cut off the entire Department of Commerce, both its head (another of eight Kent faculty who had sought the presidency) and its two instructors, on the grounds of "insufficient [student] demand" for the program, though it had grown by 1,500 percent in two years.[7]

The fear virus that had infected the whole faculty spread to the students. What was happening? Some talked boycott, some strike. When the *Red Flame*, a satirical student newspaper, appeared in May, Anderson immediately expelled the editors, one of whom, the fearless Margaret Hayes, had been famously grilled as coeditor of the *Searchlight* and, later, had served as the *Kent Stater*'s first editor. Hayes's banishment squelched all talk of striking, but many students signed a petition pledging not to return to Kent.[8]

And so, throughout most of the academic year 1927–28, the campus went from crisis to crisis. Rancor and resentment poisoned faculty relations. While faculty and administration circled each other warily, the students scorned an administration that ruled by fiat and fear and a board too aloof and autocratic to care about them.

Meanwhile, Rockwell and Cluff had their eyes on loftier matters. Undeterred by the groundswell of antagonism against them and Anderson, they were divvying up two buildings under construction. The library had taken Rockwell's fancy from the start. He took a hand in its conception, exhorting the architect to "dream a work of art." He saw it as an outer expression of his inner devotion to the school and thought it should bear his name. Cluff, a short-necked, high-waisted man of business, was untrammeled by aesthetic longings; for him, having one's name on a building was simply one of the perks of being a trustee.

Throughout this period, the campus generated as much news as war-ravaged China, according to the *Akron Beacon Journal* of June 14, 1927, and it was the "same sort of news too—war correspondence." What makes good newspaper copy, however, was bad news for an institution still trying to get its fair share of state funds. Bad news throttles enrollment. Once again the public school superintendents fulminated over Kent's disarray and threatened to discourage their students from attending Kent and to refuse to hire its graduates. Enrollment in the 1927 summer and fall terms plummeted.[9]

In June Anderson axed three more instructors, demoted three others, and replaced several long-serving professors and administrators, some immediately and without warning.[10] But two weeks later he went too far. He asked the trustees to let him discharge three veteran staff members. One of them was the most beloved campus figure, Alex Whyte, groundbreaker, custodian, coach, teacher, and fraternity adviser. Anderson accused him of leaving several campus buildings unlocked. The trustees, who had been growing increasingly disturbed by Anderson's actions and their effect on campus morale, balked at this. Even Rockwell decided that Anderson had to go. Cluff, exercising the same machine-gun style he used in the McGilvrey coup, charged Anderson with 140 offenses.

Despite the urgency for a fast resolution of the matter, Anderson's "trial" limped along from August 22 to September 19, 1927, concluding with the traditional academic face-saving compromise that conceals the real state of affairs from the public, which has a right to know about the conduct of its institutions: Anderson was permitted to resign, and the board declared all 140 offenses resolved.[11] Presumably, despite the laundry list of charges and the long "trial," Anderson just up and resigned for no good reason after only two years in office.

During Anderson's term, a man-on-the-street survey by the *Beacon Journal* on June 14, 1927, found that an overwhelming majority of Kent citizens wanted a completely new board of trustees and the return of John McGilvrey. The paper concluded that the school's greatest need was for leaders "versed in the problems of education, untied by politics and not athirst for the glory of having their names carved on expensive buildings."

Probably because of the daily dose of bad publicity, only thirteen aspirants for the presidency sent applications when the board announced its search early in 1928. Fortunately, one was eminently qualified by experience, education, and temperament, James Osro Engleman, who was selected on April 10, 1928. A fifty-five-year-old native of Indiana, Engleman was a veteran teacher and administrator and a prolific writer. After graduating from an eight-grade rural school, he had principaled local high schools while earning a two-year normal school degree at Terre Haute and a bachelor's at Indiana University. After several stints as school superintendent, both before and after earning a master's degree at the University of Chicago, he had won a national reputation (and an honorary doctorate) for services to the National Education Association. He left Indiana for Ohio in 1927 partly to do doctoral work at OSU and partly to escape the wrath of the powerful Ku Klux Klan, which he had courageously denounced.

"Big Jim" Engleman was, in the parlance of the day, a fine figure of a man, standing well over six feet with a big-boned, well-fed, shambly body, an important nose, and gentle eyes. A lover of poetry and the classics, he had the appearance and presence of a Roman senator and was an orator in the grand tradition. Pious and scrupulously upright, he disdained cussing, strong drink, and the New Deal as much as he delighted in a good cigar and an indulgent audience. Both as lay preacher and public lecturer, he loved nothing better than to hold forth on moral education and classical values. As man and administrator, he was McGilvrey's opposite. Whereas McGilvrey was inclined to leap before he looked, Engleman would look and look but never leap—though he could be gently nudged forward.

Engleman's path to Kent had been made smooth by an Ohio State friend, John L. Clifton, who replaced Riegel as superintendent of education in 1927. This gave Engleman something McGilvrey never had, a powerful advocate (instead of an enemy) in Columbus. Nor would Engleman have to cope for long with the meddlesome Cluff, who resigned from the board in August 1928 after his business, health, and reputation went south; or with Rockwell, who rotated off the board, unlamented, the next year.

So as if opening a new door onto a brighter future, on March 22, 1929, Kent State staged its first full-regalia inauguration ceremony for Engleman. For the grand event, some 1,600 guests, among them representatives and dignitaries from sixty colleges, came to campus. And the governor came, too, whispering in Engleman's ear the good news that he would soon sign the Emmons-Hanna Bill that would grant Kent a liberal arts college.

After ceremonies dedicating the Cluff Teacher Training School building (without Cluff) and the Rockwell Library (with an emotional Rockwell), Engleman delivered a heartfelt statement of his view of education's moral dimension. To become effective, knowledge "must become wisdom," he said, and to that end a normal school must educate teachers to pass on "their vision of life as a unity" by interpreting "the meanings, the hidden implications," of facts and showing how they bear "upon eternal verities." His paean to normal school education was doubtless tinged with melancholy, for he already knew that Kent's days as a normal school were numbered.

. . .

A grassroots campaign for a liberal arts college started in Kent in January 1929 probably at the urging of John Edward McGilvrey, who gave a talk to the Ravenna Rotary on January 22 trying to enlist it in the cause. Kent State's trustees officially welcomed the idea, and after that an energetic assortment of Kent service organizations formed the Liberal Arts Committee chaired by Chamber president William Reed but led by McGilvrey. Volunteers sent thousands of letters and telegrams and made hundreds of phone calls to rally support among service organizations, business and political leaders, and schools and colleges from across the northern and central sections of the state, urging them to press state legislators to lend their support.

Akron-area senator V. D. Emmons offered to submit a bill calling for both Bowling Green and Kent to be changed into state universities empowered to offer graduate work as well as award bachelor degrees in arts and science.[12] Once again, the coupling of Bowling Green and Kent in an education bill paid off when Bowling Green's president added his powerful voice to the growing chorus calling for the bill's passage.

In Kent, however, though the move had strong support among most townspeople, students, and faculty, a significant minority of professors quietly opposed it. And so did President Engleman, very quietly. Like them, he feared that a university with a liberal arts college would dilute the school's original mission to train teachers for the public schools. He opposed it as well because of his ingrained conservatism—he disliked change—and because he had come to Kent to head a teacher-training school, a task for which he believed he still had the requisite energy and skills—for consolidation (to build on McGilvrey's groundwork) and for accommodation (to pull in harness with state officials)—to be an effective leader. He understood enough about the complexities of a university, with its metastasizing curricular and personnel exigencies and budgetary nightmares, to sense that grafting a university onto a normal school would inevitably compromise his loyalty to teacher training while diffusing and overtaxing his resources.

After the introduction of the Emmons-Hanna Bill late in January 1929, the pressure on Engleman to declare himself built steadily. Alumni, civic leaders, and citizens, as well as his own board and many professors, expected him to declare his support, while a sizeable number of teacher-training faculty urged him to speak against it. The longer he remained silent, the more uncertain both sides became, and the more he dithered. He knew full well that he could not go on saying nothing about something on which so many looked to him for leadership. Yet he could not bring himself to say what he really thought for fear it would weaken his presidency.

At last, on February 1, 19129 he sent students and alumni an open, but far from candid, letter. Writing from a vantage point far above the pro-and-con forces, he loftily summarized the arguments for the bill but conspicuously said not a word concerning the opponents' arguments or his own views. The letter fooled no one, pleased some, puzzled others, and irritated the rest. When the Senate education committee learned that Kent's president had withheld his endorsement, it erased the controversial word "university" and sent the amended bill to the full Senate, where it was approved.

During the tense days preceding the final debate and vote in the House, supporters and opponents beset Engleman at every turn, some pleading with him to speak out and kill the bill, while others, guessing his personal preference, talked up the benefits the bill would bring to campus and town. To speak or not to speak—it was a painful predicament for a man so fond of public speaking. The president's nerves beginning to fray, friend and physician A. O. DeWeese, fearing for Engleman's health, insisted that he hide out on the top floor of DeWeese's house (next to the Robin Hood bar). There, while his secretary told callers he was out of town, and with his meals cooked and carried up the stairs by Mrs. DeWeese, he holed up while legislators wrangled over the bill, finally passing it on March 19, 1929.

Ultimately, the changes wrought by the Emmons-Hanna legislation reached far beyond those authorized by the bill. Strictly interpreted, Emmons-Hanna changed Kent from a normal school to a college, authorizing courses leading to a B.S. in education and giving trustees authority, on the faculty's recommendation, to confer honorary degrees of the sort given by "colleges of liberal arts in the United States."[13] All these powers, however, had already been assumed and exercised by Kent's trustees. What was new was a provision authorizing courses leading to bachelor degrees in arts and science and permission to hire additional instructors to teach them. To this the trustees applied their maximalist principle of interpretation and construed the authority to offer courses in arts and sciences as license for establishing an arts college—which they told Engleman to do immediately.

If the board interpreted boldly, however, Engleman proceeded cautiously. And if the board could not leash the greyhound McGilvrey, neither could it hurry the tortoise Engleman. Between 1929 and

1931 he introduced just nine new arts courses: four in Latin, two in philosophy, and one in psychology. His first catalog stated the arts college's purpose negatively (to train those *not* planning to become teachers) but later accented the affirmative as the college gained traction. In 1931 he split the school into two administrative divisions but let another year pass before naming their deans: Oscar H. Williams in Liberal Arts and John L. Blair in Education.

Thereafter, Kent State developed in the classic academic fashion, by parturition: for example, the philosophy, journalism, and speech departments grew out of English and education; the French department added German and Spanish; the economics and political science departments sprang from history and sociology, respectively. As the curriculum grew, so did the number of instructors with doctorates, and an honors program began in 1933 as part of a campuswide focus on scholarship. In recognition of Kent's scholarly progress, two important accrediting agencies accepted Kent into full membership: the Ohio College Association, in 1931, and the North Central Association of Colleges and Secondary Schools, in 1932.

Yet it was history, far more than Engleman's caution, that stalled Kent's progress in the 1930s. In the spring of 1929, Coolidge-Hoover prosperity had been at flood tide, with stock prices giddily high as bankers emptied their vaults to finance stocks purchased on margin. The gap between the very rich and everyone else yawned wider than ever before in American history. Then, in October 1929, stock prices had nose-dived. The economy collapsed, and with it the dream of boundless, endless, effortless wealth. Among the most expressive symbols of the Great Depression were the clusters of jerry-built shacks cobbled together from flattened tin cans, odds and ends of pine crates, tarpaper, and cardboard set up under bridges, in garbage dumps, along railroad sidings, and on vacant lots. Named for the man who presided over the catastrophe, they were a daily reminder of the disparity between national pretense and performance.

Kent State's Hooverville appeared in 1931 when some hard-up students moved into a tumbledown outbuilding once part of the old Kent farm in the woods behind Moulton Hall. This gave school officials a wince of embarrassment, but when in succeeding months more students moved in and named it "Bachelor Hall" and the press reported it, they did what city officials often did with their Hoovervilles: evicted the occupants and tore it down. The Great Depression affected all aspects of campus life. It halted all progress toward advancing McGilvrey's fifty-year building plan. In fact, Engleman's only building achievement was putting the classical façade on the front of the Administration Building (1931). Even the curriculum was affected, with the elimination of the once-popular agriculture program. Why would anyone train to teach agriculture when farmers could not sell what they grew? Engleman earmarked the farmland along Summit Street for future use as a sports area and decided to turn the college farmhouse at the foot of Summit Street into a dormitory for African American women. He forced the project through despite opposition from the local NAACP and other groups that charged him with Jim Crowism. Unwritten segregation of the races was endemic throughout the country, even on a campus in Kent, which had been part of the Underground Railroad.

Shrinking state support forced Engleman to eliminate one of the traditional two summer terms and cut faculty salaries. He paid faculty and staff in scrip. He hiked registration fees from $10 to $15—more than some could afford—and levied a special $25 registration fee on out-of-state students. With more than a million Ohio workers jobless, only the luckiest on-campus students could find part-time work in cafeterias or as department secretaries. He cut the cost of dormitory meals to $4 a week, but that was still too high for many students, who ended up dining on coffee and stale crullers or care packages from home.

Kent's academic year enrollments, however, climbed between 1929 and 1937 (save for the bleakest years 1931 and 1932) partly because the school's relatively low fees made it cheaper for some Ohioans to go to college than to cool their heels at home—idle, aimless, hopeless. But no doubt contributing to this rise in enrollment was the allure of the new arts and science offerings, as well as Kent's location as the hub of a wheel of large cities. It was cheaper to commute daily from, say, Youngstown or Canton or Cleveland than to pay dormitory fees. It was at this time that Kent began to change from being largely a residential to a more commuting campus.

The Great Depression was a state of mind as well as an economic phenomenon—a state of fear, gloom, self-doubt, and desperation. In April 1933, the state legislature's welfare committee released a report detailing scandalous overcrowding in Ohio's mental hospitals, which had long been inadequate and neglected, and announced a desperate remedy: convert one of the state's normal schools into a mental asylum. After all, there was an urgent need for more space to house and care for mental patients, and there was an overplus of unemployed school teachers—4,000, in fact—so why maintain a facility for training more when the facility was so adaptable to patient needs? Wasting no time, an inspection team scheduled a visit to Kent on May 4—a prophetic date in the school's story.

Nothing could have stirred the fighting blood of Kent's friends and supporters more quickly. The head of the Chamber of Commerce appointed a committee chaired by Martin L. Davey, candidate for governor in 1929, to organize the campus and town into a pressure group. As with the waving of a wand, telegrams, letters, and phone calls protesting the plan were bombarding the Statehouse, while newspapers derided the idea as chuckleheaded. On May 1 Kent students, teachers, alumni, and friends jammed into the Auditorium to hear fired-up speakers such as Davey, alumni president Otto J. Korb, and faculty denounce the plan.

Engleman's fears that the inspection tour was no more than a smoke-screen for a decision already made—Ohio University and Miami were sacrosanct, and Bowling Green had far fewer facilities than Kent—seemed to be confirmed when, at the end of the tour on May 4, he had to stand by and listen to the committee chair say that since Kent had "the most modern buildings," it was "most adaptable to welfare work." And the final nail seemed to be driven into Kent's coffin the next day, when, back in Columbus, the chair declared that one college campus looked as if it had been meant to be a mental asylum.[14]

But even as a fresh round of protests was being readied by Kent's supporters, the trustees pulled a surprise, passing a resolution that assured the community that Kent State was in no danger of being "abolished or seriously impaired" and called for a stop to all protests.[15] Presumably David Ladd Rockwell had contacted friends in the Statehouse and learned that the welfare committee was drowning in the deluge of protests. The welfare committee soon surrendered to the political demographics: college students and their parents outnumbered the state's mental patients.

But that summer, just as the campus was getting its bearings after the latest scare, the trustees put Kent back in the headlines. Readers of the June 27, 1933, *Ravenna Evening Record* were startled to read that two trustees, Lake County superintendent John. R. Williams and David Ladd Rockwell, had demanded Engleman's resignation at the board's meeting on June 20. They accused him of being a "weak" administrator: specifically, that he failed to maintain faculty support, keeping Kent State from getting adequate funding; that he failed to handle the athletic department, contributing to the dismal record of the football program.[16] The ouster attempt was stymied, however, because trustees E. L. Bowsher, Ashland schools' superintendent, and C. E. Oliver, an East Palestine newspaperman, dismissed their arguments as groundless, and the fifth trustee, Canton teacher Alma M. Zinninger (Kent's first graduate to sit on the board and its first woman member), abstained.

Rockwell instigated this attempt to remove Engleman. Though widely regarded in the area as a troublemaker when he rotated off the board in 1929, Rockwell was named to the board just two years later, in 1931, and there, under the firm hand of board president rubber magnate Charles W. Seiberling, he had sat for two pacific years, to all appearances Engleman's supporter. However, it was Rockwell's curse to be too small for a big pond and too large for a small one, like the board of trustees, where he tended to turn into a hammerhead shark. That is what happened soon after Seiberling retired following the mental asylum brouhaha.

By the time this trustee convulsion hit the headlines, *Kent* and *trouble* had become interchangeable in Columbus, so when the news reached the Statehouse, the Senate promptly appointed an investigative committee headed by Coshocton senator Will P. Haynes, who telegraphed the trustees to come down and explain themselves. Eager to seize the advantage of first impressions, Bowsher and Oliver set out immediately. Engleman and his friend Seiberling also drove down to give the committee their views. Bowsher's and Oliver's quick departure, however, played into Rockwell's hands. He remained in Kent, dodging a sheriff's deputy with a subpoena, and devised a dazzling coup de théâtre that would demonstrate his political wizardry.

And so it transpired that at 2:00 P.M., June 29, 1933, even as Bowsher and Oliver were voicing their ardent support for Engleman and Seiberling was blaming the whole mess on Rockwell's penchant for meddling, Rockwell himself, together with Williams and their recent convert Zinninger, was holding a trustees' meeting on campus, a meeting scheduled a week earlier—one Bowsher and Oliver surely assumed was superceded by the senate investigation. The three members present constituting a majority, and thus a quorum, elected Williams acting president in Bowsher's absence, then voted to fire Engleman and hire Berea superintendent Alfred G. Yawberg as president for four years (at a far lower salary than Engleman's), beginning forthwith. And on that cue the smiling new fourth president of Kent State College sprang (out of whose hat is unclear) into the room waving his signed letter of acceptance. The meeting lasted seven minutes.[17]

In Columbus, news of his dismissal reached Engleman and this gentle man of peace, who had ducked and dithered in indecision to the point of collapse over the bill to make the school a college, discovered his inner lion. Roaring that he would have to be forcibly heaved from office, he bounded back to campus and ordered a policeman to stand outside the presidential office in the atrium of the Administration Building and, at all costs, keep the usurper Yawberg from entering the presidential quarters the following morning.[18]

Later that morning another lion, far younger but from the same brave pride, began roaring. *Kent Stater* editor Glenwood Oyster signed his name to an editorial endorsing Engleman and circulated a pro-Engleman petition that eventually garnered 675 student signatures and then led a student delegation down to Columbus, hoping someone in authority would be interested in hearing their thoughts on the matter. And the faculty voted 71–1 for Engleman on a secret ballot. All through the day, caravans of campus and townspeople caterpillared to Columbus in support of Engleman.

The incident, which began as melodrama and modulated into light comedy as events began to smile on Engleman, now found its natural equilibrium as low farce. Obedient to the subpoena the deputy had finally thrust on him after the rump meeting of the trustees, Rockwell motored down to Columbus. But before he could step foot into the Statehouse, a policeman collared him, hauled him to the police station, and booked him on a check-kiting charge that had been filed, with great glee, by Hale B. Thompson, a respected Kent druggist who had grown weary of waiting for Rockwell to make the check good. Word sped to the Senate chamber where the committee on gubernatorial appointments was going over a list of nominees whose appointments required Senate confirmation, a tedious task prompted by the discovery that Rockwell's nomination as trustee had never been confirmed by the Senate. Now, all Rockwell's political connections served him naught: How would it look if the Senate confirmed a man in police custody for check kiting? The Senate voted 16–1 against confirmation. This removed him from the board. And, proving that bad news travels on faster feet than good, Rockwell was still sitting in the police station, nonplused by the passing of his parade, when he heard that he'd been tossed out of his small pond.

In Kent the next day, July 1, the abashed trustees voted 3–1 to rescind its action of the day before, with Trustee Williams abstaining. In reversing the action, the board removed Yawberg from the president's office—even before he had time to enter it—and put Engleman back in it, though he had never left it. For reasons never revealed, the board cut Engleman's salary by $700. Soon thereafter the Senate confirmed the governor's appointment of Cleveland judge Carl D. Friedbolin to replace Rockwell with the mandate to get the college off the front pages.[19]

Following Rockwell's departure and Engleman's restoration, and in response to the entreaties of the Alumni Association and other civic groups, the trustees voted, on March 12, 1934, to change the name of the training school to the John E. McGilvrey Training School Building. This would officially honor the man who had never abandoned his commitment to the school he had founded even though the trustees had humiliated him and vindictively forbidden him to step onto campus for eight years. (Cluff's name would remain, however, because it was carved in stone on the building's pediment.) They also voted to name the ironwork arch at the corner of Main and Lincoln the May H. Prentice Memorial Gateway to honor the beloved teacher who had entered the profession in 1873 and taught at Kent from 1912 to 1930. The ailing Prentice gratefully accepted the honor, which she described as symbolic of "*this* college as an entrance into the larger life."[20] But McGilvrey demurred. He feared that substituting his name for Cluff's would stoke another controversy, and he wanted no taint of vindictiveness to stain whatever honor came his way. So, on July 9, 1934, the trustees accepted another solicitation from the Alumni Association and did something far better. They awarded McGilvrey the faculty rank of President Emeritus and gave him a cubbyhole office in the mezzanine of the Administration Building, where he was often visited by admiring students.

While Engleman seems to have thought that McGilvrey's brief was to close the breach between the alumni of his era and those of Engleman's, McGilvrey, of course, interpreted his role dynamically, as nothing less than marshaling Kent's 7,000 alumni into an army that would lead the institution on a forced march into its promised future. Throughout his exile he had kept in touch with alumni and local civic groups, which he still saw as the engines for driving Kent State forward.

Thus, only a few months after returning to campus, he had cast a tight-woven network of alumni committees over all of northeastern Ohio.[21] And from these units emerged a consensus that Kent should have two goals: first, hire a "coach of prominence" who would recruit promising athletes by offering scholarships; and, second, make Kent State College into a university with graduate programs leading to master's degrees. The second idea was vintage McGilvrey, but the first represented a compromise on his part. Although like all schoolmen of his generation he subscribed to the classical ideal of *mens sana in corpore sano* and encouraged intramural competition, he saw no point in varsity sports. But now he appreciated its political value to an institution aspiring to become a university. The attempt to oust Engleman doubtless reminded him of the price he had paid for opposing it.

A small blizzard of resolutions from alumni groups endorsing these goals gained student support and eventually forced the trustees to take notice. On January 15, 1935, they told Engleman to hire an outside man who would serve as head football coach and athletic director; they also authorized twelve athletic scholarships, the first for the academic year. Word of the search went out, and a flock of applications flew in. Among them were from such well-known names as Amos Alonzo Stagg Jr. of the University of Chicago, Sid Gillman of OSU, Ray Watts of Baldwin-Wallace, Stuart Holcomb of Findley, and some locally celebrated high school coaches. At long last Kent seemed about to find the man who would lead it to football glory.

But when, on February 11, Engleman announced that he had hired Ashland High coach George Donald "Rosy" Starn as head football coach and athletic director, there issued forth from the collective throat of students and alumni the howl of "George Who?" If Starn was a "name," why hadn't anyone heard it before? Many scoffed that Starn was far less of a "name" than Joe Begala, their current and very competent coach whose name supposedly lacked Starn's luster. Outraged disappointment brought a crowd of some 400 students together on Front Campus. They paraded raucously down to the Captain Brady café, across from the Prentice Gate, where they shouted and booed in protest. When they learned that trustee president Bowsher had rejected a petition signed by 350 students because it came "too late," they stomped and shouted around Front Campus again and buried an effigy of Engleman.[22] (They did not know that the trustees did have a "name" coach in mind. True, it was a name not known to many, but it was well known to the only person whose opinion mattered, Starn's good friend trustee president Bowsher.) Demonstrations continued until Engleman called a special assembly in the Auditorium on February 14 at which he pleaded with them to give Starn a fair chance. But it was Starn's unaffected sincerity and his announcement that Begala would be his line coach that won their qualified support and eased tensions. Despite the controversy over his hiring, Starn was an effective football coach and athletic director. His "high-scoring" football teams compiled a 34–28–2 record during his eight-year tenure, while his basketball and baseball teams were equally strong.[23]

As for the goal of Kent's becoming a university, on Saturday, February 16, a month after the trustees rejected an alumni proposal for university status, McGilvrey met with the Alumni Association's central committee in the dining room of the Hotel Kent where they drafted proposals to change Kent from a college to a university, to authorize graduate courses leading to the master's degree, and, something new, to establish a business college to triangulate with the education and liberal arts colleges. Four days later alumnus and state representative from Ravenna Robert A. Jones dropped them into the House hopper, and a military-style campaign began. Influential graduates formed a legislative committee chaired by Karl Berns, while civic leaders mobilized Kent-area fraternal and professional organizations and a special committee enlisted most of Kent's 7,000 alumni. The Kent State University Committee opened offices above the Kent Theater, area newspaper editorials voiced support, and *Stater* editor Robert L. Baumgardner directed letter-writing and petition-signing offensives. All these forces generated enough heat, light, and noise to be felt, seen, and heard in far-off Bowling Green, and when the bills were amended to include Bowling Green, its supporters caught and spread the campaign fever throughout the northwest section of the state.[24]

The Ohio House passed the bills unanimously on April 6, and Akron senator Frank Wittemore guided them through the Senate with unanimous votes on May 15, 1935. Both McGilvrey and Engleman were present when the bills passed. And, proving that history has a sense of symmetry, the man who signed the legislation into law on May 17, 1935, was Governor Martin L. Davey, founder of the Board of Trade that brought the normal school to Kent.

Yet Davey's election to the governorship in 1934 proved to be more of a handicap than help to the new Kent State University. The unanimous vote that changed Kent into a university concealed significant opposition. As the bills moved toward passage, an inchoate dissatisfaction with them fermented among legislators of both parties, some motivated by sectional interests and some by personal animosity toward Davey. In politics there are no coincidences, only stratagems. How, asked his detractors, barely two months after Davey took office, did his city get its college turned into a university? The answer was obvious: Davey had mousetrapped the bill's opponents into voting for it by passing the word that, in order to protect his tree surgery school, he planned to veto it if it reached his desk.[25]

As a result of this political gamesmanship, Kent State University gained little benefit from having Davey in the governor's office. Even as the school was still adjusting to its new identity, the insane asylum threat suddenly rose up once again. The *Cleveland Plain Dealer* reported on August 27, 1935, that a special Ohio Government Survey Commission (under the sway of business interests) had concluded that because the cost of bringing Kent's plant and faculty into line with university standards could not be justified, it might recommend the institution's "discontinuance" and conversion into "another type [of facility] so badly needed." *Kent Courier-Tribune* publisher Albert C. Dix described the idea as a blatant political ploy to browbeat KSU into lowballing its appropriation requests.[26]

Dix was right. It was all about politics and money. For the 1935–36 academic year, OU asked for $389,000 and got $364,000, while Kent asked $501,000 for new construction and got a grand and gagging total of $975. And when Engleman went to Columbus to demand fairness, he was met with what the *Plain Dealer* described as "extremely rude and disrespectful treatment."[27] But the fierce intercession of Dix and Engleman did persuade Governor Davey to erase all building funds for OSU and OU, thus rendering to Kent a negative measure of justice—and thereby intensifying toxic interuniversity relations.

Engleman already had in hand a basic program for the new Graduate School. Much as he had opposed the college idea, he dutifully prepared the school for some of the necessary changes to come. He chaired a faculty committee that devised a curriculum of graduate courses that included four in education, three in physical education, and one each in manual training and advanced drama and theater education. The almost exclusive emphasis on education was evident in the Graduate School's mission statement: to provide the student with "a more comprehensive understanding of the nature and function of education and a greater effectiveness in teaching or in administration," a "more fundamental understanding and more thorough mastery of his major field's basic purpose," and a "furthering of his preparation for technical or professional pursuits."[28]

Graduate majors were authorized for the departments of biology, education and psychology, English, geography, health and physical education, history and social science, industrial arts, mathematics, and physical science (chemistry). Minors were approved for art, commerce, home economics, social science, and speech. Instead of creating new courses for the graduate program, however, Engleman's graduate council moved cautiously by piggybacking onto select upper-level undergraduate courses in various departments, denominating them as split-level classes and asterisking them to indicate graduate credit for extra work.

Still, many administrators and professors knew that Engleman's curriculum did not anticipate the painful wrenchings, the chill estrangements and dislocations, the rigor of new standards of performance exacted by the scholarly ideal. In fact, four days after the governor's pen turned Kent into a university, liberal arts dean Oscar H. Williams sounded this note of warning in the first Honors Day address. If Kent is "to attain the scholarly ideal" on which the "full stature of a real university" is predicated, he said, it "must devise something more intellectually stimulating" than it had thus far.[29]

The College of Business Administration did not open for business until the fall of 1936, when 185 students enrolled, but it responded with admirable creativity to the challenges. This was largely because of the farsightedness of Dean Arden L. Allyn, who had joined the faculty two years earlier. Convinced that a successful business career was grounded in an understanding of the human condition, he radically reoriented the business curriculum set up in 1924 away from the training of commercial public school teachers toward one devoted to preparing young men and women for business careers. Under his leadership, four departments and their curricula, leading to a B.S. in commerce, were established for accounting, banking and finance, general business, and marketing, plus one for a degree in secretarial science. Rejecting the principle of specialization inherent in professional schools, he sought to widen and enrich the students' range of knowledge and understanding by requiring all business students to take almost half their courses in the liberal arts, including a pioneering and highly influential course in business ethics conceived by philosophy head Maurice Baum.

There were other curricular innovations, including one in industrial organization and management (factory management) spearheaded by Goodrich executive and KSU trustee Joseph B. Hanan and another in personnel management designed by Donald E. Anthony and Hersel H. Hudson of the economics department. Enrollments increased so rapidly that within a few years the business college was one of the nation's largest and second only to OSU in the state.

For Kent, ahead was the great challenge of expanding and altering the school's mind-set as well as its curricula, of somehow changing an institution primarily keyed to professional training and only secondarily to subject matter. This would mean moving from asking and telling *how* something is done to asking the unpredicated *why* or *what* of human experience and the nature of reality. Kent faced the supreme educational challenge of developing an institution in which both undergraduate and graduate programs would progressively expand and deepen while faculty and students alike strove to reach the level of scholarly activity and performance intrinsic to the ancient tradition of a community of scholars from which the great universities of western civilization arose.

Kent as it was in 1910, at the intersection of Main and Water streets.

The Frank A. Merrill farm in Twin Lakes, the scene of the bluegill lunch.

Right: Cleveland architect George F. Hammond's plan for the normal school.

Below: Hammond's drawing of the facades of the first buildings.

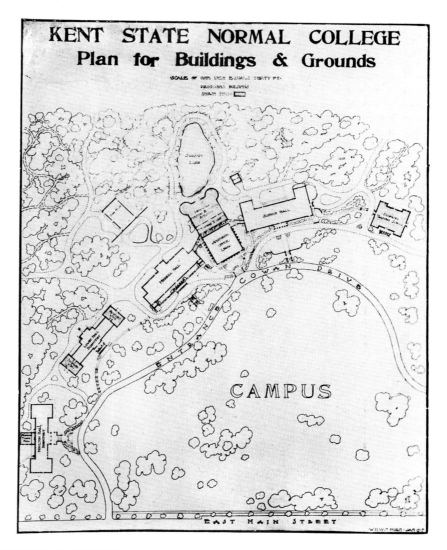

KENT STATE NORMAL COLLEGE
Plan for Buildings & Grounds

Left: A crew from the Davey Tree Company clears trees from the site where the school's first building, Merrill Hall, would be built.

Below: The Kent Farm's cottage and barn, future site of Rockwell Hall. Merrill and Lowry halls loom on the horizon; the dirt road in the foreground is East Main Street (1913).

Right: Lowry Hall, under construction in 1913.

Below: The school's first classroom building, Merrill Hall, named for trustee Frank A. Merrill. Summer school faculty and students gathered for the 1914 photo.

Left: Students learning in "The Tabernacle" (1914).

Below: A panorama of Kent's first buildings, ca. 1915. Left to right: Lowry Hall, Merrill Hall, the Administration Building, and Kent Hall.

Above: President McGilvrey
stands with his faculty and the
normal school's first graduating class in front of Merrill
Hall in 1914.

Right: Alexander Whyte
coached the school's first intercollegiate athletic team, the
Normal Nine, pictured here in
front of Merrill Hall in 1914.
Jack-of-all-trades, Whyte was
custodian, coach, play director, teacher, and fraternity
adviser.

Columbia University
in the City of New York

OFFICE OF UNIVERSITY ADMISSIONS

November 19, 1925

President John E. McGilvrey
Kent State Normal College
Kent, Ohio

My dear President McGilvrey

I take pleasure in advising you that the Kent State Normal College at Kent, Ohio, has been placed upon the list of normal schools and teachers colleges approved by Columbia University for admission to the Teachers College of Columbia University.

While we shall request that complete records be supplied for each candidate for admission the natural assumption is that every such candidate will be able to complete the minimum residence requirements for a Master's degree in a normal period of one year, assuming that the work done by the student has been completed in the institution whose degree the candidate holds. Our regulations do not permit the recognition of correspondence work nor of advanced credit assigned on the basis of state examinations or state certificate only.

Sincerely yours

Adam Leroy Jones
Director

P.S. It should be understood that paragraph 2 above refers to candidates who have received your Bachelor's degree.

COPY

The important letter to President McGilvrey from A. L. Jones, director of admissions at Columbia University, informing McGilvrey that Kent's graduates were "approved for admission" to Columbia's prestigious graduate school of education.

AN IDEAL SUMMER IN EUROPE

75 Days—June 19th to Sept. 2nd, 1926

EUROPEAN EDUCATIONAL TOUR

Organized by
KENT STATE NORMAL COLLEGE
Affiliated With
THE STUDENTS' TRAVEL CLUB OF AMERICA, INC.
1476 Broadway, New York
Including
ENGLAND, SCOTLAND, FRANCE, SWITZERLAND,
ITALY, GERMANY, HOLLAND.

European Tour Scene—Tourists Arriving at Hotel in London.

ALL EXPENSE PLAN   EXPERIENCED CONDUCTORS

Three Weeks' Course at Cambridge University (Optional).

Cost Without Course at Cambridge, $605.00.

Cost With Course at Cambridge, $655.00.

Write for detailed itinerary and further information to
EUROPEAN TOUR DEPARTMENT
Kent State Normal College
Kent, Ohio

Above left: An announcement for the educational tour to Europe in 1926, one of President McGilvrey's many innovative programs he inaugurated in 1922.

Above right: T. Howard Winters, McGilvrey's "watchdog" and Kent State's first acting president.

Right: A montage of some of Kent's student publications: *The Red Flame, The Kent Stater, Searchlight, Kentonian.*

Far left: Ruth V. Atkinson had a long tenure as head of the Department of Physical Education, in which capacity she directed most athletic programs for women.

Left: David Allen Anderson was Kent's second president. His appointment was controversial and his tenure short, 1926–28.

Below: James Osro Engleman, Kent's third president, poses at his installation with (left to right) N. W. Senhauser (Board of Trustees), Alma M. Zinninger (first woman and first Kent graduate to be a member of the Board of Trustees), Engleman, John L. Clifton (director, State Board of Education), William A. Cluff (Board of Trustees), and Charles Seiberling (president, Board of Trustees).

Above left: John Edward McGilvrey, Kent's first president, was a man of personal warmth, visionary power, noble spirit, and great integrity. He is shown here in 1935 at his desk, which was situated under a copy of architect Hammond's drawing for the semicircle of Kent's first buildings.

Above right: Governor Martin L. Davey, prominent Kent citizen and strong supporter of Kent State.

Right: James Osro Engleman, Governor Myers Y. Cooper, and David Ladd Rockwell, Board of Trustees, on the occasion of Engleman's inauguration in 1929.

Right: Football coach and athletic director George Donald "Rosy" Starn with assistants Ray Novotny (left) and Joe Begala (right). Starn was a winning coach with a record of 34–28–2 from 1935 to 1943. Begala became a Kent legend as a very successful wrestling coach.

Below: Renovated in 2009, the May H. Prentice Memorial Gateway at the corner of East Main and Lincoln streets is named for the professor who served Kent from 1912 to 1930.

Four

THE LEEBRICK REVOLUTION

{1937–1944}

The very word *university* seemed for a time to have talismanic powers. Kent State's enrollment in the fall of 1934 was 1,197, but after it became a university in 1935 registration jumped by increments of roughly 300 in each of the next four years. Modest numbers these, by later standards, but impressive ones during the Great Depression years, when so many colleges suffered deep enrollment drops. In 1937 the journalism program in liberal arts became the first four-year nonteaching major. Thanks in part to such new undergraduate and graduate programs, the *New York Times* called Kent State the "fastest-growing university in the nation."[1] And the enrollment surges meant hiring additional instructors. Between 1934 and 1938 the faculty increased from eighty to 123. During that period the number of Ph.Ds doubled from twenty-five to fifty. For the first time in the school's history, the faculty had more men than women, most of the new members coming from liberal arts backgrounds. Biologists Ralph Dexter (1937) and J. Arthur Herrick (1938) were just two of the numerous Ph.Ds whose storied careers began during this time.

If the state had made a reasonable attempt to meet Kent's annual building requests during the 1920s, when its coffers were full, Kent could easily have made room for the enrollment increases of the 1930s. But no ground was broken for new dormitories between 1915 and 1937 and none for new classrooms between 1914 and 1938. As a result, with 2,000-plus enrollments, students had to scrounge for rooms in town and cram into classroom buildings intended for 600, with locker rooms, hallways, basements, storerooms, even large broom closets doubling as classrooms.

Yet between 1934 and 1937 ample funds for classroom buildings and dormitories were readily available and were being spent gladly by universities across the country. Engleman, however, whose political principles were cut on the economic bias of Herbert Hoover, mulishly rejected all urgings to apply for grants from the Public Works Administration (PWA), the New Deal agency that built, among other things, dormitories and classroom buildings for hundreds of universities. Largely because of his stubborn conservatism, new classroom construction at Kent lagged well behind that of other state schools during most of Kent's first half-century.

The building hiatus ended abruptly in 1937 when a newly elected state senator, KSU professor Herman D. Byrne, drafted a bill that cut the Gordian knot of funding dormitories in state educational institutions. He proposed that boards of trustees be authorized to borrow funds for dormitory construction and amortize them by renting the rooms to students. His bill quickly won the support of Miami and OSU, ensuring its passage. And on August 7, 1937, KSU's trustees issued notes for $300,000 for a new dormitory and for an addition onto Lowry Hall. At the same meeting the trustees decided that all new construction to the east and south of the campus crescent would use red rather than yellow brick for reasons of economy and, some would say, aesthetics.

And they voted to name the new dormitory after President Engleman, who, at their meeting on March 16, 1937, had informed them of his desire to leave office no later than July 1, 1938, citing the approach of his sixty-fifth year. Age was not the only factor in his resignation, however; there was a note of remorse for the heavy price KSU had paid for his political principles when he told the trustees his departure would free the school to carry out a "much needed building and planning program." Still, few rejoiced at Engleman's leaving. His emollient personality, kindliness, decency, and sympathetic nature had long ago earned him the respect and affection of students and faculty alike.

The trustees wasted no time starting new construction projects. In the fall of 1937 they secured $387,000 from the Works Project Administration and $85,000 from the state to construct a football field, a baseball field, and parking lots on the site of the unused normal school farm bordering Summit Street. The next year they received two large grants for a science building, $650,000 from the state and $525,487 from the PWA. This would be the first new classroom building to go up since 1914, when Kent Hall, originally known as Science Hall, was built. The costive legislature provided the money, however, only after a lobbying campaign orchestrated by McGilvrey had deluged the Statehouse with letters, petitions, telegrams, and phone calls. And so on March 5, 1938, the trustees honored themselves and Kent State University by naming the new building for the individual most responsible for bringing both the building and the institution into being: John Edward McGilvrey.

On February 4, 1938, eleven months after Engleman's announcement, the trustees named his successor, Dr. Karl Clayton Leebrick, liberal arts dean at Syracuse University. To campus observers, Leebrick, not vetted even by a token search-and-interview process, seemed to have materialized out of nowhere. Rumor had it that he became the sole contender after making a great impression with a talk he gave to a luncheon meeting of the Kent Rotary attended by a trustee and administration officials. With his easy manner, Leebrick struck one and all as being an affable, genial guest as well as a polished, entertaining speaker.[2] And nor had anyone expected the trustees to pick a dean of liberal arts, given that nearly all the previous Kent presidents were veteran public school educators. Most surprising, however, was the shocking signal sent by Leebrick's selection: the trustees were charting a radically new course for KSU, and a liberal arts captain, Leebrick, was to steer it full-throttle toward maturity as a university.

By background and experience Leebrick was highly qualified for the task. After attending the Tempe, Arizona, normal school, he had served as principal in several Arizona schools and taught at a private school in Berkeley while earning B.S., M.A., and Ph.D. degrees in political science at the University of California. He later taught modern European history at his alma mater before moving in 1920 to the University of Hawaii as professor and head of the political science and history department. In 1928 he moved to Syracuse and became liberal arts dean. Like Engleman, Leebrick's natural element was the public lectern, though he was more effective before small groups of like-minded people—fraternal orders, service clubs, the American Legion—than when facing a large, diverse audience. He was indefatigable; he spent his first year flying around the country giving seventy-five talks, and the students nicknamed him "the flying prexy."[3] He was adept at presenting himself as an easy-going, unpretentious, regular guy with a playful streak. Early that fall, he jumped onto the stage during a pep assembly and surprised the students by leading cheers with the abandon of an undergraduate cheerleader.[4]

The trustees launched him with an inauguration of grand pomp and circumstance. The ceremonies, which attracted a horde of academic officials and professors clad in academic habiliments, were attenuated by much grandiloquent speechifying. It was a sweltering October afternoon, and Wills Gym was packed. Perhaps unmoored by the moment, or by his newly returned lei-wearing family from Hawaii, or by the lei around his own neck, Leebrick delivered a meandering speech that wobbled with adages, epigrams, and nuggets of golden verse before reaching its theme: to make liberal arts, rather than education, the "backbone of the University" and to expand the graduate college quickly so that it would offer doctoral degrees in a dozen fields.[5]

What Leebrick did to advance his vision has been recorded in KSU annals as the "Leebrick Revolution." He moved always boldly, if seldom tactfully, to reconfigure the basic structures, programs, and academic relationships of the school. Though his dream of a doctoral-granting graduate school would be deferred for another quarter century, he reoriented the faculty's mind-set toward scholarly distinction and built the scaffolding of an excellent liberal arts college. He arranged all twenty-two departments and their faculties into three collegial divisions: the College of Education; the College of Business, which included secretarial science; and the College of Liberal Arts, which housed all other programs. He then organized the liberal arts departments into four divisions: language/literature (English, foreign languages, journalism, speech); natural science/mathematics (biology, health/physical education, biology, mathematics, physics); social science/philosophy/psychology (economics, geography, history, philosophy, political science, psychology); and fine and practical arts (art, home economics, industrial arts, music). In this reorganization, Leebrick did not hesitate to ditch programs (i.e., agriculture and library science) or break old affiliations (taking psychology from education and making it a new department in the liberal arts college) or merge old departments (Latin and foreign languages) into a new Department of Foreign Languages or create three new schools (art, journalism, and music).

Revolutions—political, military, or cultural—usually run to excess, however, and Leebrick's was no exception. In his zeal to make liberal arts the backbone of undergraduate and graduate study, he soon revealed on occasion a high-handed pettiness that would eventually undo him. This was most conspicuous—and risky—in his attitude toward the College of Education. He missed no opportunity to remind its faculty that they were no longer top dog. He not only took away one of its bedrock courses, psychology, he then bunched its twelve faculty members into three divisions—kindergarten-primary, elementary, and secondary. He also booted the training school into a limbolike state without definite academic standing and denied its staff faculty rank. To add insult to injury, the state education office decided in 1939 to abolish the two-year diploma, which, since its introduction in 1914, had educated 7,463 teachers who, in turn, had enriched the lives of countless citizens.

Although most courses added during Leebrick's tenure were, like his numerous new Ph.D. hires, in the arts college tradition, the College of Business also flourished. Two years into the Leebrick era, departments in the business college—accounting, business administration, commerce, and secretarial science—had doubled. And the Graduate College grew commensurately as well under a graduate council expanded to include three faculty representatives. Graduates with master's degrees vaulted from seven in 1938 to thirty-eight in 1941. The liberal arts and business colleges proved so attractive to men that by 1939 there were more men (1,402) than women (1,163) on campus for the first time in history.

To raise the status of scholarship, Leebrick started a tradition that for decades helped nourish a sense of community: an annual address given by the school's "outstanding scholar," who was chosen from the entire faculty by secret ballot. First to win that honor was sociologist Dr. John F. Cuber in 1939. Also that year, KSU was accepted into the Association of American Colleges, a prestigious organization of liberal arts colleges. But there was no end to the ambitious plans that, for various reasons, Leebrick was unable to realize, including sabbaticals for faculty, a faculty senate, membership in the American Association of Universities and in the American Association of University Women, and state-funded housing to be rented by national social fraternities.

Yet Leebrick believed that collegiality was the presiding genius of a community of scholars. He encouraged faculty and student involvement in decision making by setting up advisory committees on every conceivable facet of campus life. He introduced comprehensive testing of incoming freshman students and started a four-year scholarship program to attract outstanding high school seniors to study at KSU. And, encouraged by Leebrick and the Kent NAACP, the new dean of women, Dr. Mary L. Smallwood, ended the shameful practice of segregating African American women in the dormitory on Summit Street. Also telling was that Leebrick and his liberal arts dean, Earle Crecraft, demonstrated their commitment to their agenda of change by regularly teaching courses in political science in addition to their administrative duties.

One of the most positive and far-reaching developments of the Leebrick era was achieved by the state universities in 1939. Though less public and nasty than in the teens and twenties, interuniversity squabbling continued during the thirties—usually every biennium, when the divisive state appropriation formula put their teeth on edge. Following preparatory planning by officials of OSU and Miami, the five presidents and their business managers gathered in Columbus on January 17, 1939, and passed Leebrick's motion to establish an Inter-University Council that would meet regularly to deal with matters of common concern and, in particular, to formulate a "coordinated program of nurture and support" in budgetary and curricular matters that would strengthen each institution.[6] Later, despite OSU's vain attempt to persuade the other four schools to promise not to offer doctoral degrees or to set up professional schools, the Inter-University Council effectively resolved the inequitable appropriation system that engendered such ill will among the state's universities, and it did so by moving along tracks graded and laid down long before by McGilvrey at a great cost to himself.

The late 1930s and early 1940s were generally good years for KSU and the country. The economy was recovering, and job prospects for graduates were brightening for the first time in a decade. The campus now sprawled eastward along Summit Street with the opening of the new athletic fields and parking lot, much needed for commuting student jalopies. McGilvrey Hall opened, and it included a new, more spacious office for its namesake. Student pilots were scratching the skies above the Akron-Fulton Airport as part of Kent's training program under a Civil Aeronautics Administration contract, which turned out some 300 pilots in those years. (After 1942 they trained at the school's airport in Stow.)

Men and women continued to celebrate spring's greening by singing and dancing about the maypole on Campus Day as they had for a generation. The Sadie Hawkins Day and Dance tradition began that year. Inspired by the *L'il Abner* comic strip, it gave women a socially acceptable opportunity to ask men for dates. Another tradition began in the spring of 1940, Rowboat Regatta, sponsored by the *Stater* and later featured in *Life:* fraternities, sororities, and independents waged mock naval battles in rowboats on the Cuyahoga River. In 1940 Professor G. Harry Wright's radio workshop began broadcasting discussions, readings, and plays to the campus, anticipating the advent of WKSU by a decade. It was the heyday of the American songbook, when famous big bands like Gene Krupa's filled Wills Gym with couples in a dream of romance and youth gliding to the lilting measures of "All the Things You Are" and "Cheek to Cheek" and jitterbugging to up-tempo tunes.

But they were dancing in the dark and they knew it. The ominous shadow of war inched closer to Kent by the day. When Russia invaded Finland in November 1940, students held boxing matches to raise money for Finnish relief, and the Student Council formed the University Defense Council to call attention to the grim threat looming for a country utterly unprepared to defend either itself or its friends. Civilian pilot training on Kent's campus expanded that fall, and when Congress passed a conscription act in September 1940, 386 students and twenty-five professors queued up in the atrium of the Administration Building on October 16 to register. (Women were ineligible for the draft, but they could, and did, enlist and serve in the armed forces.)

In 1940 the fall enrollment was 2,702, but in 1941 it dropped by 425. More and more young people were joining the armed forces or working in defense plants. America was becoming what FDR called "the Arsenal of Democracy." To serve defense workers and increase enrollment, Leebrick set up an ambitious program of forty-six night courses in such subjects as business, education, history, industrial arts, mathematics, psychology, and English.

But in the midst of this revving up of defense production and preparation for war, fifty-four of 500 Kent students polled agreed with the *Stater*'s call on October 24, 1941, for Kent students to join thousands of students elsewhere in opposing any involvement in "Europe's bloody hysteria." This isolationism was not so much a shrinking from danger as perhaps the natural recoil of an idealism shocked by the intractability of human evil: the sickening sense that the 1914–1918 "war to end all wars" was simply resuming after a twenty-year interval. The *Stater* editorial was sparked by Ohio's isolationist senator Robert A. Taft's harangue against American involvement in Europe's war.

Two weeks later, Armistice Day services were held beside the howitzer that had stood in front of Kent Hall for twenty years—a reminder of Kent men killed in the Great War of 1914–18—and the *Kent Stater* wondered wryly if the howitzer was a tribute to the men or a mockery of democratic principles. The *Stater*'s letter columns became a battleground where students supporting isolationist Charles A. Lindbergh's America First organization and those backing FDR's preparedness policy fought a passionate war of words.

All controversy stopped, however, when the Japanese bombed Pearl Harbor on Sunday morning, December 7, 1941. In a few fast months the University hardly resembled itself, though little changed in outward appearance. The ivy-clad buildings, the undulating green, the patriarchal trees, and the great hill still retained their familiar contours and colors. But nearly all the men and women were gone into the armed services or defense work. Statistics reveal the urgency of that historic moment: two couples became engaged in the month before Pearl Harbor, but in the month after, the figure soared to twenty-four, and the number of weddings zoomed from four to twenty-three in the same span. Enrollment in the spring of 1941 shrank to 696. By 1943 more than a third of the full-time faculty had left—twenty-nine for the armed forces and ten for defense work. Before war's end, some 5,000 Kent students, alumni, and faculty were on active duty with as many others volunteering on the home front.[7]

Extracurricular activities almost disappeared. Fraternity and sorority life stopped altogether. The student-run *Duchess* died—a humor magazine had no place in a humorless time—and varsity sports ceased in 1942. That year, the howitzer was donated to a scrap drive—a memorial of the Great War recycled to fight an even greater one—and some Royal Air Force flyers from England were welcomed by Kent coeds of the Office of War Activities, which sponsored fund-raising drives, a cadet-welcome dance, and an adopt-a-soldier program and distributed Christmas gifts to soldiers. At around the same time, Dean of Men Raymond Manchester started a penny drive (later called the Penny Carnival) in order to mail copies of the *Stater* and his *Saturday Letter* to what he called the "Kent Legion" in the services (mimeographed broadsheets full of whimsical anecdotes, sage advice, and reminiscence of Kent State's early days).

In March 1943 Kent shoppers watched as members of the 336th Training Detachment (aircrew) marched smartly up Main Street and onto campus. For the next year and a half some 2,000 young men from across the country slept in the dormitories, dined in the cafeteria, drilled on old Rockwell Field behind the Heating Plant, and took classes taught by Kent's ninety remaining instructors in subjects ranging from civil air regulations to English to geography to first aid to map reading to physics. The training program devised at Kent became the model for other universities. Had it not been for the 336th Training Detachment's presence, KSU would probably have ceased to exist before war's end; there were too few students enrolled and too many faculty on the payroll.

During 1943–44 the war stamped its image on a range of new courses that were designed for the aircrewmen but were also taken by the regular student body of some 600, mostly women: army life, camouflage, firefighting, map reading, Morse code, and semaphore. And correspondence courses, a program pioneered at Kent by McGilvrey, were offered to soldiers scattered around the world. With all work and learning largely focused on the war effort, Kent chemistry students working under B. F. Goodrich scientists developed synthetic rubber in the labs on the third floor of McGilvrey Hall, a scientific breakthrough that effectively nullified Japan's takeover of Asia's vast rubber plantations.

With bombs dropping over most of the globe, Leebrick dropped one of his own in the spring of 1943. Learning that the trustees were planning to fire him at their forthcoming meeting, he decided to trump them by telling the truth. At the last faculty meeting of the year, on May 25, he astonished his audience by announcing that the trustees had decided to dismiss him but were going to publicly announce that he was resigning to take a commission in the army reserves. He also told the faculty that they had already appointed psychology professor Raymond Clark acting president. Leebrick's announcement violated academic protocol and embarrassed the trustees.

The resignation story was ostensibly designed to spare Leebrick the shame of dismissal. The trustees also hoped it would save them having to admit their error in appointing him before vetting him thoroughly and then telling him to make liberal arts the school's "backbone." He had, in fact, done exactly what they wanted, but with ruthless brilliance, making many enemies in the process, especially in the education college. He was a graceless administrator with a difficult personality and a volatile temperament. He confused disagreement with disloyalty and seemed to be oblivious to the human cost exacted by his programmatic and administrative changes. In time, the atmosphere of instability and anxiety and the fraying of faculty morale caused the trustees to doubt his stewardship as well as the new direction they had set for him.

Another likely factor leading to Leebrick's dismissal was the sad state of the school in 1943, adrift in the doldrums, with 600 students and less than half its prewar faculty. The board seems to have been of two minds about whether to stay the course already set toward what Shriver calls a "liberal arts-college university" or to steer it back to the safer harbor of a "teachers' college-university."[8] An acting president would buy it enough time to answer this key question.

When Leebrick left in 1943, it was already apparent that the Allied forces would prevail. It fell to Acting President Clark and the Inter-University Council to find ways to accommodate the returning veterans. No one knew how many to expect, but everyone sensed it would be a great many because of the GI Bill passed on June 24, 1944, but eagerly anticipated ever since President Roosevelt's "Fireside Chat" on July 31, 1943. The GI Bill would eventually transform all of American higher education, most particularly at KSU. News of its passage delivered the campus from a mood of obsolescence, restoring its sense of mission and giving it the energy of hope. Members of the Inter-University Council crunched some numbers and projected that 6,000 vets were likely to flock to Kent in the postwar era. Assuming that the state would allocate funds more generously than had been possible before the war, they drew up plans for providing more classrooms and dormitories.

These plans were still on the drafting board when the trustees announced on January 22, 1944, that KSU had a new president. The appointment of George Arvene Bowman constituted one of those rare instances when the man matched the moment, for when he retired nineteen years later, Kent State University would be poised for greatness.

Five

THE BOWMAN YEARS

{1944–1963}

In the months following Leebrick's departure, the trustees seem to have clarified their thinking and decided that Kent State University would reverse course—if their choice of George Bowman is an accurate index of their intentions. Trustee president John R. Williams told the *Courier-Tribune* on January 25, 1944, that they wanted a man with "wide school administrative and executive experience" who understood "Ohio's educational system."

Ohio born and raised, Bowman was educated in the state's public schools. He served in the navy during World War I and then, after studying at the University of Chicago and Harvard, earned degrees at Western Reserve, Ohio State, and Columbia universities. His professional experiences as teacher (starting in a one-room schoolhouse, from which he swept chicken feathers on opening day), principal, and superintendent (of Chillicothe, Marion, Lakewood, and Youngstown districts) were uniformly successful. But it was his reputation as a wise and skilled administrator that took trustees Robert Dix and Joseph B. Hanan to Youngstown in August 1943 to offer him the position.

Bowman did not jump at the offer. For one thing, it surprised him, because he had no college-level administrative experience.[1] For another, though confident of his abilities, he was not flyblown with ambition; he had some honest self-doubts and finally accepted the offer only after the trustees assured him that they wanted him because they were convinced he could do the job. Bowman was not playing coy or feigning humility. He had a high degree of self-honesty and was genuinely modest, the sort of man who is easily underestimated.

Tall, well setup, with a melodious bass voice and a military bearing, Bowman was a man of impressive dignity and presence. His strengths were the quiet, perdurable virtues of a man of sound character. He was considerate, sympathetic, and gentle, his nature free of any taint of the calculating bully or the tinsel brilliance that treats others as foils. Veteran Kent journalist Loris Troyer observed that beneath his "austere" demeanor Bowman had great personal warmth, a "keen sense of humor," and "contagious attraction to others."[2]

Bowman's administrative gifts—diligence, fair-mindedness, circumspection, and the habit of measuring his judgments—were well suited for an institution that would grow and change greatly under his hand. Mindful of the legacy of bickering and dissension from the Leebrick years, he was determined to nurture a family feeling among faculty, staff, and administrators, and to a remarkable degree he succeeded. He came to know them by face and name—the newest instructor and the most eminent scholar. And he was a reassuring, fatherly presence to thousands of students, whose names he could recall with Olympian assurance years after they had graduated.

Bowman took office on July 1, 1944, the day after the 336th aircrew marched off campus, leaving him to deal with a thornbush of prickly decisions. Funds had to be found somewhere to make the dormitories—which had been modified to house the airmen—suitable for women, and the curriculum had to be retooled from predominantly military to fully academic purposes. The 336th's departure left Bowman with only a few hundred students, far too few for the size of his faculty, half of which had been teaching military subjects while the rest was in the service or doing war work. But looming over every decision was the daunting figure of 6,000 students projected to enroll after the war. Principally because of that projection, he decided to retain the current faculty rather than trim it to fit current needs and then have to rebuild it from scratch after the war, when qualified teachers would be scarce.

The most pressing issue concerned the school's facilities. How could a campus taxed by the peak prewar enrollment of 2,700 be stretched to hold 6,000? And would the state come up with the funds for new construction? In December, the trustees approved Bowman's revision of the Clark committee's plans: after the health center and industrial arts buildings were up, there would follow men's dormitories, a student union, a gymnasium, and an airport shop and hangar at the airfield in neighboring Stow—if, of course, the state allocated the funds.

Bowman's inauguration, on November 18, 1944, was keyed to the times and to the man: it was unpretentious, serious, and dignified. A WWI veteran himself, he was attuned to the needs of returning vets. The University, he said in his brief address, would spare no effort in discharging its solemn obligations to receive and educate every veteran who came through its gates.[3]

The vets began trickling in that fall: twenty-six enrolled under Public Law 16, which granted benefits to disabled vets, and within a few weeks they formed K-Vets, a mutual-help organization for men who had served since 1940. The K-Vets counterpart, the Legion of Women Veterans, came soon after. In the first summer term of 1945, after Germany's surrender, fifty-six vets enrolled. That summer Lieutenant Dewey F. Barich returned and resumed his position as professor and head of industrial arts; Bowman put him in charge of veterans' affairs. Then, soon after Japan capitulated, the floodgates lifted and increasingly higher numbers began pouring onto campus: 1,299 students (111 vets) in the fall of 1945, followed by 1,460 (462 vets) more in January 1946. From then on enrollments rose rapidly as young people left defense work for college. Vets outnumbered nonvets from June 1946 until September 1949, when postwar enrollment peaked at 6,000. Before the GI Bill expired in 1956, more than 10,000 veterans of World War II and Korea would study at Kent State, more than at any other Ohio institution except Ohio State.

There has perhaps never been another moment in American history, certainly not in Kent State's history, quite so exhilarating, so vibrant with creative energies and hopes for the fulfillment of the American Promise, as those postwar years. They constituted an epoch in the fullest sense, a historical moment of victory over tyranny abroad and mammon at home for young men and women whose sole privilege had been growing up in the hardscrabble years of the Great Depression and then serving their country in a terrible yet necessary war.

Who knows what brought them to Kent in such great numbers? Surely it was something more than the exigencies of economics and geography. Perhaps it was the school's feisty reputation for having to struggle for survival against great odds. Perhaps it was the McGilvrey legacy of openness, experimentalism, independence, and belief in education as a mighty power for good in the world. Whatever drew them here, they brought with them contagious energy and desire for learning that enkindled decades of outstanding students and shone the way for the school's astonishing advances in the sixties.

But those breathtaking enrollment surges presented Bowman with an enormous challenge in 1945. Realizing he could not wait for the state to appropriate funds for new construction, which it would finally do in 1947, he decided to improvise. The three women's dorms doubled up occupancy. Dozens of men were quartered in the Davey Tree Company "barracks" on Gougler Avenue. Area householders were canvassed for rental space. And a campaign by K-Vets that garnered 800 rooms got front-page play: vets strolling up and down Main Street wearing "Bed for a Vet" sandwich boards. In March 1946 the federal government leased the University housing for 141 single vets in quarters built in Windham for workers at the Ravenna Arsenal; five months later 250 more rooms became available, fifty of which were apartments for married vets. Windham residents were bused to and from campus. And to accommodate vets who could not commute to campus, in September 1946 Bowman set up "Kent State University at Canton," with night classes held at McKinley High. With Clayton M. Schindler as director and a faculty of thirty-eight, the initial enrollment of 641 jumped to 905, half of them vets, by the fall of 1947. This revival of McGilvrey's extension system was suspended briefly in 1950 for lack of state funding, but it was the seedbed of Kent's regional campus system.

In 1946, Kent's first men's dormitory, Terrace Lodge, opened on the corner of Terrace Drive and Main Street. But that calls for a touch of nuance: it was actually five buildings (each housing fifty men), and they were not dorms but tarted-up prefab hospital units trucked from Marion, Ohio, gifts of the Federal Public Housing Authority. Still, they offered a roof, a sack, a shower, and a world of rich memories for hundreds of men until they were razed in 1952 to make way for Terrace Hall, a women's dorm.

Five more prefab units arrived in November 1946, some from the Ravenna Arsenal and some from Camp Perry near Port Clinton, Ohio. (Like the Terrace Lodge units, these were labeled "temporary structures"—but who trusts labels? One was in use, by ROTC (Reserve Officer Training Corps), until 1970.) Two were located behind the Heating Plant and used as classroom buildings, North Hall and South Hall; there they squatted, overheated in winter, stifling hot in every other season, and loathed by faculty and students alike. The third served as a warehouse and the fourth as the Terrace Lodge cafeteria.

The fifth of these prefab units became a temporary student center called the Hub because campus life revolved around it. There, in its grungy, noisy, low-ceilinged, electrically charged atmosphere, a wide-eyed freshman could sip bad coffee and smoke cigarettes while osmotically absorbing a priceless education from watching and listening to intense, vital young men and women wearing the brave souvenirs of their sacrifice—flight jackets, khaki shirts, jump boots, navy-blue blouses, olive-drab skirts, pea coats—on fire with the desire to learn and resolved to waste not one more second of life. The example they set, the extraordinary value they put on education as a fundamental necessity and right in a democracy, would sing in the memory for the rest of the century. Some drafted comedy sketches for the student-sponsored No Time for Classes and Pork Barrel. Others argued politics or talked about an exciting idea or fact mentioned in history or sociology or biology or economics classes. Some wrote stories and poems to be published in a special section of the Friday *Stater:* "Throw the helmet in the corner," wrote Cuyahoga Falls vet Lloyd Chipps, "Let the melancholy in," evoking with a lyric stroke the bass note of war's after-vacancy.

From 1944 to 1950 the size and composition of the faculty changed enormously. As President Bowman had anticipated, there was keen competition for qualified teachers. In 1944 Kent had 114 active instructors, plus another forty-one on leave, most in military service—far too few for the projected enrollment of 6,000. Every year thereafter, however, he added new names to the faculty roster, with the largest increment in 1946, when he hired a grand total of seventy-three. Recruiting Ph.Ds with college teaching experience was very hard in the tight postwar market. Most newcomers came straight from graduate school before finishing their degrees, while others were seasoned high school teachers with M.As. The number of faculty holding the doctorate dropped from the 1940–41 high of 44 percent to 28 percent in 1949–50. Though the quality of teaching was excellent, the shortage of faculty meant heavy teaching loads, and again, as in the school's infancy, the overriding obligation was to meet the immediate needs of students—in the classroom. This meant that the emphasis on scholarly activity of the Leebrick Revolution had to be largely suspended.

Soaring enrollments forced important departmental and curricular changes in high-demand subjects. For example, the physical sciences department was strained by the demand for classes in both physics and chemistry, so they became separate departments. Health and physical education split off from the Office of Student Health Services/Department of Physical Education, while mathematics became a separate department and its longtime head Raymond Manchester became full-time dean of men. Six brand-new departments emerged: significantly, five in the education college—kindergarten-primary, elementary, secondary, special education, and library science (under librarian John B. Nicholson)—and the sixth, military science, followed in 1947, a year after a ROTC unit was formed.

A university is a dynamic institution; it measures generations in four-year increments. The place endures but the people come and go, meeting and forming friendships and seldom seeing each other again after graduation. Amidst the myriad of postwar reconfigurations, many of the original faculty, who seemed to endure forever (some of their names adorn campus buildings), either retired or died and were replaced by a new generation of dedicated and creative individuals, too many to name. And a few notable changes took place in academic administration: Bowman appointed Robert I. White as dean of education and John Reed Spicer as dean of liberal arts, both in August 1946. These two quite different individuals stirred things up.

White had taught in public schools, served as a high school principal, and was teaching graduate courses at the University of Chicago, where he took all his post–high school education, when Bowman called him to Kent. An attractive, virile, forceful thirty-seven at the time, White was a study in contradictions—intense and reflective, passionate and sympathetic, yet reserved, cool, and guarded—and he was burdened yet inspired by an almost Platonic conception of a university and the desire to realize it. He quickly became a compelling figure on campus, a ribbon of smoke unspooling from his pipe, his tie flapping over his hunched shoulders as he strode purposefully, a colleague on either hand, talking and listening, sometimes laughing. Faculty, staff, and students all regarded him as a man of promise and deferred to him. He turned the College of Education upside down in remaking it after his own educational image. His academic touchstone was "standards." The purpose of the college, he held, was to measure every aspect of the curriculum by rigorous standards. He devised a Student Qualification for Professional Standards program that maddened the dreams of generations of education majors. Designed to produce high-quality teachers, its key requirements were "adequate intelligence," a "strong academic record," a "desirable teaching personality," an understanding of how children learn, skill in using teaching resources and techniques, and an ability to "use and write English properly," for which a C average or higher in Freshman English and the passing of a special English composition test were mandatory. And students with certain irremediable health or speech defects that might inhibit effective teaching would be "withdrawn from the College."[4]

John Reed Spicer did not bring the same kind of rigor and drive to the College of Liberal Arts. Spicer was tall, poised, and self-confident to a fault; he was a restless man with poetic urges. After just a year as dean at Westminster, a small liberal arts college in Pennsylvania, he came to Kent with slender administrative experience and an unconventional idea of a liberal arts college and how to administer it. Where another dean might have regarded the omnium-gatherum of courses (from industrial arts to philosophy to chemistry to speech therapy) in the college's twenty-odd departments as a promiscuous agglomeration of curricular lumber, he thought it nicely suited the college's duty "to use its peculiar resources" for the "educational needs of the young people of northeastern Ohio."[5] He disdained what he called "the conventions of traditional colleges, liberal or otherwise," and instead of grouping departments by kind into scientific, technical-professional, and liberal arts clusters, he chose, rather, to redefine the traditional degrees, spreading confusion and consternation among students and faculty alike. The bachelor of arts represented "a curriculum in which breadth takes first place and specialization is secondary," he wrote, while the bachelor of science denoted one "in which specialization takes precedence, but does not eliminate breadth."[6] This seemed to say that a journalism major specializing in, say, newspaper management would become a scientist in the same sense as, say, a student specializing in biology or physics. Spicer's heart wasn't really in academic administration but in stimulating creativity (he sponsored a creative writing journal) and informed discussion of major postwar developments in science, politics, and culture. With the latter in view, he established the long-lived interdisciplinary course "Problems of the Atomic Age," later changed to "Great Contemporary Issues." He did not stay at Kent long, resigning in 1951 to pursue a more adventurous life as an officer in the CIA. He was succeeded by Eric N. Rackham, an experienced liberal arts dean with a Michigan Ph.D.

The College of Business, still led by Dean Allyn, took a sharp turn toward specialization and concentration during this period. As enrollments grew, the curriculum became increasingly subdivided into such "fields of specialization" as "business and the public," "commerce-art," "industrial accounting," "professional accounting," and "air and general traffic management."[7] The same spirit animated the Graduate College, which grew rapidly under Raymond Clark, who assumed the deanship in 1950. Since 1935 the master of arts had required all graduate students to write and defend a thesis. That changed in 1950 when the trustees added master's degrees in education and business administration, allowing extra course work in lieu of the thesis, and professionalized the M.A. into a program for aspiring college teachers. Of the 2,203 master's degrees awarded from 1950 to 1959, some 77 percent were in education, health–physical education, library science, and industrial arts; only 2.8 percent were granted to M.As in mathematics, foreign languages, chemistry, and physics.

Meanwhile, the physical plant was also changing. Postwar construction began in 1947 when footers were laid next to Engleman Hall for the long-awaited Student Union, a recreation center (bowling, ping-pong, pool tables) with meeting rooms and a faculty dining room. Its projected cost in 1945 was $504,210; its final cost, in 1949, was $900,000—an example of the postwar inflation that ballooned all construction in this period. Soon after the Union was under way, earthmovers began gouging out the foundation for a fifty-bed health center (named for Dr. DeWeese) near the top of Summit Street. Before "Pill Hill" opened, the good doctor, cigarette in mouth, and Mitti Smith, the legendary campus nurse who had taken nonsense from no one since arriving in 1921, had treated ailing students in an infirmary off the atrium of the Administration Building. And the long-standing need for a men's dormitory, which became all the more important with the influx of vets, was partially satisfied when Stopher Hall, named for the school's first registrar, Emmet C. Stopher, was built in August 1948. Stopher housed a boisterous medley of experienced young men who had gone to war while still boys and inexperienced boys fresh from high school, some of whom would leave college in 1950 to fight and die along with 30,000 others in Korea.

While these three buildings were still going up, work started on three more. The most impressive was the men's physical education building, with offices, handball courts, training rooms, classrooms, an Olympic-size swimming pool, and a 10,000-seat basketball court. Bowman declared it "the pride of Kent State University" when it was finished in 1950. Its companion piece, just down the hill on the athletic field bordering Summit Street was a stadium with bleachers seating 5,600 football fans. In 1956, both Memorial Gymnasium and Memorial Stadium were dedicated to the memories of the 113 KSU men killed in World War II. The third building, which housed both the industrial arts and the art departments, was named for industrial arts head Clinton S. Van Deusen. State money funded all these projects save Stopher Hall, which was paid for by loans, and Memorial Stadium, built with private gifts raised by former governor Martin L. Davey.

In addition to plant construction, expansion was another of Bowman's major goals. In 1948–49 he more than doubled the school's total acreage by purchasing four parcels of land. These 125 acres would be the land on which, over the next fifteen years, the school's second great building boom would take place as the campus's center moved eastward away from the classic Front Campus.

Restoration of athletics was yet another Bowman priority. He restarted intercollegiate athletics, beginning with basketball, followed, in order, by football, wrestling, baseball, tennis, track, golf, and swimming. All were functioning by 1946 when he signed Trevor Rees to be athletic director and football coach. A former OSU All-American end, Rees proved to be the ideal man to build a vigorous and competitive athletic program. Knowledgeable and broad gauged, he was an astute judge of talent and a gifted mentor of coaches (Don McCaffrey of the Baltimore Colts, Lou Holtz of Notre Dame, and Bill Bertka in professional basketball). During his eighteen-year tenure, Kent fielded so many outstanding teams that the Mid-America Conference, which had often refused Kent's bid to join its ranks, actively campaigned for it to join, which it did in 1951.

Under Rees, nearly every varsity sport improved markedly. Women's sports made a down payment on future distinctions with the achievements of gymnast Betty Jane Maycox, a member of the 1959 Pan-American team and of the 1960 U.S. Olympic team. Her career overlapped the arrival of the coaching team of Janet and Rudy Bachna, who would train two generations of outstanding Kent gymnasts. And with basketball now matching the high standard long maintained by the baseball and wrestling programs, football grabbed the spotlight. In 1946, Rees's first season as coach, the team compiled a 6–2 record despite primitive training facilities, hand-me-down equipment, and a squad largely composed of freshmen vets with little or no collegiate-level experience. The 1954 football team competed in postseason play in the Refrigerator Bowl. Rees's teams had had nine winning seasons in the 1950s, a remarkable record given that Kent has had only twenty-five winning seasons in eighty-six years.[8]

Although racial segregation would not fully emerge as a matter of national concern until the end of the fifties, it had tainted intercollegiate sports prior to 1940. This began to change in the postwar era, as segregation in student housing gradually ended as well. Track and field had always been racially integrated, but in the last half of the 1940s, racial diversity increased rapidly, though northern and midwestern schools like KSU gave few scholarships to black athletes. Yet, it is to the credit of the KSU football team that it refused to play against "segregated southern teams if it meant leaving black players off the field."[9] A symbol of the school's coming of age in sports, the Victory Bell was placed at the foot of Blanket Hill, a favorite spot for courting on the eastern edge of the Commons, in 1950.

The 1955 *Chestnut Burr*, the student yearbook, described the Bowman era as the school's Golden Years. Front Campus—when viewed from the focal point of Rockwell Library, with its bower of trees dappling the green lawn that ran up Normal Hill to the semicircle of classical buildings bearded with ivy planted long before by McGilvrey and Dean Johnson—looked like an idyllic small college suspended in the amber glow of nostalgia. The campus atmosphere was intimate and friendly, its personality warm and congenial. The student body of 5,000 or so was still small enough for people to greet each other by name. Most students were still first-generation college students primarily from ethnically rich northeast Ohio, although students from some twenty foreign countries spiced the mix, along with a vibrant peppering from such eastern states as New York, New Jersey, and Pennsylvania, which had yet to develop university systems.

One sign of the times, unthinkable in the next decade, was a robust interest in religion, the result perhaps of the students being born in the Great Depression and growing up during WWII and coming of age in its anxious aftermath—the Bomb, the Korean War, the Cold War—when the old Enlightenment assumptions and certitudes about human progress had begun to wobble. Philosophy professor Joseph Politella introduced four popular religion courses and taught Clevelander Ronald Q. Lewton and many other eager students "the great secret," which Lewton summed up a half century later as "how to live my life."[10] Religious groups of nearly every denomination appeared, and Bowman, keenly supportive, established Religious Emphasis Week, which featured eminent speakers and was on the school calendar throughout the decade.

Another phenomenon of the era was the revival of "Greek" life. Where President McGilvrey had regarded these organizations as undemocratic and had actively discouraged them, fraternities and sororities appeared in the 1930s under President Engleman and flourished until the war came. On May 27, 1947, the faculty voted to open the campus to national organizations, and Chi Omega (formerly Kappa Lambda) went national, followed by seven other local chapters. The first fraternity to go national was Kent's oldest, Kappa Mu Kappa (1922), which became a chapter of Delta Upsilon; fourteen others nationalized soon after. During the next decade, each fall term opened in a whirl of excitement with talk of "rushes," men's "smokers" and women's "teas," "little sisters" and "big brothers," and "pinnings," which were solemnized by moonlight serenades on sorority house porches. Honorary societies were also popular. Nearly every subject had a Kent chapter affiliated with a national scholastic organization. The most eminent of the service honoraries were Cardinal Key for women and Blue Key for men. Every May inductees were identifiable by the red and blue plywood keys they carried around campus.

Each fall, Homecoming, with its receptions, parties, football games, and dances, and spring's Campus Day, with Songfest, the maypole dance, and a gaudy parade of floats, were the highlights of the school's social calendar. And a lovely necklace of queens, confirming Kent's reputation for female beauty, decorated the year: Homecoming Queen, Military Ball Queen, Miss Kent State and Duke of Kent, Miss Chestnut Burr, Campus Day Queen, the Duchess and Duke of Kent, and Rowboat Regatta Queen.

The year's cultural menu had something for nearly every taste: theater productions (like *Finian's Rainbow*); Artist-Lecture Series (Karamu Theater productions, Cleveland Orchestra concerts); the Oratorio Society's pre-Christmas performance of *The Messiah;* sock hops in Wills Gym; formal gown-and-tux balls featuring the big band music of Les Brown, Jimmy Dorsey, Claude Thornhill; student-produced No Time for Classes, Penny Carnival, and Pork Barrel shows; the Shark Club's water ballets; and Professor Roy Metcalf's Twin Marching Bands (founded in 1940).

Rules governing women had changed hardly at all since the school's beginning. A woman could be confined to campus for failing to sign in or out of the dorm or for coming in after the 10:30 weeknight curfew or for smoking in her room or shaking a dust mop out her window (waving to a man?) or for riding in a car, unchaperoned, with a man on campus. If "campused," a woman was forced to spend her evening studying with sister transgressors in Merrill Hall under the watchful eyes of an unmarried female instructor. As the 10:30 witching hour neared, couples hovered outside Moulton, Lowry, and Engleman halls taking advantage of each breathless second until the parting bell rang. Weekend hours were longer, and there was always the late train as a universal excuse for breaking curfew.

Dress styles were more formal than they would become in the next decade. For classes, women wore pleated skirts, sweaters (sometimes cashmere) with pearls, bobby sox with saddle shoes or bucks. Men wore sport jackets or sweaters, shirts and ties, argyle socks with saddle shoes or bucks. Glasses were horn rimmed, hair was trim, and cigarettes were almost obligatory, though some smoked pipes for the professorial look.

Good manners, as well as decorous behavior and speech, were still regarded as grace notes in social relations. The first rite of passage from high school to college began when the professor addressed the student as Miss Smith or Mister Brown, thereby conferring the dignity of adulthood, a state much to be desired then. Professors, as authorities in their field, were treated with respect, even if sometimes groused about. And the value of ceremony and tradition was taken for granted. In 1956 students voted to quash a dean of men's radical decision to abolish dinks, the small caps freshmen were required to raise in the presence of an upperclassman during "Frosh Week," an orientation week that culminated with tea and cookies at the president's home, where Dr. and Mrs. Bowman warmly welcomed each new student into the University family. The Bowmans, who were childless, unashamedly regarded students as theirs to care for as well as educate. Some vets understandably grimaced at this paternalism, but few freshmen did. Mrs. Bowman was nearly as well known as her husband. Famously cost-conscious, Mrs. Bowman cruised around campus periodically to see if any lights were burning unnecessarily.

Though not as bland and buttoned down by conformity as later portrayed in popular culture, it was not a rebellious era either. There was, however, one harbinger of the tumultuous future. The national panty raid fad struck Kent one May night in the mid-1950s when a bumptious crowd of spring-smitten men gathered outside Lowry Hall and began talking themselves into storming the citadel and rampaging through its halls in search of lacey white trophies, which the women were not loath to lose. As campus legend has it, when a long, lean dean of men raised his arms and appealed to them to desist—"Men, listen to your leader!"—someone shouted "Crucify him!" and he was picked up and rolled unceremoniously down the hill.

Although President Bowman had adjusted the scales to restore the education college to rough parity with liberal arts, it was soon apparent that he did not intend to rechart the school's course in quite the way the trustees may have intended. He was content to let the University grow organically.

Enrollment dipped during the Korean War, and twenty faculty positions were cut. But when a cease-fire arrangement stopped the guns in 1953, vets once again flooded in, aided this time by a Korean GI Bill. In 1953–54 there were 172 WWII and 536 Korean War vets; in 1956–57, with a total enrollment of 5,717, there were just two WWII but 1,501 Korean vets. By 1959 there no WWII vets and only 798 Korean in a student body of 7,554. Surging enrollments in time created more faculty jobs, especially in such high-demand subjects as English and history. The English department grew from eighteen full-time faculty in 1952 to forty-three in 1959, while history grew from ten to twenty-four in the same span. In 1950 only 28 percent of the faculty had doctorates, a figure that almost doubled by 1959. Perhaps most telling, from 1952 to 1959 the faculty expanded from 277 to 399, a number that included thirty training school instructors given faculty rank in 1953.

In 1959, Bowman took seven departments from the College of Arts and Sciences (A&S), and formed the school's fourth major academic unit, the College of Fine and Professional Arts (F&PA), which housed architecture, art, home economics, industrial arts, journalism, music, and speech. Though this lightened the A&S administrative load and restored some of its curricular integrity, the move simply switched the curricular organization problem to the new college. It was now F&PA administrators, under the leadership of Dean John J. Kamerick, who crossed their fingers and swore they saw unity among their widely disparate offerings (some of which were technical, some artistic, some hybrids). But that unity was chimerical, and the new college was soon compelled to offer four separate degrees (bachelor's of arts, of architecture, of fine arts, and of science).

As the fifties waned there was a perceptible bustle and stir in the atmosphere, a thrumming sense that the school was gathering strength to soar into higher realms. Faculty and administrators alike buzzed about plans for doctoral programs taking shape on drawing boards. New professors with doctorates and research records were bringing new perspectives and expertise to departments; graduate and research scholarships were increasing annually, leading to a rise in publications in learned journals; modest reduction of the heavy teaching loads was improving both scholarly activity and classroom performance; funds for attending professional conferences were growing; and library holdings were heading toward 200,000 volumes. For undergraduates, academic scholarships leapt from just twenty-nine in 1944 to more than 140 by 1960. Honors study burgeoned, with a pilot program of independent study leading to an honors thesis. Students were winning Fulbright and Woodrow Wilson scholarships for graduate study, and half of Kent's chemistry and physics majors were doing graduate work.

Despite presiding over an era of unparalleled physical expansion, Bowman wanted above all to instill an "intellectual hunger," especially in students, and hoped his presidency would be remembered as one marked by excellent classroom teaching. The "greatest compliment anyone could receive," he often said, would be to be "considered a great teacher."[11] He seldom concluded a meeting without reminding the faculty that it was the good teacher in a classroom of hungry students that was the school's most important activity.[12] He also encouraged "intellectual hunger" by protecting the academic freedom of students as well as faculty. True, he did insist, gently, on "good taste" and mannerly behavior, but he was neither shrew nor censor. Though expected to adhere to good journalistic practices, *Stater* editors were not hobbled by burdensome restrictions. And when on one occasion Bowman summoned editors of *The Kent Writer* to his office to suggest that the phrase "screw Plato" in a poem by student David Elliot was inappropriate, he did not insist on its removal but ended the meeting with a handshake.

Despite abundant signs of academic vigor and advance, some professors fretted that the University was losing its bearings and perhaps its identity. Their concern arose within the context of a trend, newly sprung from the exigencies and dislocations of World War II, involving a steady turning away from the traditional purpose of a liberal education in a democracy—to cultivate the powers of the mind in order to prepare responsible as well as productive citizens for public service—toward vocationalism and workplace training. Many Kent professors feared that this steady shift away from the search for knowledge and the increasing emphasis on specialization and technics meant that the school was abandoning its responsibility to introduce students to the life of the mind. Some proposed a core curriculum of classic mental disciplines for all freshmen students, but there seemed little likelihood of that happening in the foreseeable future.

While the question of education versus training was being bandied, the state passed two bills that proved to be landmarks in Kent's development. Senator Ray Manchester, former dean of men, together with two Kent alumni, Akron senator Oliver Ocasek and Jackson County representative Fred Rice put a rider on a piece of related legislation that empowered KSU and Bowling Green to award any and all degrees "customarily conferred by colleges and universities in the United States." This opened the door to a doctoral program. Later, Manchester and Ocasek coauthored a bill that increased Kent's trustees from five to seven, hoping thereby to widen the board's perspective and make it less susceptible to domination by a few powerful individuals.

Other administrative changes continued on various levels throughout the 1950s, all imperatives of surging enrollments. For example, when the decade started, student affairs had a dean of men and a dean of women, a residence hall adviser, two assistant deans, and four counselors. When it ended, it had a dean of students, a dean of men, a dean of women, and eight assistant deans and twenty-eight counselors; directors of student housing, of orientation, and of Terrace Hall; and an adviser of international students. To compare gross numbers: in 1949–50 the University had twenty-seven administrative officers; ten years later that figure had doubled. At this rate, went the faculty joke, by 1980 there would be 25,000 students and 50,000 deans.

Bowman's third building phase started in 1953, when Terrace Lodge was razed and earthmovers began excavating for what would become the largest women's dormitory, Terrace Hall, which housed 720 students, three to a room, when it opened (unfinished) in 1955. The second phase of Memorial Field also began that year with the construction of the North Stand. The next year, training school operations moved from Franklin Hall into the University School, a vast structure on the corner of Morris Road and Summit (today the Michael Schwartz Center) with state-of-the-art facilities and marathon-length halls. Two more dormitories—Verder for women and Johnson for men—came in 1956. And work began in 1958 on Dunbar and Prentice halls for women, located on Midway Drive and overlooking what was fast becoming the new center of the campus.

The names on these buildings represent a significant change of policy, one for which Bowman deserves some credit. All seven honor professors or administrators. Not one bears the name of a trustee. By contrast, of the nine buildings erected before World War II, the trustees named five for themselves, two for former presidents, one for a legislator, and one for a benefactor. Of the seven built in this phase of Bowman's tenure, six were named for professors (Verder, Johnson, Prentice, Dunbar, Van Deusen, Nixson) and one for an administrator (Stopher).[13] The trustees' practice of putting their names on new buildings had long rankled alumni, press, and the public. It speaks well for Bowman's tact that he was able to persuade the trustees to recognize the valuable contribution distinguished teachers make to an institution of higher learning.

Also in 1958, a sizeable addition to Rockwell Library greatly increased its capacity to store the new books and journals being acquired for the much-anticipated doctoral programs. The automobile's voracious appetite for parking space, however, devoured the library's spacious west lawn, over heated protests from a group of professors concerned about aesthetics.[14] But the most talked-about project was also the school's most prodigious—the Music and Speech Building, with its scores of practice rooms, studios, classrooms, offices, 350-seat recital hall, broadcast studios, speech and hearing facilities, and 500-seat theater. It was set so close to the campus's eastern border that faculty and students called it "the Ravenna Campus."

As the school's semicentennial year of 1958–59 dawned, Bowman decided to dedicate it to the future. Acknowledging that the presidential workload had grown too complex and burdensome for one person, he named education dean Robert White to the new post of vice president for academic affairs. White was charged with shifting the doctoral project into high gear. In April he had Bowman invite three well-known educators to evaluate the school's readiness for a successful transition into doctoral study. The experts' recommendations included implementing all-university planning for curricular development and teaching improvement, tightening admission requirements, giving faculty a voice in policy matters via an elective faculty senate and graduate council, curtailing course proliferation, reducing reliance on split-level courses for graduate work, and decreasing the imbalance between professional education and subject-matter courses in graduate study. The next month distinguished scholar Ira L. Baldwin of the University of Wisconsin came to survey the situation from a broader perspective. He cautioned against offering doctoral work before the program was ready to do it well; it should move in measured steps, he said, offering first a few carefully selected fields taught by qualified faculty. He had astringent advice for administrators and faculty alike: Kent's professors would have to rethink their professional identities.

No longer could they consider themselves as a teaching faculty; they must become scholar-teachers whose research would be published in scholarly journals. This would be expensive; it meant reduced faculty teaching loads, travel grants, research and sabbatical leaves, and higher salaries to attract outstanding scholars. And graduate scholarships would have to be greatly increased to attract talented students. All this would affect the entire faculty because it would tilt the reward system sharply in favor of research over teaching and graduate over undergraduate programs.[15]

This part of the semicentennial, of course, was enacted off stage. What students saw of the celebration was symbolized by a great white, three-layered, plaster birthday cake, with candles, built by the Industrial Arts Club, that was displayed at the southeast corner of the Ellipse between Merrill Hall and the Heating Plant. Students and professors strolled past it on their way to and from the Hub from September 1959 until September 1960, by which time the seasons had soiled it into a drooping eyesore. Those curious about the look of the future campus could view the exquisitely detailed topographical map of the campus, present and future, built by architecture students that was on display in the library throughout the year.

An auspicious moment occurred a year later when a self-conscious group of students in formal attire posed for their class picture on the steps of Merrill Hall. They were the charter class of candidates about to begin their pursuit of doctoral degrees in biology, chemistry, education, English, and history, the five departments picked to light the way for future doctoral programs. All twenty-seven candidates (twenty-six men and one woman) were funded in part by the National Defense Education Administration, a government agency formed after the Soviets' launching of Sputnik in October 1957.

The energy generated by the new doctoral initiative ramified downward and outward. Graduate students on fellowships taught basic undergraduate classes or worked as lab assistants, freeing professors for graduate teaching, research, and directing theses and dissertations. Still, mindful of Dr. Baldwin's advice, the graduate council brought new doctoral programs on line only after a thorough vetting. By 1970 more than sixty candidates had earned doctorates. And doctoral programs raised interest in other graduate degrees. New master's programs appeared on every hand: in science (1961), a terminal M.F.A. in art (1962), library science (1963), public administration and architecture

(1968), and music (1970). By 1970, a grand total of 9,114 M.A. candidates had been hooded.

The Bowman building boom concluded with the massive six-dormitory Eastway Center and a major classroom-lecture building to house history, political science, philosophy, and, briefly, English, which the trustees fittingly named Bowman Hall. The decision to grace the liberal arts building with the name of the man presumed to have been hired to lead the school back to its teacher-training days was apt. Bowman had chosen, instead, to steer the school straight ahead toward full university status.

Six

BIG DREAMS

{1963–1970}

When President Bowman informed the trustees that he wished to retire in 1963, he also urged them to appoint a small committee composed of a few professors to help find his replacement. After the committee consulted with national, state, and area education leaders, faculty, and alumni, the board decided to appoint the man everyone had long assumed to be heir presumptive, the one who had masterfully overseen the school's entrance onto the doctoral scene, Robert I. White. Bowman, a man slow with superlatives, was delighted, praising White's high intelligence, integrity, sensitivity, and his dedication to Kent State.[1] White took office on July 1, 1963, chose F&PA dean John Kamerick to succeed him as provost/vice president, and then struck out on his own, determined to make Kent into a great institution of higher learning.

Kent State reached an important benchmark in 1964 when the Ohio Board of Regents' master plan designated KSU the state's regional university for the northeast. This official acknowledgment infused faculty and administration alike with new energy and enthusiasm. That same year President White, acting on a feasibility study by business dean Robert Hill and graduate dean Martin Nurmi, established the Kent State University Press: a key feature of White's ideal university was a press that published scholarly books and journals, the fruits of research that add to the store of knowledge about the universe and humanity without which a culture dies from the top down. Howard Allen, a veteran publisher, was the first director of the Press. About this same time, White encouraged faculty with Phi Beta Kappa keys to redouble their efforts to win a chapter of the nation's oldest and most prestigious scholastic organization for Kent as recognition of the excellence of its liberal arts programs. Then White, always dancing ahead of the beat, decided to stimulate scholarly activity by hiring four distinguished scholars at the new rank of University Professor with handsome salaries, secretarial support, and freedom to decide their own teaching schedules: Howard Vincent (English), Harold Mayer (geography), August Meier (history), Richard Varga (mathematics), and Elliott M. Rudwick (sociology). Some professors worried that this would degrade the professor rank, while some others caught the envy virus, always dormant in the academy. But in time most faculty felt that White's gamble had paid off. The presence of the four scholars did attract gifted graduate students.

With the doctoral programs in place by 1962, White began recruiting new faculty with great energy. Each fall, starting in 1963, seemed to bring a flock of assistant professors, newly fledged from graduate school and eager for flight. They came because Kent State promised to become a first-rate research institution of the sort they had attended—and for other reasons. For example, with a new Ph.D. from Iowa State (where Liquid Crystals pioneer Glenn Brown had worked before coming to Kent in 1960) physicist David Johnson arrived in Kent in the spring of 1966 after interviewing at other Ohio schools. The family chose Kent because of promised basic research funds and its beautiful rolling green campus.

By 1970 hundreds of new Ph.Ds had swollen faculty ranks to 1,047. Self-confident, outspoken, and full of ideas, some of them often criticized the administration for, among other things, adulterating the quality of the undergraduate program by expanding it too fast. Some worried that Kent would lose sight of its mission to educate in the scramble for prestige as a research institution. Yet White seemed unthreatened by the youthful faculty's energy and cocksureness. He relished their zest for intellectual distinction and their commitment to what he believed was the shaping of a great institution of learning and research. Most of them considered him to be a "faculty president," one who knew what a university should be. White's commitment to collegiality matched that of Leebrick.

For some time the Kent chapter of the American Association of University Professors (AAUP) had been building an intellectual scaffolding for collegiality as well as for due process. Mindful of the consultants' recommendation that faculty have a meaningful voice in curriculum and governance, he took the first significant step in that direction in 1963 by changing the title of department "head" to "chairman" (later, chair). From then on departmental decisions and policies were no longer made by diktat but by elected faculty committees working with elected chairs. But while White extended Bowman's policy of student participation on university-wide committees and established an elective Student Senate, he was wary of doing the same for the faculty. Bowman had established an advisory body called the University Faculty Council in 1963, which he chaired in tandem with an elected faculty cochair, but this hardly satisfied the need for a fully representative faculty voice. How could professors participate meaningfully in governance if they did not have the information on which to make judgments and a forum for expressing them?

For two decades the Kent chapter of the AAUP had used its good offices to resolve faculty grievances, disputes, and turf battles, but with haphazard results. In the process, those professors, most of them WWII vets, set a standard of professional responsibility and institutional service that exercised considerable moral influence on the new faculty. Pressure for a representative senate mounted steeply when these new Ph.Ds from institutions steeped in the principle of collegiality joined forces with senior faculty.

Of the many strong AAUP presidents who had sought, by tact and moral suasion, to speak for the faculty to the administration, none worked harder than art professor Harold Kitner. Two years into White's tenure, he and Kitner had developed a working relationship based on mutual respect and trust strong enough to survive Kitner's persistent nudgings for a faculty senate and a system of due process. As the faculty increased in number, faculty disputes increased in equal measure. Like his predecessors, White dealt with each on an ad hoc basis until 1967, when he surprised everyone by appointing Kitner to the new post of dean of faculty counsel, giving him an office, a secretary, and direct access to the president. Familiarly referred to as the ombudsman, Kitner had license to investigate allegations of inequitable treatment and to try to resolve faculty disputes.

Kitner's telephone started ringing as soon as it was plugged in. One professor accused another of throwing a typewriter at him; another accused a dean of trying to ruin his career by cutting off research funds; another claimed his department chairman had unfairly blocked his promotion. So they came—some trivial, some flimsy, some substantial. Even students sought Kitner's help. In fact, the growing number of student protests made some faculty wonder why White hadn't appointed an ombudsman for students first. Though helpful in individual cases, the faculty ombudsman was no substitute for a due process policy, as White soon realized, so he shook the administrative chain with an order requiring each academic unit to prepare a handbook of department policies, including viable due process protocols for promotion, tenure, and grievance, as well as faculty rights and responsibilities, setting in motion a process that would be refined many times over the next decade and a half. And, on cue, Kitner's phone started squawking complaints about obstructionist chairs. One long-time department head-turned-chair reportedly strode into a faculty meeting, waved the newly finished handbook in the air, and dropped it into a wastebasket, saying, "That is what I think of your handbook." Her department decamped from Kitner's office. Much blood was shed and hair pulled during the Handbook Wars of the sixties.

For the ombudsman, the issue of faculty morale often interlocked with the ascendance of graduate programs, as research and teaching jostled increasingly for primacy. Underlying the swerve from teacher to scholar-teacher was the unstated assumption that while good scholars are by definition good teachers, the converse may not be the case. (Neither proposition is necessarily true.) This conflict stirred tensions and resentments, especially among teachers of predominantly undergraduate classes, as salaries and promotions were tied increasingly to the scholar-teacher concept and greatly favored graduate over undergraduate education. The Alumni Association, fearing that undergraduate teaching was getting lost in the publish-or-perish shuffle, decided in 1967 to stimulate good teaching through annual monetary awards to two outstanding teachers, who were nominated by students and alumni and selected by a panel of students, alumni, and faculty. The first recipients were music professor Hugh A. Glauser and historian Lawrence S. Kaplan, who later held a University Professorship. A few years later a third award was added.

In 1968 White finally authorized a Faculty Senate composed of elected representatives of the major academic units and administrators ex officio and chaired by a faculty member elected by the Senate. Although its formal role was mostly advisory, the Senate did have considerable influence on policy and other matters because it was the voice of the faculty. Some wags cynically called it "the cave of the winds," where faculty gasbags vented in vain. Yet few would have wished it gone two short years later during the University's gravest crisis.

State support increased during the economic boom years of the 1960s, and so did enrollments. Every fall, from 1963 on, baby boomers from every point of the compass arrived in such numbers that, despite clusters of new dormitories that seemed to spring up overnight, there were always more students than housing for them. *Chestnut Burr* and *Stater* photographers of the era took stacks of pictures of men quartered in Wills Gym and basements and of hallways crammed with women hanging blouses and slips on water pipes and sleeping chockablock in rows of army cots. White pressed the legislature hard for building funds and drove contractors even harder. Classrooms were overcrowded, too. It was during this period, when new classroom buildings featured large lecture halls, that Kent adopted the widespread practice of teaching certain basic courses in large sections of several hundred students. Unless the teacher was a talented lecturer, this practice was more satisfying to the budget than to students, many of whom complained they were being processed rather than educated.

Like Bowman, White was a builder as well as an educator. In swinging the gravitational center of the campus to the southeast, he supervised a prodigious expansion of the physical plant from some thirty structures in 1963 to more than 100 in 1971. The great majority were dormitories erected to house the spate of baby boomers, including the Twin Towers-Eastway complex named for professors Manchester, Fletcher, Allyn, Clark, and Beall, as well as trustee McDowell. The high-rise Tri-Towers unit was named for Professor Wright, President Leebrick, and alumna Judith Koonce, who died trying to save a child from drowning. To balance the high-rise structures, there were eight Small Group dorms for men and women. Enrollment reached 22,000 in 1971. In addition, seven major classroom buildings were constructed: White Hall (education); the science complex of Williams (chemistry), Smith (physics), and Cunningham (biology); and Taylor (journalism and architecture) and Satterfield (English and foreign languages) halls. Like most of the dorms, the majority of these classroom buildings were named for distinguished, long-serving professors, but the trustees did revert to their former habit of honoring former trustees: the chemistry building was named for trustee John R. Williams and the physics building for trustee Roy Harmon Smith. In 1970 the campus stretched a mile farther to the east for the construction of the 28,000-seat Dix Stadium, named for a longtime trustee and local newspaperman Robert Dix.

As the campus sprawled ever farther away from Front Campus, students had to trot from one class to the next. So in 1968 the traditional ten-minute interval between classes was extended to fifteen, and an elaborate campus bus system employing student drivers went into action, looping the campus and ferrying commuting students to and from a wide circle of neighboring cities, including Cleveland.

White's proudest achievement as builder, the twelve-story University Library, the county's tallest structure, opened in 1970. (There is a thirteenth floor, accessible by stairs only, which, in deference to superstition, is not used.) Starting with his appointment as academic vice president, he had channeled significant funds to the library to keep it abreast of the cascade of new books and journals while trying to plug gaps in its holdings of older ones. Librarian Hyman Kritzer, who measured a president's worth by his support of the library, relished the memory of his November 1968 memo to White notifying him of the library's 500,000th acquisition, to which White tersely replied, "Congratulations. How much will it take to reach a million?"[2] About that same time, White authorized Kritzer to buy the largest private collection in history—including some 250,000 rare books—from the Gillman Brothers of Poughkeepsie, New York. The books filled so many boxes that they had to be transported by semis and stored in the Stow airport hangar until they could be processed, a feat that took several years. The rarest items were kept in the Special Collections rooms on the top floor of the tower under the eye of alumnus and rare book specialist Dean Keller, who had started the collection in Rockwell Library in 1958. For the dedication of the Library in 1971, dean of American historians Henry Steele Commager delivered an impassioned defense of the university as a bastion of liberal learning at a time when KSU was being battered on all sides.

The Library was just one part of the new campus center White projected in his 1964 building plan. Construction on the second part—the Kent Student Center—began in his final year and was finished after he left office, in 1972. This long, crescent-shaped, three-story structure facing the fountain, the centerpiece of the plaza, included a large ballroom, game room, bookstore, cafeteria, the Schwebel Garden dining room, the Rathskeller pub in the cellar, the Kiva lecture hall, a commuter lounge and food court, and a host of conference rooms.

Another of White's special projects was the Blossom Festival School, an arts program conducted in collaboration with the Cleveland Orchestra at its summer home, Blossom Music Center, which opened in 1968. Each summer music students from universities around the world competed for appointments to study with KSU faculty and Cleveland Orchestra musicians and performed before audiences under the famed Blossom "shed" or on the Kent campus. On the Blossom grounds Kent's visual and dramatic arts were displayed as well. KSU painters and sculptors, faculty and students alike, showed their work in both permanent and exhibition venues. A gift from industrialist Cyril Porthouse enabled Kent State to acquire a large tract of land adjacent to the Blossom shed for Porthouse Theatre. There, in its open-air structure, on summer nights audiences capped a picnic supper in the Reed Pavilion (a gift of distinguished education professor Gerald H. Reed and Victoria Reed) with a varied theatrical menu of comedies, dramas, and musicals. The cofounders of Porthouse were KSU theater professors William Zuccherro, alumnus and son of biology professor Peter Zuccherro, and Louis Erdmann, who designed the theater.

Far more profound and influential than changes in Kent's landscape and curriculum, however, was the changing of the ground rules of higher education that took place during the 1960s. This virtual transformation of the ethos of campus life throughout the country was brought about by the baby boomers' rapidly intensifying rejection of the assumptions and relations on which universities had traditionally operated. This was part of a larger generational revolution in attitudes and values—in many cases, even in mind-set and worldview—that profoundly altered not only the nation's colleges but rescripted the manners and morals of American society.

Kent had always enjoyed the privileged status accorded every seat of higher learning: a sanctuary for study, reflection, and the cultivation of the mind insulated by its ivy-covered walls from the hubbub of everyday life. Although Kent had more than its share of disputes, most of its external battles had been sparked by sectional rivalries and had been waged in the sharp-angled corridors of state power-politics. All that changed radically in the sixties when the tremors reverberating from the convulsions shaking the "real world" over the countercultural, antiwar, and civil rights movements undermined those ivy-clad walls.

The first sign that the tremors rocking the outside world would not spare Kent occurred in 1964. That was the year when the Student Peace Union (SPU), one of several groups anxious about the nuclear arms race and domestic politics, added America's expanding military role in the Vietnamese civil war to its agenda of concerns. The SPU brought noted pacifist journalist David McReynolds to campus to speak about his recent visit to Vietnam. The event drew an audience of some 100 people, mostly students, to Bowman Hall to hear McReynolds deliver the sort of presentation one expects on a college campus—an informative and closely reasoned discussion of a complicated issue. What made the speech memorable, though, was nothing McReynolds said or did. It was, rather, the conspicuous presence of several government agents who sat at the back of the auditorium, taping and photographing the audience. This was the first evidence that the federal government took campus discussions of the war seriously.

On April 14, 1965, Kent had its first political demonstration since the isolationists' march thirty years earlier. Staged at noon for maximum effect, it took place in front of Bowman Hall, where campus police had cordoned off a ten-foot-square area. Sixteen picketers—nine students and seven professors—walked in a circle surrounded by a crowd of several hundred mostly hostile students. The students' placards denounced American involvement in Vietnam; the instructors' read "Faculty for Peace." Campus police and government agents took pictures from cars parked at the curb.[3] Violence had marred such protests on many other campuses, but, aside from verbal abuse (catcalls and shouts of "draft dodgers"), the only violence that day in Kent was some water-filled balloons flung at the demonstrators. The picketing stopped after an hour, and the professors—two of them WWII vets and one a Korean War vet—returned to their offices, shaken by the hostility of the students, the intended beneficiaries of their protest. The demonstration, sponsored by the Kent Student Committee to March on Washington, kicked off a forty-eight-hour fast that ended the following Saturday in Washington, D.C., where Kent's small contingent joined 10,000 representatives from other campuses in a rally at the Washington Monument.[4]

An early indicator of the cultural transformation occurred in 1966, when a new conduct code was worked out at a student-faculty-administrator retreat held at Punderson Lodge. The new code of conduct effectively replaced the traditional parental model of in loco parentis with the legal model of a contract between equal parties. In a few years this change would not only erase parietal regulations regarding visiting privileges of members of the opposite sex but also result in men and women living in the same dorms and students grading their professors and openly challenging their authority in class.

Fast forward to 1968, and the pendulum of student attitudes had swung sharply against the war, in large part because the war had grown exponentially larger and bloodier and seemed to have lost purpose and meaning, as does any war with no end in sight. The American presence in Vietnam had metastasized through a series of troop surges to the proportions of a full-scale war. Opposition mounted along with the daily body counts of enemy and American dead. Meanwhile, the draft was taking more and more college students into the horrors of jungle warfare, and its specter loomed at the far end of the diploma line. From 1966 on, demonstrations became almost the order of the day on the nation's campuses, and Kent students, like their counterparts elsewhere, were galvanized by such activist revolutionary groups as Students for a Democratic Society (SDS) and Black United Students (BUS), who argued that the Vietnam War and racism were but two facets of the same corrupt economic-political system orchestrated by "the Establishment," the military-industrial complex that President Eisenhower had delineated with such gravity in his valedictory address.

The Kent SDS, with a militant, revolutionary agenda, appeared after the dissolution of the nonviolent Kent Committee to End the War. The national SDS had begun with the Port Huron Statement in 1962, which articulated an anticapitalist, pro–racial justice program aimed at making the nation's depersonalized, authoritarian "multiversities" into "communities of controversy" that would carry its radical agenda into the larger world beyond the campus. By the time the Kent SDS started up in 1968, internal feuds had split the national body into warring factions, and its activist agenda was co-opted by the more militant Weathermen and other radical groups.

The stories and photographs filling the pages of *Stater*s and *Burr*s in the second half of the 1960s indicated the tenor and tone of the protests on the Kent campus. In 1966 a few students and professors picketed the presence of recruiters for Dow Chemical, alleged to be the producer of the napalm bombs devastating Vietnam's landscape and populace. In 1967 two dozen professors held a silent vigil at noontime in front of the Student Union. The next year over 100 students marched in front of the ROTC building, about seventy-five students protested the war in front of Kent Hall, and a large group of prowar students demonstrated against an antiwar demonstration organized by another group of demonstrators.

On April 4, 1968, the prophetic voice of civil rights, Martin Luther King Jr., struggling to keep his movement nonviolent against the rising tide of black despair and anger, was silenced in Memphis, Tennessee. Kent students, black and white, walked in numb grief around campus, while riots leapt like wildfire from ghetto to ghetto over the length and breadth of the land. At Kent a group of students and professors quietly picketed the Administration Building to protest the apartheid policies of South Africa, just one instance of the widening moral and political concerns of students at Kent and other schools. Then, in the late summer of that same murderous year, Democratic presidential candidate Robert F. Kennedy was gunned down at the moment when he seemed to be reviving young people's faith in the viability of American political institutions. The deaths of two Kennedys and King demonstrated how politics of the gun can change the course of history. Their deaths robbed the country of progressive leaders of rare ability and commitment to public service and immeasurably crippled the American experiment in democracy. These murders were followed by the convulsion of rage and violence at the Democratic National Convention in Chicago in late August.

In September Kent's homegrown version of the Free University Movement began offering courses in the countercultural curriculum. Both faculty and students taught the classes, which were free, open, unstructured, with ample time for "rapping," in such subjects as folk guitar, rock and roll, racism, Marxism, world peace. The aim was to provide a "relevant" education as an antidote to the Establishment-owned traditional university with its cookie-cutter education. And an academic alternative to demonstrations that also became popular at the time were teach-ins, extended conversations between teachers and students to raise awareness of a controversial issue.

The year blundered to a grim conclusion in November, when word spread that recruiters from the Oakland, California, police department were coming. The Oakland police had become anathema to African American students following a series of violent clashes with the Black Panthers. On November 13, 1968, SDS and BUS students demonstrated against the presence of Oakland representatives on campus. Dean of Students Robert Matson, fed up and frazzled after months of SDS disturbances, got tough. He had the protesters photographed and threatened to charge them with disorderly conduct if they did not disperse. To his and the administration's dismay, half the school's 600 black students walked off the campus in protest, vowing to withdraw from school unless all demonstrators were given amnesty. White, realizing that the situation was getting too volatile, decided that no charges would be filed, citing a technicality in the conduct code. The students returned. Six months later, White brought Kent alumnus Dr. Edward W.

Crosby from Southern Illinois University to establish the Department of Pan-African Studies, a multifaceted academic center offering a four-year degree program in African culture and history.

Taking the administration's capitulation to the black student walk-off as a victory for BUS, in the spring of 1969 the Kent SDS took part in a nationwide "Spring Offensive" of militant demonstrations aimed at driving ROTC off university campuses. On April 8, 1969, six demonstrators (four of them students) were arrested for assault and battery after a clash between campus police and anti-ROTC protesters. On April 16 a disciplinary hearing was held in the Music and Speech Building for two of the students. After some supporters of the students managed to enter the building, campus police chained and locked the doors, leaving a large, angry crowd outside. Meanwhile, inside the students' supporters gathered outside the hearing room on the third floor and raised a racket loud enough to disrupt the proceedings while campus police were locking all doors leading down from the third floor, hoping to trap and arrest them. Seeing what the police were up to, the crowd scattered. Some fifty-eight were eventually arrested by state troopers and bused to the county jail, but many more would have been caught if professors Kenneth R. Calkins (history) and Carl Moore (speech) had not helped them escape by elevator. Though Calkins's sympathies were already "alienated" by the SDS's tactics and "bombastic" rhetoric, he was outraged by what he saw as the administration's crude, misguided tactics.[5]

The next day cries of entrapment echoed around campus. What had the students done wrong? They had been locked in and arrested, apparently, merely for entering a classroom building. The incident provoked vehement reactions on campus, many students and faculty claiming that White was ignoring academic due process and violating the student conduct code. Many charged that the fifty-eight hauled off to jail had been deliberately entrapped by campus police, but an extensive AAUP investigation could turn up no conclusive evidence to support the charge, though it faulted the administration for abusing due process and breaking the conduct code.[6]

The Music and Speech incident marked the end of the SDS at Kent. It was banned from campus, and its four most effective leaders, Howie Emmer, Rick Erickson, Colin Neiburger, and Jeff Powell, served six months each for assault and battery. The episode also added to growing complaints among students and faculty about the difficulty of getting access to and communicating with President White. He seemed to be holed up in the Administration Building, making all the decisions, holding all the reins of power, consulting with only a small cadre of trusted aides.

Though disruptive demonstrations, some very violent, continued to roil other campuses, none occurred at Kent after the Music and Speech lock-in. But White, stung by complaints from trustees and city leaders that he was too soft on dissent and presumably alarmed by reports from undercover government agents of massive organized campaigns on college campuses, became convinced that Kent had reached a "crossroad" and was targeted for a protracted, well-planned protest that it might not survive. Such was the "unfair reward," he said, "of those institutions which have been the most open."[7] He declared a zero-tolerance policy toward disruptive activities: anyone so engaged would be arrested and suspended. But White's policy infringed on the constitutionally protected rights of free assembly and speech, putting a student in legal jeopardy simply for attending a rally. It prompted history professor James Louis to ask at a teach-in on April 22 if the real question should not be what kind of institution will survive a policy so inimical to academic freedom?[8]

What must not be lost sight of is that no serious physical violence had occurred during any of Kent's many demonstrations during the 1960s. It had, however, marred many antiwar demonstrations on other campuses, including many in Ohio, and the circumpressure of violent disruption elsewhere shaped and colored the perceptions of KSU's officials and many townspeople, whose image of protesters was the stereotypical head-banded, filth-spewing "long-haireds." This perception was hardened by the deliberately provocative language used tactically by many radicals. Language as an ideological weapon grew out of the Berkeley Free Speech movement (1964), which took the First Amendment rights of freedom of speech and assembly as license to say whatever one felt strongly about in any language at any time or place: one result was the Filthy Speech Movement, which the SDS introduced to Kent in 1968. The Filthy Speech movement featured language as a blunt instrument in assaulting traditional values, morals, and relationships, as well as on educational and political structures; its ultimate target was authority of any sort. This further widened the generational divide that grew steadily throughout the decade. Within just a decade, courtesy, civility, and decency were discarded in favor of the presumably more "sincere" (a touchstone of the time) inelegancies of contemporary discourse in which men and women use language common to army barracks.

In January 1969 American troop strength in Vietnam crested at 542,000; six months later, in July, President Nixon announced a troop drawdown. The antiwar movement took heart. Many assumed that the "secret plan" for ending the war on which Nixon had campaigned was being implemented at last. But the war ground on, and between October 8 and 11 the Weathermen launched their violent "Days of Rage" in Chicago to "bring the war home." For four days and nights television screens were filled with the ugly faces of savage riot and brutal repression, substantiating the worst fears of countless citizens and college officials that the "blood-dimmed tide" of anarchy was upon them.

Yet, hundreds of thousands of demonstrators paraded peacefully on October 15 in cities and towns across the land as part of the National Moratorium Day. In Kent 4,000 marched serenely about the town center and later gathered in Memorial Gym to hear the governor denounce the war. And in November a half-million people demonstrated peacefully in Washington, D.C. For peace seemed then as inevitable as the return of spring.

Left: Kent's fourth president, Karl Clayton Leebrick, on his inauguration day in 1938. Left to right: trustee John R. Williams, Leebrick, Governor John Bricker, and Reverend J. A. B. Fry.

Below: Engleman Hall in winter. Naming the new dormitory after President Engleman was ironic given the president's political principles, which did not allow him to accept federal funds for construction projects. No new dormitory construction took place from 1915 to 1938.

Right: Dean of Women Mary L. Smallwood and Dean of Men Raymond E. Manchester. Dean Smallwood, with the backing of President Leebrick and the NAACP, ended the segregation of African American women in off-campus dormitories. Dean Manchester, who served Kent State from 1920 to 1954, also served as mayor of Kent and in the state House of Representatives. For many years he produced his *Saturday Letter*, which students found in their mailboxes that lined the corridor in Merrill Hall.

Below: McGilvrey Hall, Kent's large science classroom building, was named for Kent's first president, John E. McGilvrey.

World War II and after.

Left: Student Julia "Peggy" Curry (front) and another coed greet Royal Air Force pilots who visited Kent in 1940.

Below: The flood of veterans returning to campus after the war caused a housing crisis, forcing students such as Gordon Thompson and George Schroeder to take to Kent's Main Street to picket for beds.

The administration responded to the crunch and, in 1946, erected prefabricated housing, known as "Terrace Lodge," visible at the lower left in the above photo, at the corner of Main Street and Terrace Drive to provide dormitories for veterans.

Above: Until 1948 when the
Student Health Center—
dubbed "Pill Hill" by students—opened, health service
was provided in Moulton Hall.

Left: In 1969 the DeWeese
Health Center, named for
Dr. A. O. DeWeese, University physician from 1924 to
1958, shown here in front of
the new building, opened on
Eastway Drive. "Pill Hill" was
renamed the Stockdale Safety
Building and houses the campus police department.

Fifties campus activities (clockwise from top): Rowboat Regatta, a rite of spring begun in 1940; Pork Barrel, a show of topical satirical sketches and musical numbers performed by student and faculty groups; photographers who worked on the 1953 *Chestnut Burr*; members of the 1953 *Daily Kent Stater* staff; the Hub, a popular student meeting place.

Facing page: Students strolling on Front Campus.

Right: Kent's fifth and longest-serving president (1944–63) was George Arvene Bowman, pictured here with his wife, Edith.

Below: Stopher Hall opened in 1949. The first dormitory for men, it was named for Registrar Emmet C. Stopher, who came to Kent in 1916.

Above: Athletic director and head football coach Trevor Rees with his staff. Left to right: (seated) Rees, Frank Lauterbur, Jacob Urchek, Don McCaffrey; (standing) Dick Kotis, Bud Haerr, Dick Paskert.

Left: The Victory Bell, pictured here in 1995, was placed on the Commons by President Bowman in 1950 to celebrate KSU's intercollegiate sports triumphs. After many years of hard ringing, it was rebuilt in 1985.

Fifties cultural events (clock-wise from top): Eleanor Roosevelt packed Memorial Gymnasium in 1954; Handel's *Messiah* was often performed by the School of Music before Christmas; violinist Joseph Szigiti (left), shown here with Kent music professor and violinist Louis Krch, gave a recital; the theater department presented several productions during the year; the 1952 production of *Medea* featured student Jackie Gelbman in the title role.

Left: In the fall, Homecoming was the big event, with receptions, parties, football games, and dances. The 1952 Homecoming King and Queen are saluted by a guard of honor.

Below: In the spring, Campus Day featured parades on campus and in downtown Kent.

Right: Kent's first class of Ph.D. candidates pose on the steps of Merrill Hall in the fall of 1961.

Below: Kent's sixth president, Robert I. White, and his wife, Edna (center front), are pictured here with a group of students.

Clockwise from top: Gymnast Betty Jean Maycock was a member of the 1960 Olympic team. Kent baseball teams of the late 1960s featured pitcher Steve Stone and catcher Thurman Munson. Stone's career peaked with his winning the Cy Young Award in 1980. Before his tragic death in an airplane crash, Munson's play on several New York Yankees championship teams placed him among the greatest major league catchers in history. Cross-country runner Pierson "Pete" Lonrandeau was Kent's first All-American track star (1966).

Top left and right: President White established the University Press in 1964 with Howard Allen as its first director. Shown here are Allen (left) and President White with Frederick B. Artz (center), the author of *Renaissance Humanism*, the first book published by the Kent State University Press. Also shown are *Another Athens Shall Arise* by Lucien Price (1956) and *Years of Youth: Kent State University, 1910–1960* by Phillip R. Shriver (1960), two books published by the University before the formal establishment of the Press.

Above: The University Press staff at their Franklin Hall offices in the early 1970s. Left to right: Carol Horner, Mary Jane Wolfe, director Paul Rohmann, Sandy Clark, and Martha Gibbons.

President White also established the rank of University Professor, with (clockwise from top) Harold Mayer (geography), August Meier (history) [here with Elliott M. Rudwick (sociology)], Richard Varga (mathematics), and Howard P. Vincent (English) as the first appointees.

Left: While the University Professorships celebrated scholarship, outstanding teaching was recognized when the Alumni Association established the Distinguished Teaching Award in 1967. The first recipients were (from left) Lawrence S. Kaplan (history) and Hugh A. Glauser (music).

Above: Another of President White's projects was the Blossom Festival School for music, art, and theater. Programs and classes were held on campus and on the Blossom Music Center grounds in the Eels Gallery and Art Pavilion and Porthouse Theater. In this photo, President White walks the site where Porthouse would be built in 1971.

Right: In an attempt to deal expeditiously with faculty concerns, President White appointed art professor Harold Kitner faculty ombudsman in 1967, giving him direct access to the president and license to cut through red tape in order to solve problems.

Facing page: President White was a builder as well as an educator. Between 1963 and 1971, the number of campus buildings grew from 30 to 100. The culmination of the building program came in 1970 with the twelve-story library that marked the new center of the campus.

The first demonstration in Kent against the Vietnam War took place in front of Bowman Hall in 1965.

Concerned over the on-campus presence of recruiters for the Oakland, California, police department, which had a national reputation for civil rights abuses, about 250 black students left campus for several days in protest.

In the spring of 1968, students marched across campus in memory of the assassinated Martin Luther King Jr.

This anti–Vietnam War protest marched past the ROTC building, which was burned by unidentified demonstrators on May 2, 1970.

Seven

FOUR DAYS IN MAY

{MAY 1–4, 1970}

On Thursday, April 30, 1970, President Richard Nixon startled the nation by announcing that he was sending American forces into neutral Cambodia to wipe out enclaves of guerrillas supporting antigovernment forces in Vietnam. At Kent, his announcement ignited a powder train of volatile confrontations that exploded tragically four days later.

A group of history graduate students led by Steve Sharoff, Chris Plant, and Jim Geary saw Nixon's decision as a violation of the Constitution and a reversal of Nixon's own policy of Vietnamization-via-troop reduction. They formed an ad hoc protest committee and, early Friday morning, May 1, spread out over the campus posting broadsides calling for a noon rally at the Victory Bell on the Commons. When the carillon chimed noon, some 500 students clustered around the Victory Bell to hear a series of speakers denounce Nixon's action. Geary, who had won Silver Stars for valor in Vietnam, burned his draft card. After a symbolic burying of the Constitution, the meeting ended with a call for another rally at noon on Monday, May 4, when the great majority of Kent's 20,000 students would return from their weekend at home. A meeting two hours later by BUS to show support for black students caught up in weeks of rioting at OSU also passed without incident. Then President White, who observed this second peaceful rally from the sidelines, decided that the state of affairs on campus was calm enough for him to catch his scheduled 5:30 P.M. flight to Iowa City, where he was chairing a meeting of the American College Testing Program.[1] He left campus, never dreaming that his university would be gone when he returned.

That evening the weather was balmy for early May in Ohio. In downtown Kent it was TGIF on the Strip, a row of bars—JB's, the Kove, Ron-de-Vou, Big Daddy's, Seaver's—strung along the west side of North Water, the heart of Kent's vibrant music scene, where students and other young people from surrounding towns flocked on weekends to party and lose themselves in the transporting rhythms of rock 'n roll. That night there was a combustible mix of the high spirits of spring and smoldering political frustrations.

As the evening ground on, the bars throbbed and pulsated, the smoke thickened, and the heat mounted. Around 9:30 P.M. people on both sides of Water Street began clapping their hands and yelling "Pigs get out of the street!" whenever a patrol car came along. The crowds on the street grew steadily as people who had been hopping from bar to bar began staying outside, where the air was cooler and fresher. Soon many who had been inside drifted outside, too, beer bottles and glasses in hand, forcing those on the sidewalk to spill over onto the street. By 10:15 a very large crowd was in the middle of Water Street chanting that the "streets were for the people" and refusing to let cars through. Although a few cars were slightly damaged, there were no police on the scene.

By 11:00 the music, the beer, the pot, and the heat had dissolved individual inhibitions, and the mood was playful but frenetic. A police car was booed as it moved downstreet, firecrackers crackled periodically, beer bottles were thrown at cars, and a human chain snake-danced in the middle of Water Street, stopping traffic. But fifteen minutes later the mood darkened and police cars were pelted with bottles as they slowly cruised North Water. Then someone started a fire in a trash can. Some revelers blocked off the street near JB's and began stopping cars and asking drivers their opinion of the Cambodian invasion.[2]

The sequence of events that night is a tangled skein, but it seems to have been shortly after midnight when the unruly crowd started moving in a body up North Water Street, breaking store-front windows on its way. Alarmed, the city police chief called the entire force to the scene and requested help from the county sheriff and area law enforcement agencies. Police in full riot gear and armed with tear gas stopped the mob at the intersection of Main and Water and kept it from advancing farther south.

Mayor Leroy Satrom arrived at the scene during this confrontation. A high-keyed man, Satrom was already in an agitated state because of earlier reports by police informants that some dreaded Weathermen had been spotted on campus—reports that seemed to be confirmed by the melee happening now in his town. After consulting briefly with the police chief, he made several portentous decisions. He declared a state of emergency, ordered the closing of all bars, and imposed an 11:00 P.M. curfew on the city and an 11:30 curfew on the campus. Then he phoned Columbus and informed the governor's administrative assistant that "SDS students had taken over a portion of Kent."[3] The assistant called National Guard commander Sylvester T. Del Corso, who ordered liaison officer Lieutenant Charles J. Barnette to Kent.

Then, defying the law of unintended consequences, Satrom ordered the police to begin emptying all the bars on the Strip. This decision quickly doubled the size of the mob on the street, greatly exacerbating an already volatile situation. Those forced out of the bars had been guilty of nothing but drinking and smoking and listening to music. Now they suddenly found themselves being pushed and shoved outside into the rowdy crowd on the street. And the more the police manhandled them, the angrier and more mutinous they became.

Meanwhile, at the intersection of Main and Water police and deputy sheriffs began using tear gas to force the milling crowd away from the center of town, up Main Street, and down toward campus. Those who resisted—or seemed to—were arrested. The gas and the rough handling angered the crowd and left an aftertaste of bitterness among many who had played no part in the riot on North Water. Many students who were enjoying the spring evening outside the fraternity and sorority houses on Main were hassled and gassed along with the mob being forced toward campus.

At Prentice Gate the mob, mostly composed of students, refused to budge any farther. They stationed themselves on campus property and on the campus side of the intersection of Main and Lincoln streets. Facing them were city police and sheriff's deputies, who, reluctant to breach the sanctuary of the campus, waited for campus officers to take over. But they were posted elsewhere, defending campus buildings from attacks by radicals reportedly gathering on various parts of the grounds.[4] The result was a tense standoff at Prentice Gate.

But that tension was suddenly dissolved by an act of good neighborliness occasioned by a timely accident. A repairman was repairing a nearby traffic light when a car accidentally ran into the electric company truck, leaving the man dangling high above the street. Some "rioters" and the police spontaneously formed a human ladder and brought him safely to the ground.[5] After that, the crowd dispersed and the officers left. It was calm on campus and downtown by 2:30 A.M. when Lieutenant Barnette arrived to consult with Mayor Satrom.

The next morning, Saturday, saw a steady stream of sightseers moving up and down North Water. Hair-raising reports of the worst night of violence in the town's history—tales of riot and looting and mayhem—had spread during the small hours of the night. While a few KSU students were picking up debris, curious townspeople gaped at the damage, which looked much worse than it actually was, according to businessman and civic booster Lu Lyman.[6]

It was, however, the appearance that determined the attitudes of sightseers: broken shop windows, bottles and cans strewn among thousands of shards of glass littering the sidewalks and street. The town buzzed all day Saturday with swarms of lurid reports—of shops trashed and looted, of $100,000 damage to downtown Kent, of North Water being "leveled," of injured cops, of an imminent invasion by "outsiders." Nearly all proved to be either pure fiction or gross exaggerations. A Chamber of Commerce study later concluded that, all told, forty-seven windows in fifteen businesses (not dozens) had been broken at a cost of $10,000 (not $100,000)—all of it insured—and that no looting had been reported.

Still, the citizens of Kent felt as if they had been rocked by an earthquake. They were nervous, edgy, angry, fearing more destructive aftershocks were coming. Students who ventured downtown were viewed with suspicion tinged with animosity: the stereotyping of all college students as dangerous radicals had begun and would intensify over coming days. At city hall calls from alarmed citizens and agitated council members jammed the switchboard. Police informants passed on hair-raising tips, including one of a planned assault on the ROTC building that night. The pressure on Satrom to do something mounted as the afternoon wore on. Early that day Lieutenant Barnette had warned him that he had to request the National Guard's help before 5:00 P.M. if he wanted it that night, adding that if it came the Guard would have jurisdiction over both campus and town.[7] Shortly before 5:00 Satrom called in the Guard. Though Vice President Robert Matson, White's stand-in, had been present when Barnette mentioned the implications of calling in the Guard, Satrom made the decision unilaterally.

Because campus police had also picked up rumors of the ROTC assault, Matson spent much of the day in the windowless "control center" (i.e., the Bunker) in the Administration Building trying to prepare the campus. He asked geologist Glenn Frank, ombudsman Harold Kitner, and sociologist Jerry Lewis to assemble the Faculty Marshals (sponsored by the Faculty Senate) to monitor developments on the Commons that night. (Uncomfortable with the connotations of the word "marshal," they decided to limit their role to fact gathering, observing, persuading, and "reporting events to the university emergency operations center."[8]) Matson also moved the curfew on campus back to 1:00 A.M. and ordered student affairs officers to set up a round-the-clock rumor-control center and arrange special all-campus activities—free movies, dances, coffee, and doughnuts—as an alternative to the downtown bar scene, which was off-limits.

The mayor's curfew clamped down at 8:00 P.M., another warm night. Downtown all the bars were closed, stores were forbidden to sell alcoholic drinks; on-campus dorm residents (a relatively small percentage of the student body) were effectively locked up. Satrom's dusk-to-dawn curfew, which was intended to forestall violence, may have had the reverse effect. On campus the curfew generated a pressure-cooker atmosphere compounded of restless energy, resentment, and defiance. Many students who got caught up in the rioting that night were initially motivated by a desire to protest the curfew as an infringement on their civil liberties.

There seems, however, also to have been a small number of militants—students from Kent and other colleges as well as free-floating agitators—who were determined to make a violent statement. But all facts, whether of the number of militants or of crowd sizes, are indeterminate, because nothing about the events that occurred on that Saturday night is beyond dispute—except that the ROTC building was attacked.

By 8:00 P.M., some 500 students, who had begun drifting onto the Commons an hour earlier, were clustered around the Victory Bell, listening to various speakers berate the war, the ROTC, the Liquid Crystal Institute, the draft, the curfew, and the administration's Mickey Mouse attempt to distract them with competing diversions and entertainments. The composition of the throng and its motives are in dispute. The crowd was a combination of "an idle collection of students" confined to campus by the curfew, in the words of the Scranton Commission, and a "substantial" group of non-Kent agitators intent on destroying the ROTC, as James Michener's investigation stressed.[9]

Sometime after 8:00 P.M. the crowd left the Commons and paraded around the dorms to the east, swelling its ranks by shouting out invitations to the students inside. By the time the demonstrators swung back toward the Commons there may have been as many as 2,000.[10] When they reached Taylor Hall and were poised to march down onto the Commons, a number of them remained on the hill, apparently choosing to watch from a safe distance. The others then strode down toward the ROTC building. Their pace quickened as they approached it, and the two dozen or so in the front rank began shouting "Burn it!" and flinging rocks toward the wooden structure. The others followed suit. It was approximately 8:30 P.M.

Here a caveat is in order. All narrative accounts of the events surrounding May 4 are based primarily on reports based on memories of impressions and perceptions registered under emotional distress and loosely sutured together with conjecture and inference. In the attack on the ROTC building, for example, things were happening on all sides of the long, one-story rectangular structure, making it impossible for anyone present that night to get a comprehensive view of what was taking place everywhere at any given moment, or to have a clear understanding of the driving order of occurrences. In the absence of an objective record, then, any narrative represents a homogenization of multiple eyewitness descriptions of a complex, dynamic, and emotionally fraught event. Thus, what follows is a rounded narrative, sanitized of most of the contradictory, ambiguous untidiness of reality, of a crucial episode in the coming catastrophe.

The assault took the form of a series of wavelike sorties led by a small group of youths standing at the front of the crowd, presumably the same ones in the vanguard of the crowd that strode toward the ROTC building across the Commons from the Victory Bell and adjacent to the Student Center. (Some Faculty Marshals on the scene concluded that these were the instigators of the action.) Someone would dash a few feet toward the building and smash a window with a rock or trash can and then retreat. Then someone would rush forward and chuck a lighted railroad flare through a broken window and then fade back into the crowd. Each sortie was accompanied by a chorus of cheers and antiwar slogans and followed by an expectant interval of quiet waiting, as if expecting the police to do something. Numerous attempts to ignite the building failed, however, and even robust blazes soon guttered out.

After a brief interval, a hailstorm of rocks, trash barrels, railroad flares, and even a fire bomb began battering the windows and roof, and an unidentified young man lit a rag soaked in the gas tank of a motorcycle and ignited some curtains wafting through a broken window, and with that the building seemed to catch fire.

At 9:00 P.M. a city fire engine pulled up on the west side of the building. When the firefighters started unlimbering their hoses, some militants wrapped them in bear hugs while others cut and hacked at the hoses with knives, an axlike stick, and even machetes. And while several other firefighters were waging a tug-of-war over a hose with some protesters, some also moved around to the east end of the structure and began dousing the flames. Stones rained down on them, knocking two to the ground. At this point campus police finally began moving in to help the firefighters, but it was too late. The firefighters, disgusted and shaken, hastily packed up their gear and left, vowing not to return unless they had adequate protection. Soon after they had driven off the fire unaccountably died out.

During the melee, when the stones were battering the building, KSU alumnus and Faculty Marshal Dennis Cooke (biology) went inside to put out a small blaze and saw a "male student" trying to ignite some curtains. "I put the fire out," he recalled. "I use the word 'student' carefully, because there were many folks in the crowd who were not students. Even after, there were folks put on various 'commissions' who claimed to be students but who were not."[11]

Meanwhile, several hundred yards away on the northeast edge of campus, but within view of the flames of the burning ROTC building, twenty highway patrolmen were forming a protective cordon around President White's house, which was not under attack. The role of the campus police is even more puzzling. Their chief explained later that his officers did not try to stop the assaults on the building when they started because he feared their intervention might provoke a riot, and, when an actual riot did start, it was too dangerous to put his men at risk.[12]

About the time the firefighters were driving away, campus police and deputy sheriffs started dispersing the demonstrators with tear gas and forcing them off the Commons. Some fled in the direction of the dorms north and east of Taylor Hall, while another, far larger group rampaged down East Main, trashing, among other things, the information booth near Rockwell Library along the way. In the meantime a Guard contingent had entered campus to protect another group of city firefighters who had been summoned back to campus when the ROTC building had mysteriously started burning with great intensity. But it was already beyond saving when they arrived about 10:00 P.M.

When ammunition stored in the building began exploding, the flames shot up above the skyline and were dramatically visible for some distance beyond the campus. Psychology professor Ed Bixenstine and his wife, Anita, who were returning to their home adjacent to the campus from a dinner party that had ended abruptly when Provost Lou Harris got a call that the ROTC building was burning, could see the flames licking at the night sky as they drove down West Main toward town center. And many householders in the vicinity of campus watched anxiously through their windows and from their front porches. The lurid spectacle of the burning building, overlaid on the image of windows shattering downtown on Friday night, crystallized much of the fear and resentment that tainted their attitude toward students and demonstrations of any kind.

Meanwhile, the mob had reached the intersection of Main and Lincoln, near Prentice Gate, and were heading up Main Street hill toward downtown when they were surprised by a formidable force of Guard troopers with massive personnel carriers and other military vehicles coming toward them. The Guard drove the demonstrators back onto campus and herded them into dormitories. The Guard may well have spared other campus buildings from attack that night, but its often brutal tactics in clearing the campus created intense ill will among many students. By no means had all those gassed and roughed up that night taken part in the ROTC attack. Many students were caught outside their dorms taking advantage of Matson's extension of the curfew to 1:00 A.M., when the guardsmen swept them up in the mass of protesters from Prentice Gate and forced them to shelter in the nearest dorm, whether or not they belonged there. The next day, a litany of Guard abuses echoed around the campus, of students teargassed, rifle butted, pummeled, threatened, kicked, and clubbed. Reports of such treatment are too numerous and too circumstantial to be discounted.[13]

By midnight everyone was corralled into dorms and calm was restored. The commanding officer of the ROTC later assessed the damages at $85,000. The building, which had served as the school's first Hub, was a smoking ruins for the next two days.

. . .

There may have been as many rumors about the presence of incendiary "outsiders" as there were actual ones in town and on campus that weekend. But Sunday morning brought one very real one to town. Governor James Rhodes, one of the state's canniest politicians, represented a new kind of danger. He arrived in a DC-3 frustrated and furious—frustrated by the failure of his campaign for his party's U.S. Senate nomination to get traction, and furious over a wave of violent demonstrations that had rioted across the OU, Miami, and OSU campuses. He saw these disorders in near apocalyptic terms, as part of a ruthless conspiracy to destroy American higher education, a matter close to his heart.

When he deplaned at 9:00 A.M. at the KSU airport, he was in a take-charge, take-no-prisoners mood and determined to convert the base metal of Kent's troubles into political gold for himself. With one stroke he would pump new vigor into his campaign by showing the state and the nation that strict enforcement of law and order was the only way to deal with campus unrest. No matter that prior to the disruptions of Friday and Saturday night, Kent's demonstrations, though noisy, had been notably free of serious violence. Once he arrived in Kent, Rhodes would talk and act as if KSU were the very epicenter of a vast antieducation conspiracy.

After a quick viewing of the ROTC rubble, he went downtown for a meeting with local officials, Guard commanders, and campus officials. He began by declaring his intention to keep the school open but abruptly changed the closed meeting into a press conference when an aide told him some reporters wanted an interview. With the media spotlight trained on his flushed face, he delivered a fifteen-minute, fist-pounding harangue on the threat to authority posed by campus protests. He said the Kent disruptions were "probably the most vicious form of campus-oriented violence yet perpetrated by dissident groups and their allies in the state of Ohio," likening the dissidents to "Brownshirts," "the Communist element," "the night-riders and the vigilantes." He said he would not permit them to use the campus as a sanctuary and pledged to use "every force of the law" to stop them.[14]

Though good political theater, Rhodes's vehement tirade misled countless people unacquainted with the actual state of affairs at KSU and effectively changed the National Guard's mission "from one of protecting lives and property" to one of dispersing "any assembly on campus, peaceful or otherwise." Rhodes ended the conference by saying that he intended to have the courts declare "a state of emergency." He told White the same thing later when their paths crossed at the airport.[15] (After learning of the ROTC torching, White had cut his conference short and returned by the earliest available flight.)

Even more destructive, perhaps, was what the departing Rhodes left trailing behind: a murky cloud of uncertainty about "rules, prohibitions, and proclamations" emitted by some of his press conference statements.[16] What was legal, and what was not? Were students forbidden to assemble under any and all circumstances? Who exactly was in charge of the campus, the president or the Guard commander? No one could agree on the answers to these questions, especially not Guard commander General Robert Canterbury and President White and his closest advisers. Complicating all these questions was Rhodes's decision, never explained, not to request a state of emergency despite vowing that he would. And apparently no campus lawyer or administrator consulted state statutes to find out what exactly a "state of emergency" meant.

As dawn broke that Sunday morning, a massive armored personnel carrier squatted menacingly in front of Prentice Gate, and guardsmen, rifles strapped on their shoulders, patrolled every campus entrance. Yet the afternoon was uneventful, and the weather improbably lovely. Streets leading into Kent were jammed with sightseers, and cars were bumper to bumper on Main Street. People were eager to view the scenes they had read about and seen on TV over the weekend. Families with food hampers picnicked on the campus. Guard helicopters on the football field were a great magnet, especially for kids. The main attraction, however, was the smoldering ROTC building. Guardsmen were told to be friendly to students, something not hard to do on a campus blooming with pretty girls. Freshman Allison Krause walked up to a soldier and, sticking a daisy into his rifle barrel, said, "Flowers are better than bullets." In another version, the soldier already had the flower in his rifle when she spoke. The sky was clear, the air fragrant, the mood seemingly lighthearted.

Many students, however, were far from lighthearted. Word of Rhodes's remarks percolated slowly among them, shocking some, amusing others. Many took his "Brownshirt" remark to mean that the Establishment intended to stamp out political dissent by eliminating freedom of speech and assembly on campus. Many were cynical about his motives. Alumnus Leigh Herington, graduate student and assistant sports information director that spring, said years later that he "always felt" that Rhodes's behavior and remarks "were for the benefit of the Senate primary the following week." Graduate teaching fellow in English Lloyd Agte agreed: "Everyone knew it was political."[17]

Only the Faculty Marshals, after taking the campus pulse, seemed to take either Rhodes or the Guard seriously. Their concern mounted as they spoke with students and tried, with scant success, to persuade them that it was dangerous to provoke soldiers armed with rifles and bayonets. They also discovered much indignation and resentment of the Guard because of its tactics the previous night. Many students said they felt helpless, that they had no countervailing authority to whom they could appeal for understanding and protection against the massive power represented by the Guard. And there was talk of a demonstration that night.

After 7:00 P.M. students began gathering in the vicinity of the ROTC ruins and the Student Union. By 8:45 there were so many that the administration anxiously decided to move the campus curfew ahead, from 1:00 A.M. to 9:00 P.M. And at 9:00 an official told the crowd that it had five minutes to disperse or they would be arrested. Few left, however, and five minutes later tear-gas canisters began falling among them. One large group dashed toward White's house but was forced back to the Commons by tear gas fired by guardsmen assigned to protect the ruined ROTC building.

The main body of these protesters apparently later headed down to Prentice Gate and joined a crowd that, by this time, had grown so large that it spilled over onto the intersection of Main and Lincoln streets, stopping all traffic. City police and deputy sheriffs took up positions facing the demonstrators, blocking them from advancing downtown, while guardsmen moved down East Main and lined up behind them.

The standoff that lasted for the next hour bore only the most superficial resemblance to the one on Friday night, when there were no guardsmen boxing them in. Another difference was in the character of the crowd and its purpose. One investigation concluded that its composition defies easy description because it seems to have been animated by no single purpose but that it did have a dominant mood or disposition—a strong antipathy toward the Guard.[18] It also had at least one goal—to talk to someone in authority.

Shortly after 10:00, a spokesman for the demonstrators asked to talk with Mayor Satrom and President White about several demands: abolishing the curfew, removing the Guard, granting all BUS demands, reducing student tuition, abolishing ROTC, and granting amnesty to students arrested on Saturday night. Police then permitted a spokesman to use a police cruiser's public address system to announce that the mayor was coming to talk with the students and that White was being contacted.[19]

In fact, Mayor Satrom had agreed to come, but Matson and Vice President Ronald Roskens, both of whom opposed "negotiating in the streets," said later that because the Guard had charge of the campus, they had advised White not to talk with the students and that White had concurred. White, however, later told the Scranton Commission that he could not recall Matson's discussing the matter with him.[20] In days to come, many students and faculty would have trouble excusing, if not justifying, the administration's unwillingness to send someone to at least talk to a crowd of Kent students.

An hour later the students were still sitting on the ground waiting for Satrom and White to appear, when the police abruptly announced that neither man was coming and that the 11:00 P.M. curfew was now in effect. Then, after a reading of the riot act, they ordered the students to move off the intersection. But before most of the crowd could withdraw onto the campus, guardsmen advanced on them, bayonets at the ready. Many people were injured in the ensuing confrontation. Innocent bystanders as well as demonstrators were manhandled; at least two students sustained serious bayonet wounds, and several guardsmen were bruised by stones. The students at the intersection, sure that they had been tricked or betrayed, became incensed, cursing and pushing back as they were herded back onto the campus and toward the dorm areas. The guardsmen, in turn, became vindictive and often made unrestrained use not only of tear gas but of their rifle butts, bayonets, and batons. The frightening sounds of the confused struggle outside trapped several students and professors inside Rockwell Library, until a librarian negotiated a "forty-five-minute grace period" during which the Guard permitted them to leave peacefully.[21]

The Guard, driving the protesters in the direction of Music and Speech and Tri-Towers, was relentless in its pursuit of anyone unlucky enough to be outside a dorm. Helicopter spotlights pinpointed them from above. Noise from the melee brought many dorm students outside to see what was going on, and many of them were clubbed and gassed when they were swept into the chaos. That night some sixty-eight students were arrested and bused to the county jail, where they joined the thirty-two arrested in earlier disruptions. All were charged with failure to disperse and curfew violation.

Earlier that evening Harold Kitner had persuaded a handful of professors to field calls from students at the campus radio station in Music and Speech. Student callers brushed off all the professors' warnings about baiting guardsmen with bayonets on their rifles. They seemed incapable of understanding that those rifles might be loaded with real bullets; some insisted that the rifles were loaded with blanks. In the students' moral calculus, soldiers would never shoot or stab someone just for throwing a stone or shouting an obscenity.

When the six professors left the radio studio around midnight, they walked through an acrid miasma of tear-gas smoke while a helicopter tilted overhead and picked them out of the darkness with its spotlight. They had no sooner driven by Terrace Hall than they were stopped by a roadblock at the corner of Crain and Luther avenues. A visibly nervous young guardsman approached the car and, thrusting his bayonet through the driver's open window, demanded their names and destinations. They felt then just like their students—citizens of a country under foreign occupation.

Monday, May 4, added one more jewel to the flawless string of fine spring days in that mildest of Mays in memory. By midmorning the temperature was in the mid-sixties, the sky a polished dome of pastel blue. The just-budding leaves of the great oaks and elms shimmered in the occasional breeze, and puffs of spring blossoms basked in soft sunlight.

The pastoral appearance of nature was belied by the human reality. Shortly after 11:00 A.M. students began gathering in the vicinity of the Hub and the former ROTC building, some getting their first look at the ruins. A number of professors canceled their midmorning classes because so many students had cut. Students newly returned from the weekend and hearing reports of the Guard's brutal behavior on Sunday night were caught in the tide of acrimony rising against the Guard's presence on their campus and were determined to defy administration notices prohibiting the antiwar rally announced the previous Friday. Administration efforts to inform the campus had been haphazard at best, and an untold number of the 20,000 students, like many of their professors, were unaware of the ban.

Earlier that morning, at 10:00, Guard general Robert Canterbury had convened a critical meeting in the fire station downtown. Present were White, Matson, a highway patrol representative, and Satrom, accompanied by two city officials. All that is known with certainty about what transpired at the meeting was that they discussed the noon rally. The key figures in the room, Canterbury and White, left the meeting with sharply different memories of what had been said and who had said what. Canterbury swore that White said the rally would be dangerous. White denied taking part in any discussion of the rally, adding that, though he had not known that a rally was scheduled for Monday, if his opinion had been asked about permitting it, he would have answered in the "affirmative." Yet the testimony of others in the meeting, James J. Best concluded, "tends to support Canterbury's view that a 'consensus' of the meeting emerged, with none of the university officials voicing strong opposition to the proposal that rallies not be allowed on campus."[22]

Hovering over this discussion—and conditioning it—was the general misunderstanding shared by all parties in the room that the campus was under a state of emergency, which implicitly bans all rallies. This may account for White's and Matson's failure to argue against stopping the rally.[23] No one at the meeting knew that, in fact, there was no state of emergency. Because of this misunderstanding, White probably assumed that Canterbury had legal control of the campus and so it was up to Canterbury to decide whether or not to permit the rally. Still, White's equivocating circumspection is puzzling. Shortly after the meeting, White and his top assistants drove to the Brown Derby a mile east of campus to eat and prepare for a Faculty Senate meeting that afternoon.

It was about 11:30 when Canterbury arrived on campus and judged that the crowd was still orderly. But fifteen minutes later, when he saw "about 600 students massing not far from his troops," according to one authority, he "became justifiably concerned" and gave "a clear order" that the students be dispersed. "This order was given before any rocks had been thrown." A few minutes later the Victory Bell started ringing while students poured onto the Commons from every direction, the majority coming from their 11:00 classes, which had just ended. Seemingly within minutes, upward of 3,000 people—students, professors, staff members, and townspeople—materialized on or around the Commons.[24]

Looking across the Commons, Canterbury now saw a restive crowd of several hundred students milling about the Victory Bell, some waving flags and chanting antiwar and anti-Guard slogans. Immediately behind the bell, several hundred more were spread up the thinly treed hillside and over the wide terraces of Taylor Hall looming on top of Blanket Hill. A far greater number of what were obviously spectators was gathering along the long south-sloping shoulder of Blanket Hill and on the terraces of Johnson and Stopher halls. The largest number, however, may have been behind the ROTC ruins and strung along both the western and northern borders of the Commons.

As noon approached, the students near the bell became more boisterous, seeming to get a shot of adrenalin as more students joined their ranks at change of class. Their anti-Guard and antiwar shouts and chants became louder and shriller by the minute. At 11:49 a campus policeman with a bullhorn announced the order to disperse, which applied to the bystanders as well as the demonstrators. Canterbury assumed that everyone present knew that the rally had been banned; the campus radio had broadcast the ban earlier. He probably did not know, however, that the dorms had no effective intercom system, and only a few classrooms had speakers. Consequently, not many of the 3,000 there knew they were assembled illegally.

A minute later, the rope barrier in front of the ROTC ruins dropped and a jeep drove slowly onto the Commons and circled the perimeter of the crowd three times while a campus policeman with a bullhorn ordered the crowd to disperse. No one dispersed. Some demonstrators tossed stones at the jeep as it passed. The jeep drove off the Commons after a few minutes.

Meanwhile, Canterbury told his approximately 100 enlisted men and ten officers to "lock and load" their weapons and prepare for a "gas attack"—to don their gas masks.[25] Because of the clamor, many people were unable to hear the dispersal order, while others assumed that the rifles were loaded with blanks instead of live ammunition. Canterbury did not tell the policeman in the jeep to announce that fact. This failure to warn them of the potentially lethal consequences of defying the dispersal order might not have deterred the most militant, but it would surely have warned off many spectators, some of whom were there only out of curiosity or a desire to receive official information about the situation on campus.

At one minute before noon, Canterbury ordered his troops to prepare to "move out and disperse this mob" and then told his grenadiers to fire their "elephant gun" grenade launchers.[26] Seconds later dirty streamers of tear gas arced up and over the Commons. Some canisters landed among the protesters near the Victory Bell, some overshot the bell and landed in the crowd on Blanket Hill, and some, caught in a cross breeze, fell among the bystanders spread along the terraces of Johnson and Stopher. Everyone immediately began scrambling to escape the stinging fumes, the great majority heading up Blanket Hill on the south side of Taylor. Others fleeing the gas and the oncoming guardsmen ran up around the north side of Taylor Hall, and some ran into the building, which was already filling with noxious fumes sucked into the air-conditioning ducts. When the students reached the front of Taylor, they scattered across the lawn and parking lots and waited, perhaps thinking they were sufficiently dispersed to satisfy the Guard. It is doubtful that anyone had any notion of how to determine when they were legally dispersed; few could have known the number that constituted an illegal assembly.

In the meantime Canterbury, dressed in mufti and striding behind his troops—with rifles at port arms—sent a small detachment around Taylor's north side to deter anyone from circling back down to the Commons. The detachment formed a skirmish line anchored on the northeast corner of the building. Meanwhile, with the majority of students fleeing up the south side of Blanket Hill ahead of them, Canterbury's main force trekked up the steep grade, once site of a toboggan slide. Canterbury halted his troops at the top of the hill, between the southeast corner of Taylor Hall and the Pagoda sculpture. As he was surveying the situation, his troops were greeted with a barrage of curses, rocks, and chunks of concrete thrown by the students in front of them. Most of the rocks and concrete chunks fell harmlessly short, because those students were too far away, but by then students were scattered over the entire area—in front of Taylor, Prentice and its paved parking lot, and an adjacent unpaved lot. Using the voice emitter in the special masks worn by officers and noncoms, Canterbury ordered his troops to drive the crowd off the large football practice field several hundred yards east of the Pagoda. With that order he sent his troops into a trap. "What none of the Guardsmen apparently realized," Michener commented, "was that along the eastern side of this field, ran a sturdy six-foot-high chain-link fence, topped by three strands of heavy barbed wire. What was worse, at the baseball end this fence took a right-angle turn to the west to form a catcher's backstop; it would be difficult to find on the campus a more perfect cul-de-sac."[27]

By this time the grenadiers had discharged so much tear gas that the whole area was fitfully shadowed by large clouds of drifting smoke coalescing into a thin, disorienting fog. As the guardsmen marched down the thirty-foot grade in front of Taylor Hall, a large segment of the crowd gave way, let them pass, and then re-collected behind them. Many others retreated, waiting to see what the Guard would do next.

Adding to the pandemonium, students were crossing the area on their way to and from classes, and they, too, like the demonstrators near the Victory Bell and the thousand or so spectators driven by tear gas from the Johnson-Stopher area, found themselves being drawn by the centrifugal forces of circumstance and passion into the vortex of the impending catastrophe. Thus confusion was compounded. The guardsmen could distinguish only a few of those they had been ordered to disperse (who were, by any commonsense definition of the term, already dispersed) from the bystanders who had fled the tear gas, let alone from the passersby present by sheer happenstance, many of whom sympathized with the demonstrators' opposition to the presence of the Guard. Nearly all the protesters were KSU students, some even wearing headbands as statements of fashion rather than ideology. The tear gas converted many hitherto uninvolved spectators and bystanders into angry opponents of the Guard.

As the guardsmen marched down toward the practice field, they were baited and harried by some of the more foolhardy militants, who dared them to shoot, called them "fascist bastards" and "pigs," and, most maddeningly, threw rocks and gas canisters at them, then retreated.[28] The guardsmen halted when they came up against the fence several hundred yards east of the Pagoda, formed a loose skirmish line, and waited for further orders. While they stood there, now under a heavy hail of stones and curses, their anger and animosity toward students, building steadily since Saturday night, flared into something like hatred. Yet there is some reason for doubting that they were closely pressed at any time or that many of the stones hit them.[29]

But they were hot and winded from the arduous climb up the hill and frustrated to find themselves caught between the fence and the shape-shifting throng of students blocking their path of withdrawal back to the Commons. Moreover, because of their gas masks, they had only a hazy understanding of the actual circumstances in which they were operating. The masks not only made it hard for them to breathe, they also severely restricted their peripheral vision and made it virtually impossible to see anything behind them, while the mist condensing on their goggles made it hard to see clearly straight ahead. This fog of uncertainty intensified apprehensions of being in imminent danger and undoubtedly played a part in what was about to happen.

During the roughly ten minutes they stood by the fence, a dozen or so guardsmen dropped to their knees into firing position and aimed their weapons at the crowd but did not shoot. (A photograph of this incident catches student-activist Alan Canfora standing a short distance from kneeling guardsmen, taunting them to shoot at him.) One weapon was actually discharged on the practice field, however; an officer fired a .22-caliber beretta pistol into the air. "The act of kneeling and pointing their weapons at the crowd without firing," Best concluded, "may have seemed to the crowd to be evidence that the guardsmen had no ammunition, or, if they did, they wouldn't use it."[30]

At approximately 12:20 P.M. Canterbury, realizing his error in positioning his troops with their backs to the fence, ordered them to form an inverted wedge and move back up Blanket Hill to the Pagoda and then down to the Commons.[31] As the students, bunched in small groups in front of Taylor Hall, saw the troopers moving toward them, they scattered, some heading back to the Commons, while most of those in the parking lots were content to watch. But a small number of hardcore activists, interpreting the withdrawal maneuver as victory for the students, began harrying the troopers, cursing and mocking them and following closely on their heels for part of the way up the hill. This infuriated some of the guardsmen, who were tired and hot and scared. The troopers most affected by the harassment may have been among the last to reach the Pagoda at the southeast end of Taylor.

There, after a brief pause, twenty-eight guardsmen wheeled around, faced in the general direction of the abstract iron sculpture down the hill that sweeps along the front of Taylor Hall toward the dorms and parking lots. They lifted their weapons and, at 12:25 P.M., began shooting. During the next thirteen seconds, they fired off fifty-five rounds from rifles, five from pistols, and one shotgun shell.[32] Two seconds into the shooting, two officers frantically began trying to stop the shooters, striking them on helmet and shoulders with batons. By the time the shooting stopped, thirteen students had been wounded, four fatally, dying either where they fell or soon after.

Sandy Scheuer, a speech therapy major on her way to class, was killed by a bullet that pierced her neck and broke her windpipe. She died in a pool of her own blood about 390 feet from the Pagoda. Close by, 382 feet from the Pagoda, lay William Schroeder, a psychology major on a ROTC scholarship. He was killed by a round that tore through his chest and destroyed his vital organs. Somewhat closer, but still 343 feet from the Pagoda, was Allison Krause, a freshman honors student who bled to death after a round of gunshot shattered her heart and lungs. With her in the ambulance when she died was her friend Jeffrey Miller, a junior psychology major, killed by a round that entered his mouth and splintered the back of his skull. He was felled 250 feet from the Pagoda. He was the only one of the slain known to have harassed the guardsmen.

The nine other casualties were also Kent students. One, Dean Kahler, was about 300 feet from the Pagoda when a round struck his back, leaving him permanently paralyzed. The closest was twenty yards from the Pagoda, the farthest about 250 yards—two and a half football fields—from the shooters. Still, their lives were charmed, considering that the M1 has a killing range of at least two miles.

Charmed as well was journalism student John Filo. As one of his photographs records, a guardsman aimed his M1 directly at Filo, but the bullet missed and punched a perfect hole through a panel of the iron sculpture before speeding unimpeded on its way. Most of the shots were apparently fired randomly, but all were potentially lethal, even those aimed above the heads of the students close at hand. This may explain why most of the casualties were far from the immediate vicinity of the shooters. Shooting accurately downhill requires skill.

When the shooting stopped, there was a deafening silence, which was rent by the sounds of screaming and sobbing. Then students rushed to help the wounded, giving mouth-to-mouth resuscitation, stanching bleeding holes with headbands and shirts and towels, any handy thing. Some locked arms and formed protective circles around the injured, fearful the Guard was not finished with its work. Some fell apart, and some ran to call for help. Within minutes the University's Centrex telephone system was so taxed it shut down.

Soon a university ambulance pulled up near the metal sculpture, and then rescue vehicles from three area towns came screaming onto the killing field. Some students, blinded by grief and rage, had to be physically restrained from assaulting the ambulance crews trying to help the victims. Anyone in uniform was the enemy.

Outside "the War Room" the Guard had set up near Wills Gym, a WKNT reporter overheard a Guard officer reporting "two dead" in front of Taylor Hall and immediately phoned the United Press International news agency in Columbus with a bulletin stating that two National Guardsmen had been killed.[33] That was the first word the world heard of the tragedy, and it was dead wrong. So was the first word the world saw: the headline on the *Record Courier* that jumped out at 7,000 readers that afternoon blazoned that two guardsmen and one student had been shot dead. The paper stopped the run when it discovered its error, but newspaper corrections always lag errors, and the dye of first impressions leaves permanent stains. Long after students had been officially identified as the victims, the mind-sets of countless people were tainted by the false reports that students had shot guardsmen, for they confirmed the worst fears associated with the stereotype of the student radical. And, in the sophistry of prejudice, this false news, even after it was exposed as false, morphed into emotional confirmation of the older generation's darkest fears of radical youth: if they damage property, they'll soon kill us.

Once the officers managed to stop the shooting, they led the guardsmen in a long straggled line back down the steep slope of Blanket Hill and across the interminable 100 yards of the Commons to their starting point, the ROTC ruins. The troopers were dazed, scared, and shredded by what they had done. "I just couldn't believe it," one Sergeant Antram said later. "I remember my first thought, I'm getting out of the Guard. I'm C.O. [a conscientious objector]." "Nobody talked about it," said Mike Chizmadia, a guardsman from Orrville. "Some threw their weapons to the ground and started to bawl," another said. But before long, fear of possible prosecution for murder, as well as advice from their officers, took over, and, almost to a man, they refused to talk publicly about what had happened and why. A couple said they feared being shipped off to Vietnam if they talked. Many hired lawyers when they got home.[34]

In the following months a blurred picture of the feelings and motives at work among the guardsmen on the hilltop during those few minutes would be developed in numerous investigations and hearings. Most were anxious, confused, and seething with anger and resentment when they reached the Pagoda. And almost all were scared. Some said they had been surrounded by students. Some said they were afraid they would have hand-to-hand struggles with students trying to stab them with their own bayonets. Some said they had been bombarded by rocks, though others said that few, if any, rocks were thrown just before the shootings. Many were adamant that their lives had been at risk. Yet investigations of photographs taken of the scene show no evidence of students near the troops immediately before they turned to shoot.

One who insisted his life was at risk was the commanding officer. At a press conference later in the War Room, General Canterbury was visibly rattled by his first taste of actual combat. In answer to what remains one key question, he told reporters, "Our only reason for pursuing the students [across Blanket Hill] was to dispel the crowd," he said, and, feeling the crowd "had been dispelled" after the shootings, he "gave the order to return to the Commons."[35] This implies that he was unable to judge that the crowd had been "dispelled" until thirteen of them had been shot, which makes as much—or as little—sense as anything else that happened that sad, mad, terrible day.

A chaplain with the guardsmen that day, Captain John Simon, who talked with several of the men afterward, said they had been misled by Canterbury and other "Columbus" officials, presumably Guard commander Lieutenant General Del Corso and Governor Rhodes. The killings "never should have happened. I think they [the guardsmen] were angry, they were scared," Simon said, "and that something caused them to fire. What, I don't know." After the shooting, he told a reporter later, he went home and got drunk.[36]

As the dead and wounded were being removed, several hundred students followed the guardsmen, shouting and screaming, back down to the Victory Bell, where, in a nihilistic rage, they began talking about throwing themselves at the Guard and following their friends into death. Canterbury had put the guardsmen on the ready after seeing the shouting, chanting crowd coming down onto the Commons.

At this point, some Faculty Marshals, who were still stunned by what they had witnessed on the killing field in front of Taylor Hall, began trying to talk the students down from their hysterical high. One was psychologist Seymour H. Baron, who tracked down the officer in charge: "I said, 'General, for Christ's sake, I beg of you. There is going to be a slaughter. Tell your men to put down their guns. For Heaven's sake, do something.' And the general said, 'I've got to do my job. Take this man away.'" Baron then sprinted back across no-man's land to the students near the Victory Bell. They were still dangerously overwrought, and, speaking through a bullhorn he picked up along the way, Baron shouted, "You've got to survive! I don't want you to die! It won't help! You're going to get a bullet in the belly if you stay."[37] Though most students did sit down, many tried to shout down Baron and his colleagues, who implored them to calm down and discuss the situation rationally.

A few minutes later Glenn Frank joined Baron, honors dean Mike Lunine, and French professor Gerald Camber, who were talking to Canterbury, asking for time to persuade the students to leave the Commons. The professors' pleas worked this time; Canterbury gave them permission—and time—to try to persuade the students to leave. But not much time. While the professors were pleading with the students, many of whom were too rage filled to listen to reason, Frank spotted a squad of guardsmen, led by a major, creeping down the hill behind the demonstrators. Still reeling from what had happened, and stunned by the memory of seeing "a person with a black flag jumping up and down" in the blood pooling from one of the fallen students, he bulled through the seated students, stepping on some, and confronted the officer: "For GOD'S sake, don't come any closer." When the major said his orders were to move ahead, Frank stood between the troops and the students and said, "Over my dead body," and the guardsmen withdrew.[38]

After almost twenty minutes of tense negotiations, during which the professors, hearts hammering, shuttled back and forth between the general and the students, Canterbury's patience began to run out. He left the Commons in a jeep and went to the Administration Building, where he probably spoke with Rhodes in Columbus, because when he returned his manner was truculent and peremptory.[39] Captain Ron Snyder, within earshot of these negotiations, heard Canterbury refuse one of Frank's requests and then add, "They're going to have to find out what law and order is all about." The phrase has a distinctly Rhodesean ring and probably echoed the views of Canterbury's superiors in Columbus: the students had to be taught a lesson. The students already knew what law and order meant, of course; it was those things that came, apparently at random, from the barrel of an M1 rifle, whether or not you were a protester or a bystander or a stone thrower. And it was precisely that ghastly lesson they could not accept. An hour after the crisis, Frank overheard Canterbury asking his superiors in Columbus to change his orders.[40]

Major Donald Manley of the state highway patrol was also in earshot of the negotiations with Canterbury. With him was a contingent of 181 troopers, in their Smokey Bear hats and with their 22-inch wooden clubs in hand and their revolvers conspicuously holstered, models of professionalism whose arrival soon after the shootings had been cheered wildly by some students. When Canterbury finally and grudgingly said to Frank, "I'll give you five minutes," Manley told Frank, "Take all the time you need." He had told Baron essentially the same thing earlier, but Frank, Baron, and the others realized that it was Canterbury's orders that counted. And he seemed dead set on attacking in five minutes.[41]

Frank's heart was in his throat when he and his colleagues hurried to the students to make one last desperate appeal, which someone captured on audiotape: "We've got to leave or we'll be slaughtered," Frank said. "Please, please, please, listen to me right now. I don't care whether you've never listened to anyone before in your lives. I am begging you right now. If you don't disperse right now, they're going to move in and there can only be a slaughter. Would you please listen to me!" This was followed by a short pause and an exclamation: "Jesus Christ! I don't want to be a part of this!" And at this cri de coeur, the students, "almost beyond miracle," as Frank remembered it, got slowly to their feet, and, some lugging a few protesting diehards against their will, "they started to leave." By then Frank's legs were almost too weak to bear him up. He broke down and had to be helped off the Commons.[42] It was now almost 2:00 P.M.

Lunch was halfway over when a phone call brought President White speeding back to campus, hearing a sound like fingernails screeching on a blackboard in his head. Although he didn't yet know the mess of horrors awaiting him there, he must have been staggered by the phone call. Among the welter of thoughts and feelings rioting in his mind during this journey of a few minutes, he must have been beset by misgivings and self-doubts, not least about his career and reputation. With a temperament, character, and ability almost ideally suited to academic leadership, White had always been a golden boy, his career a string of solid achievements. Assuming Kent's presidency at a young age, he had almost single-handedly created its graduate program and, within a few years, fixed its place among the state's leading doctoral institutions.

Now he, never having tasted failure before, was racing back to face a calamity beyond the experience of any university president in American history, one for which no academic curriculum or administrative experience could have prepared him. And, for the second time in four days, he had been absent when violence ripped his campus—once too often, surely, for it to be attributed to ill fortune or some perturbation of the stars. Given the events of the weekend, and knowing as he did the symbolic importance of the Commons to his students, even as he left for lunch he must have felt some premonitory intuition that banning the rally was more dangerous than permitting it. Feelings of dismay and injured pride over having had to cede control of the campus to Canterbury doubtless played some cozening part in his decision to leave rather than stay on campus and suffer the humiliation of having someone else do his job. And at some level he must have sensed that it was a mistake to leave, for having unwillingly forfeited control, by leaving it he had willingly relinquished the power to influence events at the rally.

Back on campus, at roughly 12:45 P.M., White was briefed by Roskens and ordered the campus closed. There was nothing more he could do to stop further bloodshed. Roskens sent Glenn Frank in an ambulance around campus announcing over its public address system that the students were to go to their dorms, pack their belongings, and leave the premises by the shortest route as soon as possible. Meanwhile, five miles away in Ravenna, county prosecutor Ron Kane, after failing to persuade Rhodes to close the campus on Sunday morning, prepared a brief which, later that afternoon, persuaded Judge Albert Caris to issue an injunction closing it indefinitely.

For the 1,800 dorm residents, those two hours were frantic. Prodded by anxious resident advisers and not knowing if they'd ever return, they jammed clothes and books into luggage and boxes and hurried off, most on special buses, marshaled with surprising speed by the administration, to every major city in the state. One eighteen-bus caravan transported 1,000 students to the Rapid Transit terminal near Cleveland and left them to find their own way home. Some hitchhiked and some traveled home in impromptu carpools. By 4:00 P.M. there were only about 300 students on campus—those who lived in married student housing and international students. And an hour later the only people to be seen on the vast rolling campus on the hill above town were National Guardsmen and law officers. Every gateway to the campus was blocked by troopers and military vehicles. The doors of every classroom building were chained shut. Every parking lot was as vacant as the moon.

Local public schools began closing almost as soon as the campus, so swiftly did the contagion of shock and fear spread. Guardsmen even stopped a bus returning some elementary students to their homes on Kent's western border, walking up and down the aisle, their bayonets unsheathed on their M1s. Every vehicle approaching the city limits was stopped and searched for "outside agitators" and weapons. Daily newspapers and the U.S. mail went undelivered to much of Kent because the Guard blocked delivery trucks from entering the town. Vigilantes with bullhorns cruised some sections of town, excitedly warning householders of imminent attacks by student radicals said to be lurking in wooded areas and abandoned barns outside of town and telling mothers to "get your children off the streets." As the soft spring evening sidled down, police cars—riot guns sticking out of windows taped to prevent shattering—cruised city streets, and officers warned people to stay inside after dark or "they might be shot." Armored Guard vehicles moved along the empty streets.

Tempers were at hair-trigger. A vigilante fever infected normally sensible businessmen; some shopkeepers armed themselves and stayed in their stores downtown overnight, drinking coffee and smoking, determined to protect their property at all costs. One armed group was said to have spent several nights on the roof of a shop across from the Strip. Throughout that long first night, like every night that week, state highway patrol and Guard helicopters scythed the night air in widening concentric circles over campus, town, and countryside. The pulse and throb of their motors and the sudden down stabbing of their spotlights reminded many residents of news footage of Vietnam villages.

The Guard controlled campus and town until May 8, when it was withdrawn, despite the loud protests of county prosecutor Kane. Feeding the fear, he refused to lift the injunction to open the campus, worried that it would be an invitation to radical terrorists hell-bent on revenge.

Many were pierced by pangs of remorse after the shootings. Surely some who, in their ideological zeal, had thrown rocks and curses at police and guardsmen suffered some trial of conscience. Even some professors who had taught their students to think critically, to cultivate the life of the mind, to exercise their democratic freedoms, and especially those who had stood in peace vigils and marched in nonviolent antiwar demonstrations, setting examples for their students, surely some of them pondered in the dark, third-degree hours of the night the possibility that they may have been at one end of a moral continuum that led by insensible degrees to the four dead and nine wounded students at the other end.

There were doubtless some whose passion for revolution had made stones of their hearts, as there were also many people in towns small, like Kent, and large, across the state and nation, who not only stridently blamed the students for their own deaths but, taking counsel of their fears and prejudices rather than their consciences and their charity, hot-bloodedly declared that the Guard should have killed even more students. The parents of Sandy Scheuer, grieving for their only daughter, were tortured by anonymous hate mail for weeks after her death. Among a host of other consequences, the tragedy of May 4 served as a catalyst in the process of demonization that cast all college students into the same radical mold. Yet it also, in some sense beyond reason, helped bring the Vietnam War to an end by bringing it unbearably home.

Eight

THE AFTERMATH

{1970–1971}

The next morning, Tuesday, May 5, Harold Kitner and Martin Nurmi (the newly elected Faculty Senate chair) summoned some two dozen professors, mostly members of the outgoing and incoming executive committees, to an emergency meeting at psychology professor Ed Bixenstine's home a few blocks from campus. The purpose was to discuss ways of completing the term, to enable seniors to graduate and to keep the school alive while the campus was closed. All were deeply shaken, and many were grieving, especially those who had witnessed the tragedy, like Sy Baron and Glenn Frank, who stared disconsolately at the floor and said little. All knew viscerally that the longer the school was closed, the greater would grow the inertial energy to keep it closed for good—or ill—and few had any confidence that the administration could be counted on to act with decision and dispatch. Their overriding concern was the students, for whom they felt a moral and ethical imperative to finish the work of the term scheduled to end in five weeks.

Several reported getting calls about students leaving their homes, moving in with friends, and joining groups of Kent students reportedly taking refuge at Akron University and Oberlin College. The poignant theme of estrangement from family and home would resound often during the months following the shootings. Homecoming for many students after the shootings was a bitter parody of a genuine homecoming. Instead of open arms and warm hearts at the door, many were confronted by angry parents whose sympathies were entirely with the Guard. Instead of feeling that a grave wrong had been done, many parents said the Guard should have killed more students. The generational divide could hardly gape wider.

After an hour's discussion, the group agreed that the entire faculty should meet as soon as possible with President White and Provost Lou Harris. But where? The campus was off-limits, and the city was under a state of emergency, though no one present knew exactly what that meant. After a few phone calls, a Unitarian Church in Fairlawn offered its sanctuary for a meeting later that day.

That afternoon found about half the KSU faculty and some teaching fellows seated in the church, with White and Harris facing them from the chancel. In hindsight, this moment marked the beginning of the university's regeneration. And regeneration is not an extravagant metaphor. For, existentially, few, if any, of those present felt confident that the school would survive. And there were many reasons for doubting it that day, what with the injunction; the spreading antagonism toward the students, faculty, and administration; and the not-so-remote possibility that the legislature would either convert the school into an insane asylum (a rumor already stirring in the county) or starve it to death by cutting off funding.

There was little inclination to cast blame. Too much was at stake. So, setting aside their reservations about the administration's role in the catastrophe, the assembly gave White a round of applause. The image of him at that moment was not soon forgotten: a man once vigorous, confident, and assured stood before them now, sheet white and stooped, as if about to break.

After some discussion, it was agreed that the administration would provide the faculty with the class rosters, home addresses, and phone numbers of their students. The faculty also passed two resolutions that, when published the next day, turned much opinion against them in the county. Reaffirming students' right to dissent, the faculty declared that it would not teach "in circumstances which are likely to lead to the death or wounding" of students and, while condemning the protesters' acts of violence "to person and property," said that Rhodes and Del Corso, rather than the guardsmen, bore heaviest responsibility for the tragedy.[1] Later, many administrators blanched at such "impolitic" statements, which offended a great many citizens, who thought that in defending students' right to express dissent, the professors were excusing violence.

The shots that felled the Kent State students on May 4 were heard round the world. This time, though, it was American soldiers, not British soldiers, shooting American students demonstrating on an American college campus against the Vietnam War. Virtually overnight some 500 international reporters and television crews descended on Kent and began sending out reports that would dominate world news for weeks. Kent State found itself, where it never expected or wished to be, in the tragic spotlight of world history. In the wake of the shootings, angry protests and demonstrations rippled across college and high school campuses in America and Europe. And, after two black students at Mississippi's Jackson State campus were shot dead by police during a protest against racial discrimination, campus demonstrations increased exponentially in number and vehemence. Eventually some 800 American colleges would suffer serious disruptions and several hundred colleges would shut down entirely.

Meanwhile, on May 7, two days after the church meeting, the Faculty Senate convened formally. And, together with White, they directed the academic deans to complete the instructional obligations of the quarter by the best means possible. Later that day, the administration won the first of a series of modifications of the county court's injunction that eventually made it possible for seniors to graduate in June, on time.

That Sunday, May 10, the Guard permitted White to meet with the trustees at the presidential residence (Williamson House) on the northern border of campus. White reported that, although the school would be closed for the rest of the term, coursework would be completed, thanks to what he described as "the splendid response of the faculty."[2] Because he couldn't in good conscience yet assure parents that the campus would be safe for their children, he would hire off-duty police and deputies to augment campus forces. The Guard and the highway patrol had been transferred to OSU, where campus disruptions continued. The trustees passed several resolutions, among them condolences to the victms' families and commendations of White and the faculty.

While a horde of local, state, and federal investigators combed the campus in the days following the shootings, rumors were spreading throughout the city and county. According to one, it was communists dressed up as guardsmen—not real guardsmen—who had killed the students in order to start more riots. The day after the shootings, Kent resident Mary Vincent struck up a conversation with some students who felt they were being ostracized by townspeople. They asked her help in getting together with some reasonable people to talk about forestalling future trouble in town. This chance encounter gave birth to an idea, which, with Lu Lyman's help, started a series of cottage discussions in private homes that went far to restore a measure of civility and mutual respect to town-gown relations.

Meanwhile, on Friday, May 8, White and the administrative staff were allowed onto campus, and the faculty returned the following Monday, though they had to leave by 5:00 P.M. each day. The linchpin of White's "phased plan" for restoring the campus to normal operations by getting the injunction removed would be the faculty's success in completing the quarter's coursework in time for June graduation. They did this through a combination of correspondence work and teaching students in private homes, churches, libraries, public parks, river banks—in any and all available public venues—shades of the school's early days, when McGilvrey sent his faculty to the students because the students could not come to campus. Teachers of small classes had the easiest time, especially if their students lived close enough to Kent to meet in the teacher's home. Teachers of book subjects, like history and literature, had it far easier than those who needed lab facilities or special equipment.

Some professors traveled great distances to students scattered far from campus; one science teacher drove hundreds of miles in a circuit that included areas around most of the major cities in Ohio as well as sites in Maryland, New York, New Jersey, and Pennsylvania. Even more meaningful, perhaps, for faculty and students than the educational value of holding classes in such extreme circumstances were those moments when what had formerly seemed routine, instrumental transmission of knowledge from instructor to student suddenly became re-centered and re-grounded in an open relationship between vulnerable human beings ambushed by history.

In addition to teaching, many professors spent their evenings that May carpooling to neighboring campuses to meet with Kent-in-Exile groups and listen and plead with bewildered students not to give up on their school. These encounters were disquieting, because the students' naked disillusionment seemed so deeply disabling, as if their props against chaos had broken underfoot, pitching them into freefall. Yet they were clearly desperate to talk to someone who would listen to their anger and fear and frustration, someone who would show them that their school had a human face and a human voice.

Communication was the key—or so it seemed to many professors—and the lack of it had greatly contributed to the tragic shootings. As student protests were proliferating in the late sixties, White had become increasingly worried about the difficulty of communicating in an ever-expanding institution. The larger the student body, it seemed, the greater the need for the personal touch common to small colleges: quantitative changes when great enough produce changes in quality. He discussed this with his advisory board on external relations at the Twin Lakes Country Club on May 22, 1970. "How large can a university get to be and still do what it ought to do?" he asked; "can it become too large for the community in which it exists?"[3] He offered no answers but his posing of such questions suggests that he suspected he had lost touch with students, failed to find a way to talk with them. Insiders said "it wasn't his style" to rap with students. Others said he was the prisoner of his academic rhetoric and culture.

Along with completing the term, administrators and professors wanted to restart the school's neuromuscular system, so that when the campus reopened it would be perceived as different from its present ugly image—in White's words, the "Mecca" of student protest. The first step in the direction was to repair relations with Kent State's constituents. In neighboring communities there were many people who, though upset by the violence, were willing to give faculty members a hearing. In the days immediately following the shootings carloads of professors set out in the evenings for such places as Akron, Cleveland, Canton, and Hudson to talk about the school and the shootings.

Feelings were tightly wound and tempers touchy, at least at the start, and the opening questions were often hostile, implying that the professors were responsible for the disorders, by either inciting or failing to squelch them. The professors, for their part, soon realized that a soft answer does at least soften, if not always turn away wrath, and these sessions usually ended on a note of mutual understanding and in a spirit of tremulous good will. This is what happened one night in the Hudson Library, where a handful of professors found themselves one night trying to field, with tact and grace, some nasty curveballs thrown by a testy audience that included industrialist Burton Morgan, who sat in the front row red faced and thunder browed, steaming disapproval. He later became a generous benefactor of KSU.

On May 13 White established the Commission on KSU Violence to investigate the circumstances and causes of the violence. University Professor and geographer Harold Mayer chaired a small committee of students, faculty, and administrators. One of the two students was senior Kathy Stafford (of Tipp City, Ohio), who had been on the student High Court and on the vice president's advisory committee. Instead of going home on May 4, she had hitched a ride to New York City, where she was staying with friends, when a phone call from Kent summoned her back to serve on the commission. She was just one of many students who helped in the school's regeneration. The commission worked intensely for ten months, under increasing strain as differing perspectives, presumptions, personalities, and interests clashed. They interviewed scores of witnesses and pored over reports, news accounts, records, and every available document bearing on the four days. In the end, however, they were unable to agree on what happened and why or on whether the report should criticize certain decisions and behaviors. Yet they did collect and preserve for the historical record numerous valuable firsthand accounts of the tragedy that would otherwise have been lost. And the commission published the penetrating "Minority Report," written by English professor Doris Franklin, which evenhandedly and eloquently did most of the things expected of the majority report, which was never written.

On May 14 the Faculty Senate passed a carefully worded resolution against violence, which pleased White, mollified the trustees, and perhaps reassured townspeople. And on May 27 White appointed a second presidential commission, the University Commission to Implement a Commitment to Non-Violence, to be led by alumnus professor Charles Kegley. The Kegley Commission was tasked with proposing measures to secure the campus in time for a nonviolent reopening in the fall. Pressed by a short deadline, the members recommended a number of changes, many of which were enacted and helped materially when the fall term began. Among them were reducing the visibility of ROTC (which was to be moved to Rockwell Library months later), setting up a twenty-four-hour desk operation in all dorms, providing students with new identification cards, appointing a new student ombudsman, and heightening sensitivity to black students' concerns.

. . .

Getting the wheels turning to finish the quarter's work and prepare for June graduation exercises and reopen the University in the fall was but only part of White's agenda. For a week or so after the shootings, Kent was the news center of the world. Along with flocks of investigators from the FBI and other government agencies, about 500 members of the national and world media overran campus and town after May 4, overtaxing campus news service personnel and dogging White with requests for interviews, most of which he refused. He did not like the spotlight, and he had better ways to spend his time.

Following the SDS and BUS disruptions of 1968–69, White had become hardened to most hostile criticism, but he was not prepared for the indigestible fare that now became part of his daily diet. Along with the predictable personally abusive letters, there were many springing from the narrow yet deep tradition of American anti-intellectualism, from people whose opposition to higher education was exceeded only by their ignorance of it. Bitterest of all, perhaps, was the mail from people whose lives had curdled over time and left them unable to forgive young people for being young. Even alumni mail, while largely supportive of White personally, often decried "permissiveness" and blamed the school's troubles on a minority of "trouble-makers."[4]

White was perhaps most upset by the anti-University letters that appeared each day in the *Record Courier*, the major news source in Portage County. Its owner-publisher, Robert Dix, was White's friend and president of the Board of Trustees, the school's only legal buffer against the storms now battering its gates. Each edition seemed to feature a strident chorus of hate mail, aimed at him and his school, singing variations on the theme of "they should have shot more students." Though there were many pro-University letters, he was especially troubled by the splenetic letters from people of the town that had campaigned so ardently, first for a normal school and later for a liberal arts college and a university, the institution in which it had vested so many of its hopes for a prosperous, enlightened, and cultured future.

In his few public statements, White was grittily upbeat about town-gown relations, in the same vein as his remarks to his external relations advisers on May 22, but his mood was far glummer in a candid "Informal Review" he sent the trustees on July 7. A deep "schism" divided campus and town, he wrote, because of community "wishes that the University, faculty, students, and all were removed." Save for a few exceptions, he went on, no community official had "given encouragement to me or to any other major officer," and many personal friendships had been "either severed or strained," while "venomous talk" had robbed him and his wife of any desire to live in Kent.[5]

Still, not everyone in the county and town was estranged. Later studies found an almost even division between pro- and anti-White/ KSU opinion, but it was the naysayers, full of passionate intensity, whose voices were loudest and most penetrating. And, as anyone who lived through those dark days can attest, there was a pervasive atmosphere of suspicion, ill will, and animosity that cowed many pro-school voices into silence for fear of reprisal or further fracturing civil life in the community.

On May 31 the Faculty Senate and the Educational Policies Council (EPC) appointed the Ad Hoc Committee on Innovative Curricular Change, a thirty-member group of students, academic administrators, and faculty chaired by English professor William H. Hildebrand. Charged with making the curriculum more relevant to student concerns, the committee adopted a brilliant proposal by honors dean Mike Lunine of adding an experimental component to the Honors College in which subjects of current interest, like those offered in the Free University, could be tested for possible inclusion in the permanent register of courses. Teachers would work pro bono; there would be no prerequisites and no fees. Over the years of its existence the Experimental wing of the Honors College creatively engaged students, and faculty, in contemporary educational, social, political, and cultural issues. A committee proposal aimed at helping students avoid large lecture sections was also adopted: requiring departments to publish the maximum enrollment number for each class in the schedule of classes. But the EPC rebuffed a requirement that everyone holding faculty rank teach at least one class every two years, a proposal aimed at protecting high-level administrators—presidents especially—from the dangers of dwelling exclusively in the abstract world of meetings, budgets, and planning by forcing them back to a classroom or a lab with students. The EPC dominated by administrators, decided that administrators could not spare the time from more important duties.

Meanwhile, opening campus for summer classes and resuming full-time operation in the fall were predicated on getting the injunction lifted, which required convincing Judge Albert Caris that the campus was safe and secure. The cost of extra security personnel was ruinous, draining the University's reserves at a time when enrollments were expected to plummet, along with state support. Also, all employees were required to get new IDs before the single mass registration for both summer terms. And on registration day, June 23, the University set up six special information centers at the major gateways to the campus to hand out visitor permits, answer questions, and provide information.

One grace note of that season in purgatory must be recorded as a demonstration of art's uncanny power to ease the warring tensions and wounded feelings that tormented town-gown relations. Robert Shaw, then conductor of the Atlanta Symphony and by consensus the world's preeminent choral conductor, had grown fond of KSU during the early years of the Kent-Blossom Program when he was associate conductor of the Cleveland Orchestra under George Szell. Convinced that the shootings were a national tragedy and wanting to help the school, he enlisted his friend and former colleague Clayton Krebiehl, Kent's choral director, and the Cleveland Orchestra in a plan to bring the community together in a ritual of public mourning. Shaw flew to Kent from Atlanta, at his own expense, and on the night of June 3, before 600 "mourners" in the United Church of Christ on the eastern edge of campus, he led a chorus of 180 and an orchestra of thirty-seven townspeople, university people, and students in a moving performance of Luigi Cherubini's *Requiem Mass in C Minor*.[6]

A matter of much concern to the Class of 1970, and of great symbolic significance to White, was being able to hold graduation services on campus. Thanks to White's phase-in plan, Judge Caris lifted the injunction on June 5, returning the school to the trustees just in time for spring graduation. On June 14, 1,200 seniors received their diplomas in a ceremony that testified to the school's resilience and vitality. In his address, White promised to pursue four goals: improving communication within the campus and with the community, instilling the principle of nonviolent action, encouraging a belief in the possibility of constructive change, and establishing KSU as a center of research into "peaceful resolution of conflict."[7] During the ceremony he received a telegram that, he told the audience, informed him that President Nixon had appointed a May 4 investigative commission to be chaired by the widely respected William Scranton. This was exactly what White had hoped for: a high-level panel of distinguished public servants tasked to find out what happened and why it happened and to deliver an objective report on their findings. The Scranton Commission, as it came to be called, was also charged with investigating the Jackson State killings.

Summer school got under way on June 22 without incident—to a collective sigh of relief that life once again was moving to the reassuring measures of the academic order. Enrollments for the summer almost equaled 1969's. The weather seemed to smile on campus—sunny days and warm nights throughout a summer unmarred by violence. Administrators worked at the stretch, and many professors did double duty, teaching during the day and at night helping plan for a peaceful return to full-time operations in the fall.

Yet that initial sigh of relief soon condensed into anxiety about what would happen when the entire student body returned for classes in September. Save for a few harmless bomb threats, the campus was notably tranquil during both summer terms, as if the convulsions of May had happened somewhere else. But everyone knew that they had happened here and that the Kent shootings, far from discouraging demonstrations, had increased the number of young people who were disillusioned with the political, economic, and social order of the country. Disruptions and demonstrations broke out periodically across the country, but they tended to be nonviolent, if more vehement and militant than before.

The Scranton Commission started public hearings on campus on August 19, 1970, before moving on to Jackson State. Many campus administrators, faculty, and students testified under the cold, appraising eye of the television camera, most eager, even anxious, to help the commissioners understand what had happened here. With reporters and microphones and television cameras on campus for three dramatic days, Kent State was once again at the top of the national news.

Summer school ended shortly afterward, leaving the campus empty again. Then, after a brief interval, as the fall term approached, the campus filled once again—first, with new freshmen for a week of orientation, then with the entire student body, the exuberant vitality and the welcome sound of their voices reminding faculty of one of the unsung gifts of their profession. More students than ever before—21,365—were on campus that fall.

Rumors and threats floated like autumn leaves. There were raucous demonstrations by larger crowds than in prior falls, and the students were more radical in their views and more aggressive and defiant in expressing them. But unlike the SDS activists, they were nonconfrontational and nonviolent, perhaps because the large infusion of moderate students into the peace movement after May 4 diluted the sway of those committed to direct action. False alarms and bomb threats, mostly targeting classroom buildings during midterm and finals, were common. The alarm would ring, campus police would clear the building, students and teachers would cluster in groups at a "safe distance," smoking cigarettes and chatting, until the all-clear sounded. Then classes would resume as if nothing had happened. After the first wave of threats, few teachers or students took them seriously.

As if cued by the school's reopening, the Scranton Commission released its report on September 26, 1970. Its findings were drawn from the sworn testimony of dozens of witnesses, its own staff findings, and the FBI's secret report to the Justice Department of its extensive investigations. Among the key conclusions, the commission found that those who sparked the violence that brought "havoc" to the town on May 1 and those who burned the ROTC building on May 2 were partly responsible for the May 4 tragedy; that the noon rally on May 4 was primarily a protest against the Guard's presence on campus and only incidentally against the war. The commission also deplored the Guard's decision on May 4 to disperse what had been a peaceful demonstration, its marching tactics, and its policy of using rifles loaded with live rounds in crowd-control situations. What was doubtless its most stunning and memorable finding went to the heart of the matter: "The indiscriminate firing of rifles into a crowd of students and the deaths that followed were unnecessary, unwarranted, and inexcusable."[8] The report raised the spirits of students, faculty, and administrators, chiming as it did with the prevailing opinion on campus.

But only briefly. A few weeks later, on October 16, the state special grand jury, convened earlier on September 14, issued secret indictments against one professor and twenty-four current or former KSU students, charging them with a total of forty-three offenses. Its conclusions were at odds with the Scranton Commission's. The grand jury found, among other things, that the guardsmen were justified in firing their weapons because they sincerely thought they would "suffer serious bodily" harm if they had not fired. It put primary responsibility for the shootings on the administration for encouraging "an attitude of laxity, over-indulgence, and permissiveness" toward students and faculty, leaving the school "vulnerable" to attacks by "radical elements within the student body and the faculty." The report also found that the administration had "fostered dissent" and encouraged an attitude skewed to ignore the "positive" aspects of American history in favor of the "negative." The most troubling aspect of the report for the faculty and administration was the threat posed by the grand jury's view of academic freedom, due process, and First Amendment rights.

The teaching of critical thinking is one of the central responsibilities of a university education.[9] Then, in a vain attempt to keep grand jury testimony secret, the judge issued a court order forbidding witnesses to comment on the report.

A great howl of protest rose up from the campus, from professors and students alike. Some of the indicted students were enrolled in classes, and they, along with a large number of their sympathizers, had been waiting with nervous bravado for weeks to hear what the grand jury would do. There was a certain cache, a swagger about having testified; those who had not been honored with a summons were accused of having "subpoena envy." Veterans of Blanket Hill talked about the paranoid atmosphere, a pervasive feeling of being watched by Big Brother—frequent ID checks, uniformed police in dorm lobbies, video cameras in hallways. Ohio senator Steven Young charged that fifty undercover FBI agents were enrolled at Kent, and rumors spread of a pilfered FBI document in which J. Edgar Hoover bragged about creating an "atmosphere of such extreme paranoia on campuses—as if there's an FBI agent behind every mailbox."[10]

Student reaction followed the choreography of dissent in that period. An angry crowd of some 2,000 stormed up to the Administration Building and stood outside White's office, demanding that the ROTC and the indictments be dropped. The first request was unacceptable to White for many reasons—not least being fear of political reprisals—and the second, which would have delighted him, was beyond his doing. (In a screwball way, the demand that the indictments be dropped betrays their continued clinging to the tattered ideal of the campus as a bastion of academic freedom and civil liberty.) The protesters were loud, profane, disrespectful, but studiedly nonviolent. Told that White was unavailable to speak to them, they hooted and jeered then dwindled away. He knew the University had a communication problem, but he seemed unaware that it started with him.

For weeks White made no public statements about the county report. But a trip to Washington, D.C., for a meeting of the National Association of State Universities and Land Grant Colleges gave him a national stage on November 6. There he held a press conference at which he denounced the grand jury's findings. Its attitude toward fundamental academic principles and the Bill of Rights, he said, must be seen as a "local manifestation of a national problem." Charges of "permissiveness" and inability to control students can be leveled at "all higher education," he said, and their ultimate target is nothing less than the "constitutional safeguards of American democracy."[11] His remarks may have been stimulated by historian Henry Steele Commager's address at the dedication of the University Library the next April.

It was on a cold midwinter day, February 13, 1971, that White told the trustees of his intention to leave the presidency on September 15. He had long planned to retire in 1970, he said, but May 4 had made that impossible. "The presidency is now totally consuming and had been for some time," he said. "Its unending confiscation of all time and thought destroys home and personal life." Always a hard worker—his workday began at 5:00 A.M.—White, though only sixty-two, had been driving himself relentlessly since the shootings, and its debilitating effect on his nerves and body was showing. His shoulders slumped, his face sagged, and his collars gaped around his neck. And as if recovering from May 4 weren't a sufficient challenge, he sensed that he would soon be facing something he'd never faced before: a major budget crisis.

In November 1970, the voters had rejected Republican James Rhodes in favor of Democrat John Gilligan, who, though a strong supporter of higher education, discovered that Rhodes had emptied the state's storied reserves built up by Frank Lausche, for whom spending money ranked as a mortal sin. Rhodes used much of that money to expand the network of state schools by placing community colleges and state universities within easy reach of every resident. Nationally, the economy was heading toward a recession, and Ohio's revenues were shrinking along with its industrial base. This meant, for White, that campus belts would have to be tightened. But whose belts and how many notches? Everyone, of course, offered someone else's stomach. White knew that any serious reduction of the academic budget would further undermine faculty morale, already low, and cripple graduate programs just as they were getting a sound footing. This factor may have outweighed all the others in his decision to resign.

The shootings had sapped White's health and community support. The event had turned local opinion against him and the school, and it had even weakened his support among the trustees, particularly some conservative members who privately agreed with the grand jury charge that White was too permissive with radical students and faculty. White knew that without the board's full backing, he could not continue making the difficult and unpopular decisions he believed necessary to keep the school on track to becoming a great university, especially with the state's faltering economy. At the same time, anything he might do to appease his critics, such as further curtailing academic freedom, would rile the faculty, whose support he also needed as well as desired. When asked about the trustees' role in presidential departures, one experienced academic administrator observed ruefully that a smart president "learns to read the tea leaves." White hints at his reasons for leaving in an essay he wrote later.[12]

Sometime before White announced his retirement, he had reason to think his dream of memorializing May 4 with a center for peace studies would be fulfilled. He accepted a proposal drafted by Raghbir Basi (economics) that would make peace studies part of the curriculum by involving all three of the professorate's traditional academic dimensions: teaching, research, and service. Dismissing objections from his top aides, White gave the center modest start-up funds and quarters in North Hall, near the ROTC ruins. After the EPC gave it academic moorings in the curriculum, the Center for Peaceful Change (CPC), which was founded as "a living memorial" to the slain students, began operating. Its main energy source was a group of talented instructors and graduate students—Mike Turner, Jon Begala, Paul Keane, and Dennis Carey, who soon led CPC during all its chameleonic forms in subsequent decades—a creative if not always favored witness to the tragedy of May 4.

The CPC came on line just in time for the first memorial ceremony of the May 4 shootings, which White must have anticipated with fear and trembling. For this, the culminating moment in his academic career, White was determined to strike a proper balance between observing the constitutional safeguards and avoiding a repetition of the mayhem of 1970, while always bearing in mind that the great majority of students were sincerely concerned about the state of their world and were committed to peaceful change. He decided that the ceremony of May 4, 1971, would be essentially a campus family event. This was consistent with his desire to keep the campus safe from disruptive outside influences. All elements of the ceremony would be carefully controlled.

Trouble struck four days early, on Saturday morning, May 1, and at the same place as the year before—downtown on the Strip. Around 11:00 P.M. Thursday evening, a crowd of about 1,000 became rambunctious after a student was struck by an errant motorcycle. Shouting antiwar slogans, the throng blocked the street. Police ordered them to disperse and then swept the street, arresting thirty-six people on a variety of charges. The crowd marched back to campus and surrounded Rockwell Hall, ROTC's new quarters, where they listened to impromptu speeches until about 1:00 A.M., when most left. About 200 students, however, migrated to the vicinity of the Student Center, on the Commons, where they were eventually arrested and bused off to city jail, most charged with failure to obey a police order. A host of Faculty Observers, as they now called themselves, spent that long night moving among the students, trying to keep things peaceful.

On the night of May 3, 1971, a large group of students, faculty, and townspeople gathered around the Victory Bell and, with lighted candles, processed with great solemnity around campus for about an hour, finishing up at the Taylor parking lot, where half-hour vigils were held throughout the night at the four sites where students were slain. The idea for the vigil originated with sociology professor Jerry Lewis, a Faculty Marshal who had witnessed the shootings, and his student Michelle Klein, and the idea of the candlelight procession was student Jeff Auld's. When President White was told that perhaps 2,000 would take part, Lewis recalled, all of White's objections to having people gather on the hill crumbled.[13]

The next morning, May 4, some 6,000 solemn mourners, including White, assembled on the Commons at 11:00 A.M. for the memorial service for the slain students. It was held under University auspices. White concluded his brief remarks with a reminder of what brought everyone to that place: "If any one thing unites us, the desire for memorial does just that; that and a craving for peace. We grant to them their green peace and rest, and offer a legacy of commemoration by those left behind." The Reverend Jesse Jackson was the featured speaker, and there were two representatives of Jackson State as well as several from Kent, including shooting victims. The ceremony ended with the tolling of the Victory Bell.[14]

Student activists, however, refused to cede ownership of May 4 to the administration, beginning a struggle that would go on for years. The ad hoc Mayday Coalition staged an alternate program an hour after the official one was over, with a sit-in at Rockwell Hall. A crowd of 1,000 to 1,500 surrounded the building, blocking all doors. Over the long afternoon and night they sat there while a series of speakers denounced, among much else, the war, racial and economic injustice, and police repression in the nation's capitol.

Coalition leaders ensured that the sprawling building was encircled by a chain of demonstrators at all times to keep anyone from getting in or out. At one point new student body president Craig Morgan instructed the crowd on how to protect themselves against tear gas and advised them that if arrested, as seemed imminent, to call the Student Senate office or the Kent Legal Fund.

What no one told the demonstrators was that some faculty members, hoping to avoid a repetition of the shootings, were in the Bunker trying to keep the administration from overreacting. They urged White, Matson, Roskens, and others to go down the hill and talk to the students, to listen to them and try to reason with them, to show them at least that someone in authority cared enough to listen.

At least one official did. Board chair Robert Dix surprised the students by strolling down the hill and talking to them through a bullhorn. Identifying himself, he told them that the school meant a lot to him as well as to them, and he urged them to think carefully before doing anything rash, because, he said, "if you cool it, then we can build a great institution."[15] A few booed and jeered, but most gave him a respectful hearing. Dix's action may have convinced White to let the demonstration wear itself out. And it did, with no damage, no violence, no arrests. This set a pattern that prevailed (save for a few incidents) for the next several years, until the divisive war in southeast Asia finally ended.

Nine

TROUBLED TIMES

{1971–1977}

The new president of Kent State University made a memorable entrance onto the scene. He purred into town at summer's end behind the wheel of a Thunderbird and, as he later recalled, with "just twenty bucks in my pocket."[1] He and his wife soon discovered that the situation in town was memorable, too, if in a "bizarre" way. They were staying that first night at the University Inn when he was accosted by two couples who recognized him as the new president. "Well," one of the men leaned toward him, "I hope you're going to be a hell of a lot tougher than the man you're succeeding; they should have shot 400 of them, not 4."[2] Such was his unofficial welcome to town.

There was also a touch of the bizarre about the process that brought Glenn Olds to Kent. Though the campus had witnessed several dustups between trustees and presidents in the past, such academic unseemliness had been pleasantly absent during the Bowman and White eras. But the post–May 4 tensions among trustees over the institution's management and mission bristled with thorns after White announced his retirement, and the trustees' first priority became finding his successor.

On May 9, after the first May 4 ceremony had passed in relative peace, the board formally appointed a nine-member search committee: three trustees (Dr. Kenneth Clement, Robert Baumgardner, Cyril Porthouse); three professors (Drs. Ray Heisey, Martin Nurmi, Thomas

Moore); undergraduate president Craig Morgan; graduate student president Jack Eyman; and alumni president John C. Young. By then the committee was already eye-deep in resumes, having been at work since the beginning of March. Fourteen candidates were in the pool by the end of March, among them Vice President Ron Roskens and John Kamerick, a former administrator at Kent and then president of Northern Iowa University. Olds was tossed in sometime in April. By May 23, 1971, his and Roskens's names were on a list of fifteen candidates board secretary George Urban recorded as already interviewed.[3]

Eventually the committee worked its way through over a hundred applications, winnowing the chaff from the wheat until it had a small handful of the choicest prospects for the board to consider. The complexity of the task was exacerbated by the importance of the final choice at that instable period in the school's history. Anxiety on campus grew with each passing week, as the committee went about its work with such proficiency and regard for confidentiality that no credible report of its doings dribbled out. Would a new president be in place come September? If so, who? If not, what then? No one relished beginning a new academic year without a sitting president.

Sometime early in July, with the search in its final lap, faculty committee member Tom Moore got a phone call from a trustee not on the search committee. The caller said that Canton-area "conservatives on the board" were maneuvering to scuttle the whole process and unilaterally appoint Roskens president. Moore immediately alerted the other faculty members on the committee.[4] No word of this reached the ear of the public.

Then, on July 19, 1971, another confidential conversation took place. Over lunch, trustee president Robert Dix told Glenn Frank, newly elected Faculty Senate chair, "in no uncertain terms" that the board "wanted Roskens" as the next president. Both Dix and Frank knew that the trustees had already formally accepted the search committee's report, and in Frank's view that committed the trustees to making an honest effort to select one of the candidates vetted and recommended by its own committee, which had eliminated Roskens as a candidate. So, when Dix asked Frank to "facilitate" Roskens's appointment by giving him his support, Frank bluntly refused. It would be improper for the board to violate its own procedures, said Frank, and he intended to report his "concerns" to the full senate at a closed meeting on July 26. Faced with Frank's hard-jawed intransigence, Dix then responded that, "minimally, Roskins [*sic*] would be named the interim vice president and Executive Vice President before a new president was selected."[5]

On July 25, 1971, the day before Frank was to trumpet his alarm to the senate, the Sunday edition of the *Akron Beacon Journal* detonated a bomb on its front page, under the headline "Presidency for KSU's Roskens?" A "split" among the trustees, the paper reported, could result in the appointment of Roskens as the school's next president. Word of the "split" had leaked out following a five-and-a-half-hour executive session at Twin Lakes Country Club on July 24. According to the paper, two "Canton area trustees," Clayton Horn and Robert Tschantz, were said to be pushing Roskens, who was not "one of the five men selected" by the search committee from the pool of candidates.

When the *Beacon Journal* reporter asked Dix to comment on the leak, Dix replied that Roskens was "not a serious candidate but is under serious consideration." At least three trustees, including Horn and Tschantz, strongly favored Roskens, according to the paper, which also quoted an unnamed campus "spokesman" (probably George Urban, the board secretary) who said "a group of college professors" had urged the trustees to appoint Roskens. Of the five committee-recommended applicants, the paper said, Glenn A. Olds, a former ambassador to the United Nations for social and economic affairs, ranked first.

The next day, hoping that going public with the planned end run would force the trustees to abide by their own rules, Frank delivered his "Statement to the Faculty Senate." He told the senators that the board was "on the brink of rejecting" the slate of candidates nominated by the search committee. While the trustees had the legal power to select the school's president, he said, it would be "inappropriate, if not unethical," for anyone to press the board to consider anyone who has not been fully vetted by the search committee according to established procedures.[6]

Frank picked his words with care, hoping to make his case without naming names, but his meaning was clear. The board was about to circumvent its "established rules" by interjecting a candidate the search committee had already "studied and eliminated." Although Frank didn't say it, what he meant was that Roskens, having been thrown out the front door by the search committee, was about to be smuggled in through the back door.

Coming hard on the heels of the *Beacon Journal* exposé, Frank's statement crackled across campus with electric speed. Its effect on the trustees became clear a week later, on August 2, 1971, when they passed an ungainly but revealing motion, presumably extorted by rack and thumbscrews during an executive session. The first half of the motion appointed Glenn A. Olds to the position of president, beginning September 15, 1971, at an annual salary of $40,000 plus a $5,000 annual expense account; the second half established the new position of Executive Vice President and Provost and urged the new president to offer the position to Roskens, as if the new president would have the temerity to refuse the urging.

These events briefly lift the heavy curtain of executive sessions behind which trustees customarily decide matters of great moment to the entire university community. They not only afford a glimpse of board dynamics and internal politics, they remind us of the faculty's historic responsibility to speak truth to power. For the board was in danger of mistakenly equating its legal powers with authority, which is a matter of morality and depends on the consent of its subjects—in this instance the faculty, students, and alumni—and adherence to due process.

Glenn Olds was the most academically distinguished president in the school's history and brought to the job presidential experience and significant involvement in the world beyond the academy. He held an earned doctorate in philosophy from Yale, was an ordained Methodist minister, had served under four different U.S. presidents (an adviser to two of them), and had been an ambassador to the United Nations. He was also Kent's first and only president who had been a professional boxer before he was out of knee britches. As if that weren't enough, he and his wife, Eva, seemed to have been sent from Central Casting for the roles of president and first lady of the university.

Olds was a man of striking bearing and dignified presence who moved with an athlete's supple ease. He had an expressive voice, a trained intellect, and extraordinary rhetorical skills. His disposition was buoyant, he thought well on his feet, his impulses were generous, and his temperament had a strong visionary ply. Possessed of such conspicuous gifts, he almost "glittered when he walked," though he was haunted by no secret sorrow.[7]

Olds was born into a hardscrabble family in Sherwood, Oregon, on February 28, 1921. His father, a hard-luck farmer, taught him to box when he was six. In his preteen years, at the bottom of the Great Depression when his father was earning just a dollar a day at odd jobs, Glenn and his brother boxed and wrestled for pennies at curtain-raisers. Because his father preached that money was best earned by the sweat of the brow, Olds had no plans for college until, as high school valedictorian, he was offered a scholarship to Willamette University in Salem, Oregon, where he got his B.A. in 1942.[8] Three years later he graduated with a divinity degree from Garrett Theological University, in Illinois, and moved next door, to Northwestern University, for an M.A. in philosophy. He then went to Yale for his doctorate in philosophy. With help from scholarships, friends, and money earned as a dishwasher, he was hooded just three years later, in 1948. After a year as assistant professor of philosophy at Depauw University, Olds spent three years as visiting professor at Northwestern and associate professor at Garrett, where he developed an integrative curriculum in philosophy involving science, culture, and politics. He was chaplain and professor at the University of Denver from 1951 to 1954 before moving to Cornell University to direct its large inter-religious program. In 1958 he assumed the presidency of Springfield College, in Massachusetts, where he instituted a new liberal arts curriculum and extensive international programs in Africa, Asia, and Latin America.

A revealing anecdote survives from his Springfield days. When Martin Luther King Jr.'s fame and force were reaching national proportions, Olds took a phone call from Senator Leverett Saltonstall, Massachusetts' venerable aristocrat and political leader, asking a favor for J. Edgar Hoover. Convinced King was a secret "commie," Hoover had secretly mobilized the agency to sully King's reputation and silence his voice. Saltonstall asked Olds to cancel a speech King was scheduled to give in two weeks at Springfield, thus denying him a prominent platform. Olds refused.[9]

Olds left Springfield to become dean of international studies in the SUNY system (1965–68). His work for Nixon in the 1968 presidential campaign was rewarded with an ambassadorial appointment to the UN's social and economic council. His referees for the KSU presidency included U Thant, secretary-general of the UN; the secretary of the Department of Health, Education, and Welfare; and Ernest J. Boyer, chancellor of the SUNY system. All noted his intelligence, energy, and rhetorical skills.[10]

Olds came to Kent hoping to bring peace to the campus. To do that, he knew he would have to promote a culture of communication and open discussion and participation, especially between the administration and students. His communicative skills were one of the reasons he got the job. As one member of the committee said, "This guy can talk to anyone, and listen too. He can rap with the kids."[11] Early in his tenure he signaled the kind of president he wanted to be. He took student leaders of a petition drive to Washington, D.C., where they lobbied for a federal grand jury investigation of May 4, an imaginative stroke that helped humanize the presidency for many students and stored up much goodwill. Olds was eager and willing to talk and listen to the faculty as well as the institution's numerous other constituencies. Though he had come with at least two other major goals—strengthening the faculty and increasing funding for student recruitment—bringing peace by nurturing a campus ethos of reasonable discourse and shared responsibility was foremost.

But what he found when he took office was something he had not planned on—the first major budget crisis to hit the school since World War II. The economic surge of the 1960s had spent its force by the end of the decade, in no small part because of the ruinous costs of the long war in southeast Asia. Rising oil prices jacked up energy costs, starting an inflationary spiral at the same time that the economy was sputtering, wages were stagnating, and jobs were shrinking. In Ohio the economic downturn was steep. There was a revenue shortfall in Columbus, and enrollments were dropping in private and public universities, putting their balanced budgets in peril. Fall enrollments in 1971 plunged sickeningly; Kent's fell to 20,194. Sharpening the plight of public higher education was the traditional opposition of Ohio voters to supporting public education, a disposition that gained new muscle as a result of the campus unrest of the late sixties. Another source of opposition was the state's numerous private colleges and universities, which claimed they were losing students to the inexpensive public schools. On July 15, 1971, Kent's trustees had sought to ease the budget crunch by raising student fees for the fall, but a month later President Nixon, invoking powers given him by the Economic Stabilization Act of 1970, imposed a ninety-day freeze on wages and prices.

It was against this grim background that Olds spent his first day in office, on September 15, drafting a letter to the faculty. He started by noting that the traditional honeymoon that a new president hopes for was over even before it began. A budget shortfall of between $1.3 and $3.5 million was projected, and to wrench it into balance would require cutting expenses and finding new sources of income. Aware that nothing was likelier to make faculty nerves judder more than the dreaded phrase "cutting expenses," he offered them an anodyne: once the freeze ended, all contract obligations, pay raises, and promotions would be honored.[12] Still, a malicious fate could hardly have dealt a worse hand to a new president, making his opening gambit in the intricate game of collegial relations with his faculty.

Through a combination of budget cuts and a ride-to-the-rescue allocation of funds ($1.5 million) from the Board of Regents, the school muddled through most of that academic year.[13] On January 17, 1972, Provost Bernard Hall sent the first official warning of possible retrenchment in a letter detailing professionwide due process guidelines that deans and department chairs were to follow in implementing it. From then on "retrenchment"—shorthand for freezing hiring and salaries and cutting entire academic programs and their staffs, including tenured faculty—was in the air and on the lips of faculty and administrators alike.[14]

One of those new sources of revenue Olds had in mind became evident on April 3 when he announced a $30 quarterly fee hike for undergraduates. Ten days later, though, the trustees raised undergraduate quarterly fees just $10, graduate fees $30, and out-of-state students' fees $50. Bucking against any fee increases, students quickly collected 1,200 signatures on a petition against the hike. They also set up their own committee to investigate the budget, and on April 19 student government elected five representatives to serve on Olds's investigative budget-cutting committee. Some professors interpreted this to mean that students were beginning to focus their attention on their school, seeing it as a collaborative enterprise in which they invested their money as well as their educational expectations and seeing student government as giving them a potent voice in determining how their money was spent. If true, this would mark a positive inward turning after years in which students had devoted their energies to trying to reform the world.

But that world wouldn't go away. Nor were the students yet ready to give up trying to set it right. It was an election year, and Nixon, hoping to force North Vietnam to negotiate, had resumed bombing raids, despite massive public and congressional opposition. On April 29, 1972, Kent students staged a strike, part of a nationwide demonstration to protest this expansion of the war and the draft. Shortly after the strike, which was peaceful, activist Renee Davis, one of the demonstrators charged with a variety of offenses during the Democratic National Convention riots of 1968, spoke to a large throng of students on the Commons. Afterward, the crowd moved en masse to Rockwell Hall, sat down in a ring around the building, and demanded the removal of

ROTC. The sit-in ended when campus police bused 125 demonstrators to jail. This did not augur well for a peaceful May 4 memorial service just three days away. And things got worse.

On April 27, 1,000 noisy but nonviolent demonstrators blocked traffic at the intersection of Main and Water streets, and a bulked-up city police force drove them back onto campus. The next day the state government filed a restraining order prohibiting further disruptions through May 10. On May 2, people passing by the front of Rockwell Hall were startled to see 300 white tombstones, which turned out to be part of a vigil against the Vietnam War. On May 3 the American Civil Liberties Union filed a suit to vacate the state restraining order, and that night the candlelight vigil opened the May 4 service. Thousands huddled solemnly in the chill night air in front of Taylor Hall, the flames of their candles illuminating the significance of the event with greater clarity than the artificial lights of the building and parking lot.

The second May 4 commemoration was coordinated by the Center for Peaceful Change (CPC) and featured a talk by Olds's guest, the famous scientist and thinker George Wald, whose original research in physiology and medicine won him the 1967 Nobel Prize. Wald was the sort of figure Olds hoped to attract to Kent in order to promote his plan to open up the campus to the world by making it an academic center for international studies. The activists formed a coalition called the May 4 United Front and sponsored an alternate program. They objected to the CPC involvement, claiming it was a tool of the Establishment and charging that it was the National Guard, not protesting students, who needed to study peaceful change. Though May 4, 1972, passed without disruption, five days later some 200 students staged a peaceful sit-in at Rockwell.

And the month ended with the largest sit-in of the year. Renee Davis was back on campus. On May 31 a huge crowd of students encircled Rockwell, leaving twenty ROTC instructors and seven cadets stranded on the third floor from early afternoon until after nightfall. Students crammed hallways as well as ringed the building. Olds walked around the building, talking to the demonstrators through a handheld microphone, answering questions while trying to persuade them that they had made their point, that no good purpose was served by holding their hostages any longer. He later imposed a 9:00 P.M. deadline for dispersing, but they stayed, and campus police arrested 129 for trespassing.[15] Such demonstrations would end only when the war and the draft did.

Olds's first address to the Faculty Senate revealed his vision of the institution; it was the suggestive but nebulous vision of a man of fertile mind, quick enthusiasm, and high ambition who moves by intuitive leaps and bounds rather than by careful, step-by-step measures. It also suggested that he may not have had a clear understanding of the objective reality he was facing—a faculty and student body restive, wary, and insecure, still struggling to recover its equilibrium and self-confidence after the tragedy of May 4. Moreover, he had a passel of more urgent problems, principally the financial crisis, which continued unabated throughout the decade and greatly exacerbated the feeling of insecurity and vulnerability that had begun with the closing of the campus on May 4, 1970. Few professors present in the months after the campus reopened can forget the chilling rumors emanating from Ravenna that the school was going to be turned into an insane asylum, the very same idea bruited by a committee of the legislature thirty-five years earlier. Small wonder the faculty was suspicious, untrusting, and indisposed to give Olds the benefit of any doubt almost from the start of his presidency.

One of Olds's earliest initiatives was to give faculty and students a meaningful role in university governance. For him, this meant a place at the tables of power. He brought the chair of the Faculty Senate to trustees meetings and, along with the undergraduate president, to cabinet meetings. He also projected streamlining the upper administration and reducing its size, a pleasing prospect to professors who were constantly being reminded that money was tight. He talked to the faculties of the various colleges and visited each of the departments to introduce himself—a novel experience for professors, having a president come to them. And, to encourage informal relations with his faculty, he and his wife invited small groups to their home for dinner and conversation. A decorative therapeutic sandbox they had installed at the foot of the stairs off the living room became the subject of much professorial gossip.

Olds took one look at the briar patch of thirty-odd university committees, each preparing a weighty report, and decided they were a waste of faculty time and cut the number by half. He wanted to make planning and governance more efficient and representative. To that end he also charged the Institutional Planning (IPC) and University Governance committees with preparing a long-range plan for discussion by the faculty in a meeting in September 1972.

Here, Olds was tackling the same hairy beast that had defeated his predecessors, as it would his successors: rationalizing budget planning while building a representative governance structure articulated throughout a multilayered institution scattered over eight campuses with some 30,000 students and 1,300 professors. From the faculty viewpoint, their new president was contemplating a costly, large-scale renovation of the institution at a time when it had barely enough food in its larder for the next meal.[16]

Equally troublesome to faculty, Olds wanted to make KSU undergraduate education into a personal educational experience, to coordinate it to the interests and needs of students and their oft-expressed desire for "relevance." This led to some creative experiments in dorm living. He had the ground floor of Stopher Hall converted into a coed Living and Learning Community for arts students. There they studied, "rapped," turned their walls into canvases, and partied together. In time, the living-learning concept would become a popular feature of residential living.

Residence halls had undergone significant changes during the 1960s. By the early 1970s Kent, like most public institutions, had stopped treating college students as children—which they weren't quite—and started treating them as adults—which they weren't quite either, leaving them to find their own way through the bewildering labyrinth of moral ambiguities and temptations excavated by the cultural and sexual revolutions. Some dorms became officially coed, while many others were de facto coed, since a policy of free access to dorms and the virtual abandonment of check-in/check-out policies in women's dorms meant that no one in positions of responsibility knew who was in a dorm room at any given time of the day or night. Because conduct codes were effectively scuttled, dorms became so free and open, so unfettered by traditional restraints as to be virtually uninhabitable Animal Houses. Many parents understandably worried about the safety of their children. Fear of violent crime and rape was so endemic that security services were set up in the Library and other gathering places to escort students back to their residences after dark.

Olds personally disapproved of the changing scene on campus, but, like other university administrators of the day, he was unable to withstand the swelling tide of the cultural revolution that crested during the first half of the 1970s.

When students grumbled that he too was not sufficiently open and available, Olds started a series of open forums on October 25, 1972.

Only about 150 students showed up for the first one, but he was not dismayed or deterred. He was friendly and approachable, and he enjoyed talking with them. They liked him and his wife, whom they found intriguingly unconventional. They especially appreciated that Olds saw himself as a professor as well as a president. He began teaching an introductory course in philosophy soon after taking office, the first Kent president since Leebrick to relate to students on these terms. And in the spring he played intramural softball with them, playing as he taught, with skill and zest.

Olds's reforms of the undergraduate program, which had languished in the sixties' scramble for graduate prestige, did not involve altering its basic structure but, rather, giving it new dimensions. He projected a "new kind of curricular design," one he hoped would make sense of the undergraduate experience by putting *uni*ty back in *uni*versity education. One promising way of integrating or amalgamating the smorgasbord of offerings was to give it a significant interdisciplinary component. With that in view, he encouraged a variety of proposals for integrative education and a "universal" or "general" college, as well as one for international studies, and sought advice from experts familiar to him from his previous university appointments.

His desire to integrate the undergrad curriculum, not a new one at Kent, sprang from a conviction that dividing knowledge into various fields of study (centered in departments, with their majors and minors) of ever greater specialization and professionalism led inevitably to an ever narrower and limited understanding of the human condition, producing students ill equipped to understand the world and their place in it. The questions raised over a decade earlier still abided an answer: What is the difference between training and education? What is the purpose of an education? Of a university?[17]

As part of the integrative thrust, for example, in the 1972–73 academic year the Arts and Sciences dean, Bruce Harkness, appointed a committee of a dozen professors from A&S and F&PA to come up with ideas for possible interdisciplinary courses to be cotaught by, say, historians and sociologists or political scientists and speech communication professors. The committee met monthly that year, mulling over various proposals, their viability and their educational value; those whose interests dovetailed formed subgroups and met more often. Near the end of the academic year, the committee gave its report, which included several promising proposals, with supporting data, to the dean. After a few weeks he convened them and thanked them for their service, regretting that there was not enough money to support any of the proposals, and informing them he was disbanding the committee.

After the IPC came out in favor of "interdisciplinary communication and programs," the Office of Research Administration gave it a one-thumb-up approval in 1974, with the important caveat that "basic disciplinary research" should be protected.[18] Nothing came of that initiative either. Olds also sought to emphasize continuing education as a part of the school's mission to the public and as a largely untapped source of new students. Proposals for a College of Continuing Education drew opposition from faculty who feared their own programs would be trimmed to pay for the new unit. Trying to make innovative changes in times of financial exigency is usually an exercise in futility.

Over the course of his presidency, Olds's fertile mind, his prolific imagination daily churned out new ideas that alternately amused and irked the faculty. An administrator who worked closely with—and liked—him observed wryly at the time that Olds would get a dozen new ideas during his morning shower and bring them to the office for his staff to implement. But this wealth of new programs and ideas rang hollow in faculty ears being told simultaneously that the school was too poor to support existing programs.

Olds's talk to the Faculty Senate on June 5, 1972, stoked much faculty opposition. He declared that the old days of simply adding new programs were gone, squeezed out by budget pressures. "If program A is to be increased in number," he said, "it's got to be at the price of program B."[19] Only four days earlier, however, he had appointed Raga Elim as director of the Center for International and Comparative Programs, another of his long-term projects. Because this promised to be a major new program, with potentially serious budget implications, it made professors already fretting about the prospects of their own programs wonder if Olds's left hand knew what the right was up to. Nor did their concerns abate noticeably when, on October 10, 1972, he announced that CPC had won a $30,000 grant from the National Endowment for the Humanities. The program was already rumored to be costing far more.

Even more than such seeming cross talk, however, what most spooked the faculty was Olds's mention of adopting a cost-benefit approach to budgeting. They knew that, when weighed on a quantitative scale, most areas of study would be found wanting. The life of the mind is, by its very nature, extravagantly wasteful. Speculative thought, which underlies all fields of learning, is essentially shooting in the dark. It spends most of its energies unproductively getting lost in its own meanderings, walking up blind alleys and stumbling over trash barrels. Even hard-nosed science proceeds by trial and error, which, according to bookkeeping standards, makes it wasteful.

Reports of Olds's senate talk sowed anxiety among the faculty, fears of major changes being considered by the IPC. Keenly aware of their frozen salaries and suspecting that new-fledged doctoral programs might be cut back or even cut out, graduate professors in particular were upset over Olds's ambitious agenda, not least about proposals for reconfiguring undergraduate education along interdisciplinary lines, for a "universal" or "general" college, and for internationalism—all of which they viewed through the bleak lens of budget shortfalls and program "trade-offs."

What a former administrator has called a "culture of aspiration" had taken hold at Kent during the 1960s. Olds underestimated its importance.[20] The move toward a strong graduate program in the 1960s had attracted a large number of talented, research-minded scholars with first-class degrees and high ambitions for themselves and the school, which they were impatient to make into a great university. As long as undergraduate reform did not take away funds needed to fuel the upward trajectory of graduate programs, these professors were not, in principle, against it. They did not fancy being part of an institution, however, in which undergraduate education was largely "touchy-feely-squealy" experimentation; they wanted "strong" programs. Olds's most determined opponents would emerge from among their ranks.

Research faculty were not the only worried members of the professoriate. There were numerous untenured assistant professors who sensed they would be the ones expected to pay for curricular initiatives. They shouldered the major share of the undergraduate teaching load, and they knew that teaching new courses, perhaps in a newly configured departmental unit, would make it harder for them to find time for the research necessary to win pay increases, tenure, and promotion from senior professors on departmental promotion committees who had jaundiced attitudes toward educational innovations. Some untenured professors took their anxieties and complaints to the faculty ombudsman rather than to their department chairs and deans.

Meanwhile, on October 23, 1972, Olds accepted Faculty Senate chair Gordon Keller's invitation to give the senate a brief overview of the school's "economic condition and outlook." The faculty needed to vent their feelings, he told Olds, over the parking fee policy and other matters. There was galloping disgruntlement over the fate of the state income tax and the national economic malaise and doubts about the administration's plans for coping with the budget problems. Olds came to the senate, accompanied by the provost, the treasurer, and trustee Robert Stopher, but not to talk about parking fees. His subject was instead the catastrophe facing the school and the state if voters passed the anti–income tax referendum on November 7. If they did, said Olds, the state budget and the budgets of all state institutions would have to be cut by 25 percent, an unthinkable proposition. Kent's enrollment was down 5 percent, he noted, leaving the administration no recourse but to cut at least $2 million from the budget to compensate for the reduction in state subsidy.

But if the income tax survived the vote, he said, the state would have a "larger resource base," and the budget planning for 1973–74 was based on the assumption that the income tax would survive. But all signs now pointed to its rejection. When asked for his opinion, Stopher said that while he too thought the income tax was "in real trouble, there was one reason for hope": voters tend to vote no when they "don't understand an issue." As it turned out, the income tax survived because enough voters cast their ballots for it thinking they were voting against it. Such is the cockeyed beauty of democracy.[21]

Then, just when the faculty was beginning to sigh with relief, both the *Beacon Journal* and the *Record Courier* carried reports of a November 9 board meeting that enraged the faculty. The headline in the *Record Courier* the next day screamed "$77,000 for 3 KSU appointees." The three appointees were a new vice president for administration (Walt Bruska, $35,000 annual salary), a presidential administrative assistant (Carolyn White, $17,000), and a presidential executive assistant (William E. McKinley, $25,000). To take the sting from the charge that he was adding to his staff in a time of belt-cinching, Olds said that the three hires would return his staff to the 1971 level, before he reduced it by $100,000. That may have salved trustees' concerns, but not the faculty's.

By present standards, the three salaries seem quite modest. Not so in the early seventies, when the budget was overstrained, faculty salaries frozen, and programs under the ax—and when a dollar was really a dollar. Bruska and White had worked with Olds elsewhere. These hires made Olds seem to be talking out of both sides of his mouth, bringing in outsiders when insiders were on the chopping block. The newness of the two to the campus activated xenophobic glands. Some new presidents, understandably, prefer to hedge themselves about with assistants whose judgment and loyalty they trust. But even if the new hires did not tax the school's finances unduly, in adding to his staff before taking measures to ease faculty needs Olds betrayed a seam of insensitivity, of not being quite in touch with a situation, that comported ill with his generally sympathetic nature and contributed to a growing morale problem.

Other items in newspaper accounts of the meeting seemed almost calculated to enflame the faculty. The papers reported that Olds also told the trustees that the school would have to cut between $800,000 and $1.5 million from its budget for the current year because of a 4.9 percent drop in enrollment. He had also predicted "a great deal of strain" would come when the IPC budget recommendations came out because they would set program priorities and costs as the basis for budgeting, though he said he would not make value judgments based solely on cost, and nor would "all high-cost, low-yield programs" be cut. "But some will," he added, "depending on the priorities and objectives of the university." He was "prepared to bite the bullet."[22]

A few days after the board meeting, someone mailed Olds a photocopy of the *Record Courier* with the following legend typed above the headlines: "Did you attend the Faculty senate [*sic*] meeting Monday? You have already lost your faculty. No one believes you."[23] And after a routine meeting with the senate executive committee on November 13, Provost Hall sent Olds a memo saying he thought he wouldn't "get out of the meeting with any skin left on me." "Morale is low and tempers are short," he wrote, because of the new administrative appointments, low salaries, and rumors "flying around" about $150,000 worth of "renovations" for the new Library.[24]

The details of the Library rumor didn't appear in the *Kent Stater* until December 8, by which time it had brought down such a Vesuvius of angry complaints from faculty members onto Olds's head that he was forced to give up the idea of moving the administrative offices, which were too few and too small, out of the Administration Building and into the Library. Since it was a proposal that would repeat itself, it's worth detailing here. The administrative quarters in the Administration Building were completely inadequate. The rooms were too small and too few to accommodate the size of the administrative staff, and there was no ventilation system. (Provost Hall was said never to have drawn a full breath in his office.)

In surveying the campus for more appropriate lodgings, Olds's eye lit on the new library, a huge structure centrally located and lavishly endowed with spacious reaches, some of which seemed wasted while waiting to be filled with new books, magazines, and newspapers. His plan was to reconfigure a prime area at a cost of $150,000. The faculty did not object to the money so much as it did to an administrative usurpation of the educational enterprise itself: the Library was for study and research, not for administrative business, an arguably useful but decidedly lower order of activity; and it needed all its available space for new acquisitions, because that's what scholarly libraries do—they grow. And since grow is also what administrations do, the two should not be housed in the same building.

On November 14 ombudsman Harold Kitner asked Olds for an urgent meeting to discuss faculty morale. He had been drafting a long memo about the need for "remedial action" when the hiring of the three new staff members hit the headlines: "I cannot emphasize enough," Kitner wrote, "that it's been a long time since I have seen so many stolid members of the faculty reacting with so much anger." Olds was "facing a crisis in credibility" and a petition was being circulated.[25]

The follow-up memo Kitner sent Olds on November 20 prior to their meeting surveyed with systematic rigor all of the points of conflict and laid out possible remedies. The memo was clearly intended to help Olds extricate himself from the quaking bog into which his exuberant tongue and high-minded intentions had led him. Because of its reasonable tone, the precision of its argument probably did not strike Olds as the indictment another might have felt it to be. Among its more urgent recommendations were that Olds impose the same moratorium on administrative appointments as on faculty hires; that he suspend further talk of "*major changes*" in academic programs "until faculty salaries and existing programs are properly financed"; that he accept no "master plan at this time which implies further proliferation of administrative units"; and that he tell the faculty that his major priority is to provide a cost-of-living salary increase.

Appended to the memo was a copy of the petition from "Disturbed Faculty Members"—a set of questions revolving around the gap between Olds's statements and actions and the perceived disparity of treatment between the administrative and academic sectors of the school, most of which concerned money. Why have travel funds to professional meetings been removed from departmental budgets "but not from administrative personnel?" Why a 2–3 percent salary hike for faculty and a 10 percent hike for administrators? And, more generally, "How has the reputed $800,000 surplus from last year's budget been applied to this year's needs?" The fact that some of the implied charges were off the mark in no way diminishes the seriousness of Olds's situation. As Kitner said, it was a crisis of credibility, the hobgoblin of every president.

The two men met on November 20, discussed the memo at length, and parted thinking they had had a meeting of minds on most of the items. Kitner also assumed his memo had the same confidential status as those he had sent White over the years. Olds passed the memo to the provost for appropriate action, and Hall in turn sent Kitner a frost-rimmed memo pointing out the numerous inaccuracies in the petition and detailing some of his own ongoing efforts to deal with faculty morale, which, he noted, was within the purview of his office. Kitner's memo, to his surprise and dismay, also found its way onto the desks of other high administrators, academic and nonacademic, as well as to the Faculty Senate executive and budget committees.[26]

The net result was that the messenger, the bearer of bad news, became the issue. Kitner was perceived as sticking his overdeveloped ombudsmanic nose into matters properly the domain of other officials and bodies; his recommendations for dealing with faculty morale were out of line. At the end of November, Olds wrote Kitner: "I find, alas, that both Bernie [Hall] and the Faculty Senate, with whom I met at their request, feel that you have moved from the ombudsman role of report and recommendation to policy-making and implementation."[27] It was doubtless a bitter moment for Kitner to find himself charged with violating due process, which he had worked hard to weave into the fabric of the school's culture. Of course, stepping on people's toes, getting out of line, offending people, and being misunderstood were part of an ombudsman's job, as he knew. He resigned a year after this unhappy episode and later became chief negotiator for the faculty in drawing up the master contract. The turmoil over faculty morale subsided soon afterward, but it formed a template of Olds's relationship with the faculty that would continue until his departure.

. . .

The 1972–73 academic year brought a number of famous faces to the campus. Historian Arthur Schlesinger campaigned for Senator George McGovern in the presidential election, poet Allen Ginsberg gave a reading, journalist David Brinkley and Daniel Ellsberg of Pentagon Papers fame gave talks, and jazz singer Nancy Wilson performed in the University Auditorium. In October controversial actress Jane Fonda spoke against the war before a large crowd of students. And polymath R. Buckminster Fuller gave an inspirational lecture on "inventiveness," urging architecture students to become "problem solvers" by trusting their native creativity and by using natural resources to "make more for less." Famous for his innovations in such fields as philosophy, architecture, and engineering, R. Buckminster Fuller was most closely identified with the geodesic dome, a tubular construct as strong as structures 97 percent heavier. He supervised architecture students while they built a geodesic dome on the Taylor Hall lawn.[28]

Student discontent over the fee hikes continued. On October 9, 1972, the Student Senate voted unanimously to boycott the Faculty Senate budget committee, and five days later it set up its own budget review committee, convinced that its interests and the faculty's were at odds. At the same time student leaders were struggling with the administration over control of the new "University Center," as the administration was referring to the building under construction, which students regarded as their center. In the fall of 1972 they began complaining that they had little influence in shaping policy affecting operations of a building which, they pointed out, was being paid for by their fees.

On January 14, 1973, Student Senate, deciding it needed more space for student organizations, voted to evict three staffers of Student Group Affairs from their offices on the second floor of the Center and take over that space. This bold action set in motion a series of disputes that ended in a train wreck—the suspension of student government on campus for the rest of the year. A few days after the eviction vote, a determined group led by student vice president Kathy Czujko presented Olds with a proposal calling for the trustees to set up a policy board to operate the Center. This stung student body president Bob Gage, who denounced Czujko's "confrontation tactics" and announced his own plan for the administration to give the Center back to the students. Czujko in turn denounced Gage's plan. The falling-out of the two leaders split the Student Senate into factions. Many students took sides, while others asked how students could get a workable system when their leaders couldn't work together. Before long the senators, fed up with student government's inability to deal effectively with the administration, threw up their hands and voted to suspend all operations except for funding until the fall 1973 term.

Later, in May 1973, student government held a constitutional convention. After unanimously approving a new constitution, it held a referendum election, and as a result, after two quarters out of action, the Student Affairs Council (SAC) went back to work. At the end of March a grievance system was activated to hear complaints about the university, especially the food program in the dorms. Deep-seated troubles persisted, however, and there was still no governance structure despite several attempts to bring a reform proposal to a vote in the Student Affairs Council.

In time student government returned in the form of Student Caucus, presumably in the interests of more democratic decision making. What can be understood from this troubled time was that too few students cared enough to vote in their own elections, let alone take active roles in their own government. Left unresolved by this political fiasco was an important question: does student government have any real authority over the programs and buildings financed by student fees and nominally intended for student use?

The new University Center opened on January 2, 1973. One positive result of the struggle over control of the University Center came in March 1973 when the building was officially named the Student Center, a small sign of heightened sensitivity to legitimate student concerns. The structure's boomerang-shaped design was traditional, especially when compared to the Art Building, which opened late in 1972. An exercise in the geometry of forms, a collocation of boxes, of rooms without walls, its aesthetic was the severe beauty of straight lines, open vistas, and sharp angles. It had translucent side panels that could be raised to let in natural light and give access to the surrounding lawns; heating ducts and water pipes—part of the décor—were strung high overhead like lengths of macaroni. Intrinsic to its peculiar charm was its disdain for ordinary human comfort, as shown by its paucity of public facilities, its echo-chamber noisiness, and its chill atmosphere. The new Business Building, which had opened the previous year and was much more conventional in design, vaguely resembling a computer, was set against the eastern flank of Summit Hill, where the College Barn had stood once upon a time.

What promised to be the start of a great tradition occurred on November 17, 1971, when the Golden Flashes, under Coach Don James, won the MAC football title by defeating Toledo. James and star players Jack Lambert and Gary Pinkel were later singled out for special honors. Lambert went on to become the linchpin of the championship Pittsburgh Steelers' storied "Steel Curtain" of the seventies and was later assumed into the Pro-Football Hall of Fame. Pinkel achieved great distinction as a top-level football coach after his application to coach the Golden Flashes was rejected by his alma mater. The 1973 Flashes, despite failing to win the MAC title, may have been the superior team, spawning hopes that the school was becoming a football powerhouse, perhaps second only in the state to OSU. But over succeeding decades that dream died aborning as the team never could rise above mediocrity, despite fielding a host of outstanding players who later had successful pro careers.

With the end of both the Vietnam War and the draft in 1973, the focus of student interest turned not only toward intramural sports, which became wildly popular during the seventies, but toward local causes and cultural developments as well. That sensitive concern for the well-being of others, which is the hallmark of a civilized society, was very strong at Kent, contradicting the "Me Generation" label that cultural historians later pinned on seventies' youth. Students threw themselves with energy and dedication into the cause of the disabled, enthusiastically cooperating with the school's conversion of the campus into one fully accessible to the handicapped. And in April 1974 Greek Week put a twist on philanthropic activity by staging an annual spring bathtub pull, ending with an arduous tug at Moulton Hall and a donation of $1,020 for the American Cancer Society. Sororities and fraternities revived after their hiatus in the sixties, though they, too, were changed by the ethos of social justice that was one legacy of that complex era.

A host of student groups gave energy, time, and money to serving the distressed residents of the impoverished Skeels-McElrath area of Ravenna. What began as a Greek service project eventually resulted in the construction of a two-part complex that housed a community center, classrooms, and a gym. Campus religious groups and other organizations of students, faculty, and townspeople pitched in with funds and tutoring sessions. The Knight and Cleveland foundations made key donations, and to Olds's manifest delight, the student body voted to put an optional fee donation on registration forms, making what became known as the King-Kennedy Center the only university-funded neighborhood center in the nation. Some students and faculty participated in community service projects in Akron, while others, inspired by activist Cesar Chavez's visit to campus, took up the cause of immigrant farm laborers, picketing and boycotting to dramatize their plight.

This was the decade when the women's liberation movement became a force. Kent students formed the Kent Women's Action Collective (KWAC) and moved out smartly to make known their cause. They picketed stores selling Farah pants, held CR (consciousness-raising) sessions, orchestrated a letter-writing campaign for passage of the Equal Rights Amendment, sponsored dances for "sisters" with music by an all-women band, and gave self-defense training to women through a Women Against Rape (WAR) program.

But the decade wasn't all seriousness and activism. For a brief period that embarrassment of britches known as "shooting the moon" or "mooning" was the seventies' equivalent of goldfish swallowing. But when dropping britches proved to be insufficiently shocking, it was supplanted by "flashing" and "streaking," which spread like a rash over Kent's campus in 1977, months after it had become the "in" craze on other campuses. On the evening of March 25, 1977, some twenty men stripped and sprinted self-consciously around campus to the amusement of several hundred spectators and a few local reporters. Four days later four women, not to be outdone in deeds of daring, streaked with the men but later expressed shock over their treatment. One said the fun was spoiled when "the men just started pawing all over us—girls didn't do that to the guys!"[29] Olds dismissed it wryly as a novel way of observing the rites of spring.

He had more serious concerns on his mind. The budget problem worsened after the recession hit hard in 1974. In a move away from an all-you-can-eat board plan, Olds tried to avoid raising fees by improving efficiency with a mandatory food coupon program, which included a "specials" line for students to choose a "selected" dinner tray at reduced cost. Students loathed the system, claiming it both shortchanged and inconvenienced them. Fueling this reaction was the widespread opposition to compulsory dorm residence for freshmen and sophomores, a measure adopted to fill dorm rooms that had been empty since 1970. One student became so overwrought that he publicly declared that he wouldn't pay his board bill for winter term until the coupon system was eliminated.[30] A throng of students marched to Olds's house on November 5, 1975, to protest the coupon plan. It says something about his success in changing the campus atmosphere from one of confrontation to one of peaceful discourse and dissent that students felt free to march on his house. They knew that at least he would appear and hear them out—and not arrest them when they demonstrated.

Discontent was fomenting among faculty as well. A collective bargaining movement, which had started in the AAUP in the late 1960s, gathered strength. A few representative events serve as markers of its evolution. In November 1973 the administration announced possible faculty reductions because of the tight budget. Two days later, in a show of solidarity, a crowd of several hundred students and some faculty marched to Olds's house to voice their opposition to faculty cutbacks. Soon after, a newly formed Student/Faculty Coalition sponsored a Student/Faculty Solidarity Day.

Faculty resentment at having lost sabbaticals and other benefits after May 4, fear of retrenchment, and growing doubts about the administration's ability to cope with the deteriorating situation made collective bargaining attractive to increasing numbers of professors. Early in 1975 a Faculty Senate poll revealed that a majority of the faculty favored collective bargaining, a finding that jangled administration and trustee nerves. Soon after, a Coordinating Committee on Collective Bargaining began drafting procedures for beginning formal negotiations with the trustees. And the administration began casting about for ways to drum up opposition to the movement, which they feared would make faculty and administration perpetual adversaries. A small vocal group, encouraged by Provost John Snyder, set up shop but had little success in turning the running tide. Finally, at its meeting of March 6, 1975, a bare majority of trustees, their jaws clenched, formally authorized an election to determine the faculty's bargaining agent.

At that election on October 29 and 30, 1975, by a small majority of twenty or so the faculty voted to have the United Faculty Professional Association (UFPA) as its sole bargaining agent. After the American Arbitration Association ruled the election valid on December 5, on January 5, 1976, a divided Board of Trustees voted to recognize UFPA as the faculty bargaining agent. The testiest period in the collective bargaining story began, however, later that spring when UFPA charged the administration with foot-dragging to avoid coming to the bargaining table. It was convinced that the administration was planning to derail collective bargaining by issuing individual contracts for

1976–77 with raises based solely on merit and inequity, key items for negotiation. The trustees scoffed at the charge, saying it had every intention of bargaining in good faith but that it had to follow state guidelines in preparing the coming year's budget.

Over the following months, UFPA offered several proposals that would enable the administration to stick to the state's budget schedule and still negotiate a master contract. All were rejected. Then the Faculty Senate raised its voice, unanimously passing a resolution urging the administration to negotiate. Tempers seemed to fray day by day that spring. There was talk of picketing to dramatize the faculty's frustration and the administration's laggardness. UFPA president Ed Bixenstine and other leaders couldn't determine whether Olds or the board was responsible for the stalling tactics. The trustees insisted they were calling the tune, but many UFPA members suspected Olds was doing the fiddling. In retrospect it seems clear to someone who lived through it and has now examined it through a reasonably objective lens that, while some UFPA suspicions were based less on fact than on the free-floating fears attendant on any risky venture, the board and administration were hoping by temporization to reduce UFPA's slim majority of faculty support and thus get the union decertified. And the board was almost certainly calling the tune to which Olds was dancing.

But it was Olds who paid the piper. On April 15, 1976, at the board's instruction, he sent UFPA a decertification document that, if accepted, would have vitiated the union. Among other things, it would have revived an issue already adjudicated by arbitration, and it implied that UFPA's narrow margin of victory made it unrepresentative of the faculty. On April 20, 1976, the Faculty Senate received a resolution from UFPA calling for a formal vote of no confidence in the administration, and Olds, who, having "knowingly and willfully violated their responsibility to implement the faculty's democratic decision," the resolution concluded, "no longer enjoy[s] the confidence of the Kent State University faculty."[31]

On April 27, having authenticated the 100 faculty signatures accompanying the resolution, the Senate sent out ballots for the first no-confidence vote in the school's history. In the meantime, board chairman and Kent alumnus Robert Baumgardner, still fuming over UFPA's refusal to take his word that the board intended to bargain in good faith and protesting that UFPA was unfairly holding Olds responsible for board policies, reaffirmed the board's earlier position. After the board turned down back-channel offers from UFPA to compromise provisionally on some issues, Bixenstine issued an UFPA broadside on May 5 that rehearsed the sequence of events leading up to the no-confidence resolution, clarifying what it meant and what it didn't mean. If passed, it would mean that Olds must start negotiations in the summer downtime and issue letters of intent rather than individual contracts. It would not, however, mean that the faculty or UFPA was calling for Olds and his staff to resign; but it would mean they must act in ways that would restore the faculty's confidence in them.[32]

The faculty voted no confidence, a grievous blow to Olds. Though opposed to the "adversarial structure" intrinsic to collective bargaining—because he believed in the "collegial concept of a university," which he'd tried hard to improve at Kent—he said he would try "to make it work," because he also believed in "government by consent of the governed."[33]

Despite the faculty's no-confidence vote and the decision for collective bargaining, Olds retained the support of most of the trustees.[34] Then twin scandals in the business college burst into the headlines, softening that support and causing him to lose face and, worse yet, heart. In both instances it was his ardor for innovative ventures and new departures, his propensity for becoming personally involved and leaping over channels—part of his improvisational management style—and, especially, his credulousness in judging character and motives that greatly compounded his troubles. In his private life, Glenn Olds was a generous, openhearted man and a soft touch for any hard-luck story. (After borrowing $5,000 from him, a woman left town trailing a string of unpaid bills.[35]) And in his professional life he was an easy mark for an academician peddling a promising invention that just might become a cornucopia of funds for the University.

On October 3, 1976, the *Beacon Journal* printed a lengthy exposé of questionable carryings-on in the College of Business Administration. The first case involved the Kent Econometric Model (ECM) and its inventor, Vladimir Simunek, a Czech-born economics professor who had devised what he freely admitted was the world's largest and most accurate business-forecasting model. (That he also happened to share a surname with an eminent but unrelated Czech economist didn't diminish his plausibility.) Simunek was a soft-spoken, persuasive, tenacious scholar with an entrepreneurial idea Olds could not resist. With enrollments dropping and state support shrinking, Olds seems to have begun by encouraging Simunek in a business venture and ended up pampering him beyond discretion in the fading hope that the model would become a money cow for Kent.

In 1973 the business college dean and several of his faculty partnered with Simunek to form a private business called Kent Econometric Associates (KEA), which would market the forecasting model's predictions to private business, industry, and banks, with the University footing the bill for nearly all development costs for the model. But that spring a chorus of complaints by skeptical business faculty forced Olds to ask the attorney general's office to look into the matter. The investigator found no evidence of violations, but, as only emerged months later, he hedged his findings with recommendations that the trustees put KEA at arm's length from the school's academic operation by giving it a new name—Kent Econometric Institute (KEI)—and shifting it to the University Foundation, the University's private fund-raising arm, which would market the model and share in its profits. The investigator also warned the administration that, based on Simunek's practice thus far, wherever he was permitted to feed numbers into school computers, he was likely to abuse the privilege, monopolizing the computers and running up excessive costs in fees charged to individuals and departments for the use of some of the University's more powerful computers. When the computer center director learned months later of this investigator's warning, he was flabbergasted that no one had told him about it; it was then too late to lock the barn door—Simunek's computer bill had already cost the University over $100,000.

The attorney general's investigation served only to make Simunek's critics howl even louder. In their view, his model was a hoax, and he was an academic con man. It is possible, of course, that he simply believed in his model and its powers past reason; there is no evidence that he had the bedrock cynicism of a genuine con man. But his model did have two flaws, both of which undermined his claims: it was always just two small tinkerings—two of those elusive mathematical formulae—short of predictive accuracy; and, far more seriously, it kept on not making money. Still, Simunek did win some supporters and backers, mostly from off campus. One was the influential Hudson magnate Burton Morgan, who, after witnessing a demonstration of the model in November 1976, asserted that Simunek was not a "fraud" and that the model worked. Morgan was willing to invest in it.[36]

The Simunek scandal, while never leading to any legal resolution, was a public embarrassment to Olds, to the business college and its dean, and to the whole University. It raised uncomfortable questions about the propriety of a public institution footing the bills for a private business by giving it free space and open-ended access to its expensive facilities. It soured relations between Olds and Provost Snyder, incited rivalries and resentments among the business faculty, tarnished its dean's reputation, made the entire administration look inept and disorganized, and riled the trustees. Of course, as a former trustee remarked, if the model had become the moneymaker Simunek promised and Olds envisioned, none of the complaints would have mattered.[37]

The second, more sensational and longer-running, of the two scandals during this period was the Bermudez affair, named for Puerto Rican businessman-educator Andres Bermudez, who received his doctorate in business administration from Kent in March 1976. Along with its exposé of the Simunek affair, the *Beacon Journal* reported allegations by several business professors that some members of the college's graduate faculty had waived residency and other requirements for Bermudez in exchange for free trips to Puerto Rico and other gifts, including bottles of rum. (The rum gave the story long-distance legs.) Bermudez denied the charge, and a Faculty Senate special investigation that fall concluded that, though the dissertation committee members had put themselves "in an apparent conflict of interest," they were guilty of nothing more serious than imprudence.[38] The Bermudez case then slid onto the back burner, where it simmered unnoticed for months.

Collective bargaining negotiations finally started in the summer of 1976. The administration opened tough with an offer it knew UFPA had to reject: that salary increases be based solely on merit and that school directors and department chairs who had voted in the bargaining election not be part of the bargaining unit. Thereafter, negotiations inched ahead by a series of small, hesitant agreements into the next spring. Then, in late April 1977 the trustees abruptly stopped negotiating and ordered Olds to distribute individual faculty contracts for the next academic year. Surprised and alarmed, UFPA's council summoned the faculty to a meeting in the Presbyterian Church on Summit Street, where it got authorization to invoke several sanctions, including withholding professional services.

And so a strike no one really wanted seemed inevitable. Nerves ratcheted higher when the trustees had Olds distribute guidelines for maintaining operations during an "Unlawful Work Stoppage." Then, in a sudden about-face, the trustees decided to resume negotiations, and the two parties signed an "Interim Agreement" on May 11. In addition to settling the salary issue for 1977–78 and certain vexed governance issues, this agreement effectively regularized the bargaining process. The reason for the trustees' change of mind may trace back to their meeting of the previous November.

The main action item on the November 11, 1976, agenda had been a proposal to construct an annex on the north side of Memorial Gym in which to gather all facets of the Health, Physical Education, and Recreation (HPER) unit under one roof as inexpensively as possible.[39] First mooted in 1962, a new facility had been on the KSU capital request list since the 1967–69 biennium budget. Yet, in hindsight, it seems odd that, given the administration's struggles to move beyond May 4, Olds did not sense the political ramifications of putting the addition so close to where the students were shot. The dogs nipping at his heels may have distracted him from the dragon ahead.

The first note of concern was sounded on October 5, 1976, in a letter to the *Stater* warning that the annex might interfere with the ongoing legal actions stemming from May 4. Then on November 3 the *Stater* ran an article pointing out possible encroachment by the annex on the area of the May 4 confrontation. Still, the trustees were surprised when some forty students representing such groups as the Student Caucus and the May 4th Task Force showed up for the November 11 meeting. Caucus members Nancy Grim and Scott Marburger gave the trustees a list of concerns about the proposal, including insufficient student input, damage to the site's natural beauty, encroachment on the May 4 site, inadequate justification for the project, and the need to search for alternative sites.[40] Nevertheless, the trustees approved the project unanimously.

Olds, normally acutely sensitive to anything touching May 4, was running a gauntlet of problems prior to the meeting, and his attention was almost certainly not fully focused on the annex proposal. He and trustee chair George Janik had planned to cap the meeting with a dramatic flourish in which Olds would announce his resignation effective in June 1977. He was worn out, downhearted, and in desperate need of a change of scene and a long rest. Beset on all sides—though generally respected and genuinely liked by students, he felt estranged from most of the faculty—he had lost effective control of the institution in the turbulence over shrinking funding and enrollments, the collective bargaining struggle, the no-confidence vote, plus record-setting energy costs because of harsh winters, and the Simunek scandal—which had resurfaced.

On October 7, 1976, the *Stater* reported that despite the board's March ruling denying KEI use of any facilities or support unless "authorized by the provost," the venture was still alive and well in its Wright Hall office, with Simunek himself answering the phone. When quizzed by a reporter, Provost Snyder explained that KEI was being billed and that he expected it to pay, though he could not explain why the target date of June 30, 1976, after which KEI was forbidden to use University facilities, had been ignored. Proving that troubles come not as single spies but in battalions, the *Beacon Journal* revealed that on October 11, 1976, Snyder had warned Olds in September 1975 that the University's relationship with KEI may involve it in "acts of conversion or embezzlement."

As Olds's relations with his top academic administrators stretched to the snapping point, he came to rely heavily on trustee George Janik, a passionate advocate of his alma mater who had a high but not uncritical regard for Olds personally and for his many gifts. Janik saw Olds as a man of the finest character, superbly suited by education and temperament to preside over an undergraduate liberal arts college but unable to find his footing in a shell-shocked institution heavily weighted toward graduate study and research. To Janik, Olds was a true academic visionary who produced more exciting and promising ideas than his administrative skills could muster and deploy into workable programs.[41]

Like some other close observers of the Olds presidency, Janik was convinced that if Olds had left Kent in 1975, he would have departed with laurels on his brow for having opened the campus to the greater outside world of ideas and culture; for restoring dialogue; for his willingness to converse with students; for his opening new lines of communication with the campus community; and, above all, for binding up "the deep wounds among students, faculty, and community."[42] Few recalled such contributions when he left the campus, mainly because his most trying days would come after he announced his resignation.

After the trustees approved the gym annex proposal in November 1976, the issue faded from public view for the next six months—only to reappear during the May 4, 1977, ceremonies when three fire-breathing anti-Establishment speakers—lawyer William Kunstler, comedian-activist Dick Gregory, and Vietnam vet Ron Kovic—took turns haranguing an audience of some 3,000 in Memorial Gym. Kovic set the tone and sounded the theme on which the others rang variations: "If they try to build that gym, if they try to hide that truth," he shouted, "then they're going to have to bury 1,000 students in the cement that they pour."[43] On-campus activists had been content with campaigning to have four buildings renamed for the slain students and to have classes canceled for May 4 ceremonies. After Kunstler, Kovic, and Gregory had finished their tirades, some 1,500 students marched down Main Street. They were just passing Rockwell Hall when they heard that the trustees were meeting inside—doing business as usual on the anniversary of May 4. The students charged toward Rockwell, hot with righteous indignation.

The trustees' meeting had just started when a noise drew chairman Janik's eye out the window to the unruly, noisy mob striding toward the building. Before the meeting he had cautioned Robert Blakemore about the appearance of impropriety in meeting on May 4, but Blakemore, eager to report on the search committee's progress, argued for proceeding with the meeting, and Janik deferred to him. Before the crowd reached the building, Janik and Olds managed to hurry the other trustees and spectators out a side door and then braced themselves to face the throng pouring in through the other door.

Neither man was prepared for the vehement questions and accusations volleyed at them from all sides. They may well have felt morally compromised by meeting on a day "sacred" to many students. In any case, their repeated attempts to justify the action in approving the site on Blanket Hill satisfied no one. Contemporary photos of the tense confrontation show the accusing presence of shooting victim Dean Kahler sitting in his wheelchair near Olds, which may have made moot any explanation either man offered.

After a time the protesters' anger abated somewhat as they realized they would get no satisfaction. So after a short huddle they decided to occupy the building. The group eventually agreed on eight "demands," including no construction on the site of the shootings, "official" recognition of the injustice of the "Kent State massacre," no change of status or dismantling of the Center for Peaceful Change, no classes on May 4, and renaming four buildings be renamed for the slain students.[44] The Rockwell sit-in was peaceful and long, ending some fifteen hours after it started. Janik and Olds stayed to the end, talking with the students. It was during the long hours of the evening sit-in that the May 4th Coalition was conceived.

On May 12, after a large rally on the Commons, a crowd of May 4th Coalition supporters packed the Kiva, where the trustees had earlier announced they would meet in order to accommodate a large number of students. The trustees had agreed to hear just four of the demands, and, after the students had finished, Olds responded by assuring them that the annex would not violate the May 4 area and would not affect the pending civil suits. The trustees then voted to approve the construction contract, legally committing the institution to a construction project that would disrupt the campus for months. In a conciliatory gesture, however, they instructed Olds to appoint a committee to study renaming four buildings, place coordination of May 4 activities in the hands of a University-wide body, and keep the Center for Peaceful Change an autonomous academic unit. The board also agreed to consider the Coalition's other demands. Four days later the provost announced that CPC would retain its autonomy, but shortly after that an ad hoc committee rejected the building renaming proposal.

Conciliation was far from the minds of Coalition members. As soon as the May 12 meeting ended, they marched directly from the Kiva to Blanket Hill and set up a tent they had stored there earlier. Olds phoned Janik that evening to tell him about the tent, and Janik advised him to have it taken down. Olds, however, persuaded a majority of trustees that it was wisest to let the students vent their feelings. Tent after tent popped up over the following days, however, and soon "Tent City" stood on Blanket Hill. Over the next two months it would become the center of a rolling, roiling controversy that transfixed the campus, splashed KSU all over the front pages and evening news broadcasts—again—and generated a jungle of legal actions that almost rivaled that of May 4's.

Something else happened, too. During its sixty-two days of existence, Tent City residents formed a community. Something resembling familial ties were forged through shared living and democratic decision making. It had the bracing air of camping out, of roughing it, of sharing hardships while transcending the humdrum of ordinary life via a single-hearted commitment to a purpose higher and nobler than mere self-gratification. Despite disagreeing over means, the residents agreed on one overriding end: preserving the entire May 4 site as a symbol of "our land," as Nancy Grim defined it, where "an earlier generation of students were shot down," as well as of the antiwar, anti-Establishment movement.[45] Still, most of the residents were political moderates or liberals and never embraced the militant radicalism of the handful of Revolutionary Student Brigade (RSB) members who, with their ideological discipline, exercised increasing influence in the open-ended discussions.

The May 4 Coalition and the administration, the two parties to the gym annex controversy, were divided by their different understandings of what constituted the May 4 site. For the Coalition, it was "the entire center area of the campus where the events of 1970 unfolded." For the administration and board, it was limited to the specific area where the students had been shot. Throughout the controversy the administration and board consistently maintained that the annex would not violate the "sacred" ground where the students fell.[46] Thus, what one party revered as "sacred ground" was secular property to the other.

The Coalition, having no big guns to match those of the administration, made do with brains and youth's boundless energy. They demonstrated unusual sophistication in attracting supporters, skillfully using broadsides, media interviews, classroom visits, letter-writing campaigns, legal actions, and well-publicized rallies to take their case over the heads of the administration directly to the larger public. Their strategy was to bring the administration and trustees to heel by subjecting them to irresistible outside pressures. During June and July the Coalition staged national rallies featuring speeches by well-known activists and parents of some of the slain students; public officials and celebrities publicly urged the administration to change the building site.

The administration and trustees unwittingly collaborated with this strategy by keeping their collective mouth shut. They neither defended nor explained their decision. Intimidated by the culture of legalism that had rapidly kudzu'd the administration after the 1960s' protests, they heeded the advice of their legal team to make no public statements for fear of jeopardizing their case in court. This gave the Coalition free run of the propaganda field.

Although Olds and some trustees paid informal visits to Tent City during the summer, there were no formal exchanges between the two sides. Their positions were too fixed. Neither had a realistic or sympathetic understanding of the other's point of view. Some trustees airily dismissed the protesters as mere revenants of the SDS. Most Coalition supporters stereotyped the trustees as Establishment fat cats.[47]

The absence of negotiations and the silence of the board and administration eventually generated such pressure in Tent City that on July 6 some 100 Coalition supporters steamed down to Rockwell Hall bent on finding out when the arrests would begin. Warned, Olds was waiting for them in front of the east-facing doors. He had refused Janik's offer to stand by him in what both knew would be an ordeal; he may have been a lame duck, but he was still president and no coward. There is reason to think that Olds hoped to pacify the crowd with news of a possible resolution of the site issue. At that moment, Portage County representatives Jon Begala and Marcus Roberto were in Columbus negotiating with House and Senate leaders to find funds to rotate the annex about forty feet away from the Blanket Hill site. Trustees Janik and Michael Johnston, along with treasurer Dick Dunn, were scheduled to fly down to Columbus the next day to join them.

What transpired when the crowd confronted Olds was perhaps the ugliest moment in the entire gym controversy. The protesters spewed their frustration, anger, and ideology at Olds, shouting him down with "hoots, catcalls, and obscenities" every time he opened his mouth.[48] To the mob he was no more than a thing, an object, and hence fair game for vilification and revilement. Though shaken and heartsick, for forty minutes he withstood the abuse with dignity before walking back into Rockwell Hall.

In contemplating the end of his troubled presidency, Olds had been able to find some solace in his efforts to restore civility and the discourse of reason to the campus, as he told the trustees when he announced his retirement. But after his experience in front of Rockwell Hall, he said, "I didn't dream I would see an eye-for-an-eye, tooth-for-tooth atmosphere on campus as I did just a while ago. I've worked as hard as I know how to avert it."[49] (In the autumn of 2007, at a symposium marking the thirtieth anniversary of Tent City, Coalition leader Alan Canfora expressed regret over the way he and others had treated Olds.)

Though Begala would remain convinced that the relocation funds would have been forthcoming and contractual hurdles surmounted, the rotation compromise came to nothing—in part because some trustees resisted it, but mostly because the Coalition rejected it outright. Though the democratic ethic of freewheeling discussion was a feature of Tent City decision making, some denizens wielded more influence than others. One knowledgeable observer categorized the tenters as either "moderates," who were willing to compromise, or "hard noses," who argued that anything less than "complete capitulation" by the administration betrayed "a lack of courage." By imputing cowardice to their opponents, the "hard noses" usually prevailed.[50]

It was about this time that some trustees had second thoughts about the annex. At the June 9 meeting, trustees Joyce Quirk and David Dix proposed moving the site altogether, but a motion by Robert Blakemore tabled the idea pending the removal of all vestiges of Tent City.

When the decisive moment was at hand, and construction was scheduled to begin, some 250 Coalition supporters gathered at the Student Center on the evening of July 11 and voted to stay in Tent City and to accept a nonviolent mass arrest. Two days later, campus police began the arduous job of lifting and carrying 193 protesters off the site, putting them on buses for transport to Kent city hall for booking. A large, respectful crowd sprinkled with media representatives witnessed the event, a Kabuki-like ceremony of nonviolent resistance and self-restraint. Thanks to the good offices of Dennis Carey of CPC, the American Friends Service Committee, and campus police led by Chief John Peach, all officers in the vicinity were unarmed, and the demonstrators pacifically submitted to being physically removed. It was the high moment of a controversy crosshatched by moral and intellectual ambiguities.

After the leveling of Tent City, the Coalition's communal bonds began to dissolve. Resentments and rivalries flourished. The "hard noses," especially members of the RSB, tried to impose their militant agenda on the group. This turned off the "moderates," who were committed to nonviolent dissent. Above all, there was the inescapable fact that Tent City no longer existed. It was no longer anyone's home, just a symbol that would grow in memory as former residents looked back on their season of youth through the prism of nostalgia.

National Guardsmen fire tear gas as the crowd retreats up Blanket Hill toward Taylor Hall.

Students seeking cover near the Prentice Hall parking lot as shots were fired.

Clockwise from top: Professor Glenn Frank (geology) pleads with students to disperse after the shooting stopped. Midafternoon, a Portage County judge ordered the University to be closed. This map was provided at the May 4 site into the 1980s and reproduced in *Kent State/May 4: Echoes through a Decade,* edited by Scott L. Bills (Kent State University Press, 1982).

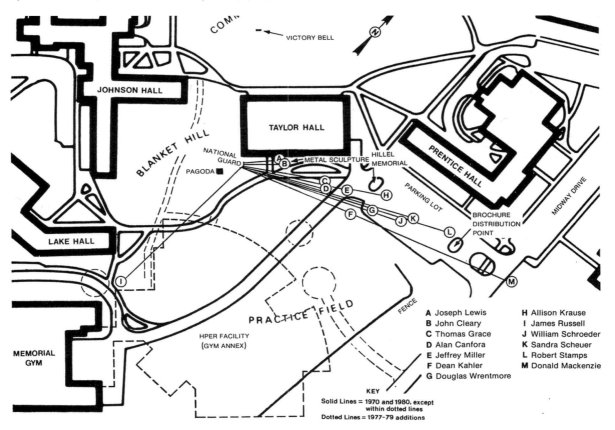

A Joseph Lewis
B John Cleary
C Thomas Grace
D Alan Canfora
E Jeffrey Miller
F Dean Kahler
G Douglas Wrentmore

H Allison Krause
I James Russell
J William Schroeder
K Sandra Scheuer
L Robert Stamps
M Donald Mackenzie

KEY
Solid Lines = 1970 and 1980, except
within dotted lines
Dotted Lines = 1977-79 additions

The 1970–71 Faculty Senate Executive Committee grappled with some of the greatest problems ever to confront an American university campus. Left to right: Stanley Christiansen (physics), Richard Heimlich (geology), chairman Martin Nurmi (English), D. Ray Heisey (speech communication), and William Fisher (journalism). Not pictured: Thomas D. Moore (education).

President Nixon appointed the President's Commission on Campus Unrest to investigate the shootings. Former Pennsylvania governor William W. Scranton (third from left) chaired what was called the Scranton Commission and held hearings on campus in late August 1970.

Trustee Robert C. Dix talks with students protesting the presence of ROTC on campus in 1971.

Above: The first Vigil, May 3, 1971. Sociology professor Jerry M. Lewis (in cap at extreme left) leads the first march commemorating the shootings. Carrying candles, the marchers walked silently from the Victory Bell down to Prentice Gate, then looped east up Main Street and ended at the Prentice Hall parking lot for a twelve-hour vigil—a ritual repeated each May 3 since.

Left: Jesse Jackson attended the first May 4 commemoration in 1971.

Right: Glenn Olds replaced President White in 1971. Olds came with impressive credentials: he held a Ph.D. in philosophy from Yale, was an ordained Methodist minister, and served as an ambassador to the UN for social and economic affairs.

Cultural events resumed on campus. Olds's friend, designer-philosopher-engineer R. Buckminster Fuller lectured on his geodesic dome; Eudora Welty, pictured here with Dean Keller, visited in 1977; and Allen Ginsberg held a poetry reading.

Far left: Sports were popular and, for the most part, successful, especially the football team coached by Don James, culminating with the greatest season in the school's history in 1973.

Left: Future Pro-Football Hall of Fame player Jack Lambert was a team leader.

Below: The new Student Center and Plaza opened in 1972.

On arriving at Kent, Golding was plunged into the controversy over the construction of an annex to Memorial Gymnasium. A large group of students and others, fearing this would destroy the site of the May 4 shootings, erected "Tent City" in protest and occupied the site for sixty-two days in 1977.

HEALTH, PHYSICAL EDUCATION & RECREATION   KENT STATE UNIVERSITY

Ten

THE GOLDING RESTORATION

{1977–1982}

Once Olds announced his resignation, effective the end of spring term 1977, the trustees started the machinery for finding his replacement. They picked trustee Robert Blakemore to chair a fourteen-member search committee drawn from a wider-than-usual range of KSU constituents, including a community representative. The committee received some 200 applications, suggesting that Kent had considerable appeal for academicians despite its troubled history. The committee worked efficiently, and by the end of March it had already entered what Blakemore called the "quarter finals" of its search for the slate of five candidates from which the board would choose the next president.[1]

Near the end of the process, Janik and treasurer Dick Dunn flew to California to interview two of the finalists. By far the most impressive was Brage Golding, a fifty-seven-year-old veteran of World War II and president of San Diego State. During the interviewing process, which spanned several days, Golding focused largely on the school's financial data, scrutinizing it line by line, to the exclusion of almost everything else.[2] His obvious percipience, impressive academic and business experience, and his decisive nature convinced them that he had the sound judgment and managerial mastery that KSU ached for at that moment in its history. The other trustees agreed, and, at their June meeting, the board unanimously voted to appoint him as Olds's successor. One can scarcely imagine two men less alike than Olds and his successor.

Golding brought to the position unprecedented breadth and depth of administrative experience in business as well as in higher education, including two successful university presidencies. After taking his B.A. at Purdue in 1938, he had been enrolled in an active ROTC program while studying in Chicago when he was ordered to active duty on December 6, 1941, the day before he was to be married. He served throughout the war as an artillery officer with the rank of major, earned his doctorate in chemical engineering at Purdue, and spent the next eleven years in private business and working part time as visiting professor at Purdue. In 1959 he became head of Purdue's School of Chemical Engineering. Six years later he moved to Dayton to take on a tougher challenge: transforming an OSU–Miami joint-branch operation into a full university, Wright State, with more than 12,000 students. That task successfully completed, Golding accepted the presidency of San Diego State in 1972.

In addition to the lure of a major new challenge, Golding was willing to take the Kent job because he was fed up with the California state system and administrative superstructure that gives individual college presidents little power. Far too little for Golding, whose autonomous nature bridled at taking orders from above—or, for that matter, from anyone. Golding's need—a combination of robust ambition and steely competitiveness—to constantly measure himself against an ascending scale of abstract challenges rather than, say, against a human opponent is revealing. It may have been simply that he had never met a man he could not best. At his initial interview in San Diego, he told Janik that under no circumstances would he stay at Kent longer than five years, his usual length of service at an institution. The implication was clear: five years would be ample time for him to straighten things out, even at Kent.[3]

Because Olds's tenure ended in July and Golding's would begin in September, the trustees appointed relative newcomer Michael Schwartz, vice president for graduate study and research, as acting president, the fourth in the school's history. Schwartz later recalled his brief presidency as "the longest two months in man's history."[4] An index of the spreading complexity of that extraordinary summer is that at one time or another three of Kent's presidents—Olds, Golding, and Schwartz—got entangled in the ropes of Tent City, which survived as a symbol long after it vanished as a fact.

In the weeks following the arrest, the Coalition members fought a rear-guard action, using legal initiatives to delay the start of actual construction. They also staged attention-getting, street-theater violations of the construction site. In the early hours of July 29, for example, sixty-nine trespassers were arrested; at 9:00 A.M. another was hauled off for crawling under the fence; and a few hours later five clergymen read a statement at the site and then four of them, and a bystander, crawled under the fence. All were promptly arrested. All told, several hundred people may have been arrested during that turbulent summer, and in some cases bail was posted by trustee George Janik's wife, alumna Nellie Lou Williams, whose sympathies lay with the protesters. This led to a visit to their Hudson home by a puzzled *Rolling Stone* reporter who wanted to find out what was going on.[5]

No sooner had construction resumed on August 1 than a federal judge in Cleveland ordered the University and the Coalition to work out a compromise, to the dismay and disgust of the administration. While these negotiations were supposed to be going on, the president-in-waiting, vacationing at his cabin in Maine, stepped unwittingly into a mess he had been assured would be cleaned up before he took office.[6] The August 2, 1977, issue of the *Beacon Journal* reported that trustees Joyce Quirk and David Dix, along with the Reverend John Adams, a representative of the slain students' families, had tracked Golding to his Maine retreat in a last-ditch effort to move the annex site. After hearing them out, Golding said he would ask the board for a resolution seeking funds from the legislature to relocate the gym annex. Golding also reportedly urged the three visitors to involve all parties to the dispute in a community-wide effort to win state funding.

But before campus authorities and board members could adjust to this turn of affairs, Golding denied the report, either because he had spoken without due circumspection or because his visitors had misconstrued his meaning. Three days later, the *Beacon Journal* reported that Golding denied the statements attributed to him by Quirk, Dix, and Adams, at the same time stating that his conversation with them was supposed to be completely confidential. The last public word on this squabble belonged to Reverend Adams, who released a forty-two-page account of the visit in which he denied Golding's denial and asserted that neither he nor the two trustees had misrepresented or misunderstood Golding, nor had they betrayed his confidence.[7]

Golding, who would soon impress the Kent campus and community as a man of unshakable self-confidence, was so discombobulated by this twist of events that he flew to Kent.[8] He was doubtless kicking himself for accepting the Kent job. It was around this same time that he told one trustee that he wouldn't have taken it if he had thought he would get caught up in the gym controversy.[9] But he had taken it, and he was too proud to walk away from a challenge, even one he had not chosen.

He reached campus on August 8 and, during the next four days, consulted with each of the trustees (presumably fence-mending with at least two), Schwartz and other top administrators, and two Coalition leaders. Before returning to Maine on August 12, he issued a report of his visit that included the following statement: "Personally, I wish the gym had not been put there. I feel strongly enough about it that I think the trustees should make one last effort to respond to the feelings against the gym."[10] Golding reportedly asked the board to try, either formally or informally, to secure legislative help to move the annex. In any event, that afternoon Schwartz and trustee Dick Dunn flew down to Columbus. But it was too late. When the Begala compromise had been a live possibility, too few administrators or trustees had supported it and the Coalition had scorned it. Timing is everything in politics, as in comedy, and bad timing in the first tends to produce a mordant species of the other.

On September 12 construction crews began gouging out the eastern flank of Blanket Hill. Though many large rallies would be staged during the next weeks, the Coalition gradually disintegrated. Yet, on the day before fall classes began, September 11, some 100 protestors, a few brandishing wire cutters, clambered over part of the chain-link fence and moved onto the site. Campus police videotaped but refrained from arresting them.

When school resumed the next day, the tide was turning, as new students and those returning to campus after vacation rejected the radical turn the protest had taken over the summer. Later that day a crew from the Davey Tree Expert Company removed two trees, much as a Davey crew had begun clearing Normal Hill nearly eighty years earlier, and two days later construction resumed, to the helpless dismay of protesters and the grim relief of administrators, including the new president, Golding, who had never believed the annex should be put on that hot spot and who was not yet home free of the gym controversy.

For when police were stoned and buildings spray-painted following a large rally on September 24, Golding donned his battle armor. He had had enough of moral ambiguities, which murk the mind and make one infirm of purpose. The controversy was consuming seventy hours of his time every week, making him by turns "angry, bitter, tired and sad," because, he said, his presidential duties put him "in a no-win situation where there is no absolute right or wrong."[11] So he ordered workers to set up a ten-foot fence around the site, told the Student Life Office to deregister the RSB, and published a "Presidential Notice and Order" setting draconian conditions for rallies, including limiting hours and location.

The climactic battle came on October 24. About 500 lovers of a lost cause, the majority apparently not Kent students, defied a county court order by gathering on the Commons at noon. After they refused an order to disperse, sheriff's deputies on horses charged them Cossack-style, scattering them whenever they began to regroup and teargassing them wherever they ran. No rally was held, no one was seriously hurt, the site was protected. But the image of the University as a sanctuary of free inquiry was besmirched. Having tried for too long to forget its history, having refused to learn from that exacting and enigmatic preceptor, it was forced to relive it—not literally, of course, but symbolically, in a more costly and challenging way. In a profound sense, human beings live and die by symbols, which can enrich life immeasurably by giving it meaning and purpose and value—or render it null and void.

The gym controversy left Kent's new president little time in the fall of 1977 to deal with his main task: putting the institution back on a sound financial basis. One could argue that Kent had no financial basis, sound or otherwise. The causes were not far to find.

There was, to cite just the most glaring, the devastating impact on state revenues of the nation's long economic malaise. This was compounded by the sad crumbling of the state's once-mighty industrial base. Then there was the racheting cost of campus security and the legal bills stemming from the shootings, which drained the school's reserves and forced it to poach money from other important operations, such as maintenance of buildings and grounds. No sooner had the security costs been paid than new bills were generated by the legal actions spawned by the gym controversy. And many parents understandably blanched at the idea of sending their children to a school that seemed to be forever in turmoil.

The months of bad publicity over the annex site caused a sickening enrollment drop between 1969 and 1978. And enrollment drops meant additional reductions in state support. The numbers are revealing. In that nine-year span, Kent's full-time student equivalent enrollment

(FTEs) grew an anemic 2 percent, compared to 24 percent at all other Ohio public universities. The 1971 freshman class was 1,000 students smaller than 1970's, causing a ripple effect that strained the school's budget until 1976. If not for a massive recruitment campaign in 1975, Kent would have experienced no enrollment increase at all during that nine-year span. During that same period Kent's competition—Youngstown State, Akron, and Cleveland State universities—grew by more than 37 percent.[12] A menacing army of such daunting statistics confronted Golding at the end of October 1977, after he had disposed of the gym annex problem.

He began his first address to the faculty by easing their fears, assuring his audience that he had "not come to Kent State to preside over either the decline or the closing of the university." But before they could settle complacently into their seats, he hit them with disturbing news: the admissions office was reporting a one-third drop in the number of high school seniors submitting their ACT scores to Kent. The implication was clear: such a huge drop in student interest threatened an enrollment disaster like that of 1971.[13]

This, however, was precisely the sort of challenge Golding relished and which he was superbly equipped to meet. During the next four years he marshaled all his experience and skills—in administrative organization and systems management, budgetary discipline, financial strategy, and sure-handed leadership—and set in motion an array of measures designed, directly and indirectly, to give the school a fresh, new, appealing image, one that would change the public's attitude toward KSU, which he believed had to be unhitched from the nightmare of May 4, 1970. This was the key to restoring the institution to fiscal sanity and putting its house in order.

The recession worsened, reducing revenues and making major problems for Ohio's public institutions: from 1980 to 1983 Ohio slashed funding for higher education by 30 percent. Instances abound of the economic instability of the period. In January 1982, for example, state budget experts discovered a huge income shortfall, which meant another cut in Kent's budget for the next fiscal year and, inevitably, another hike in student fees, which students protested to Columbus.

Thanks to Golding's vigorous recruiting campaigns, enrollment was not the nightmare problem in the early eighties that it was for most state schools, for Kent won the competition with its neighbors, Akron, Youngstown, and Cleveland State. Still, on March 16, 1981, Golding sent a letter to parents spelling out future budget realities in blunt terms. His ostensible aim was to warn of a steep reduction of state funds coming in the near future, partly because of the state's ongoing economic malaise but mostly because of post–baby boom demographic projections of drastically shrinking numbers of eligible college-age students. His letter had a subtext: parents must change their attitude toward tax-supported public education, must recognize its value not only to individual students but to the entire state; and, not incidentally, elect legislators who would make education the top priority. Only by improving its higher education system, he believed, could Ohio hope to reinvigorate the state's economy, a theme that would resound throughout the next generation and beyond.[14]

One of his first acts was to contract with a Cleveland advertising agency for help in devising a highly successful marketing campaign that focused on Kent's academic strengths, its legitimate claims to being the premier state university in northeast Ohio, as well as to its bright palette of cultural and social opportunities. Radio commercials and newspaper ads throughout the northeastern quadrant of the state featured testimonials from former students, many well-known personalities and public figures, about how their experiences at Kent State had set them on career paths and enriched their personal lives.

Golding began cutting costs as part of his larger mission of putting the budget in order. Sentiment did stay his hand. He started at the top-heavy top by reversing the long trend toward constructing an ever more elaborate and expensive superstructure of upper-level administrators. Early in 1978 he eliminated the vice presidential positions for administration, finance and treasurer, public affairs and development, academic affairs, education and student services, and graduate studies. He consolidated their functions into three positions: vice president for business affairs and treasurer, vice president for University affairs, and vice president for academic and student affairs. To the last post, *primus inter pares,* he appointed Michael Schwartz. These reductions, while perhaps having only modest effect on the budget, sent a reassuring message to the faculty and staff that every program and member of the University family would be treated equally and fairly in his efforts to deal with the budget crisis.

Incidentally, Golding's commitment to fiscal discipline was personal as well as professional. He took very seriously his duty to be a good steward of the resources entrusted to his care, particularly monies from state instructional subsidies and student tuition and fees. He was not one to waste a dollar or plunge his head and feet into the public trough. Once, when he and his wife were scheduled to fly to Europe via Great Britain on personal business, Dr. Robert Clawson, director of international and comparative programs, asked if Golding would meet with a representative of the University of Aston, in the UK, to discuss a possible exchange program. Golding agreed, and Clawson reserved a room for them in the Horse Guards, a tony hotel with a view Clawson thought would please Mrs. Golding. When the Goldings were shown their room, however, the president noticed the view of the Thames sliding majestically seaward and inquired if rooms without a view were less expensive. When informed that indeed they were $100 cheaper, he changed their rooms.[15]

As part of his overall effort to set Kent's house in order, Golding appointed an Institutional Advancement Committee, steered by representatives from a variety of campus constituencies, to solicit ideas for increasing enrollment by raising faculty and staff awareness of their critical role in shaping the public's perception of the institution. This was a healthy dose of boosterism intended to counteract the habit of pessimism and gloom ingrained by years of disorder, confusion, and instability. A reorganized and augmented recruitment staff mounted a vigorous campaign for new students, while a joint Faculty Senate/UFPA committee on enrollment initiatives pitched in as well.

Golding's programs worked. In a few years Kent was one of the few public universities that successfully defied doomsday projections of long-term declines in college-age students, proving that demographics are not destiny. Beginning with the fall class of 1979, each succeeding freshman class grew in number every year he was president, a remarkable turnabout, given that the recession didn't bottom out until 1982.

A corollary of improving the school's image was improving its performance as an educational institution. He shifted advising responsibilities from the administrative wing to the colleges and schools, putting them closer to the students and where they made their career decisions. Especially successful was his highly popular tutoring program for dorm residents in basic subjects, which was staffed largely by outstanding and eager upperclassmen under the supervision of experienced teachers. To personalize the school for incoming students, the Educational Policy Council and Faculty Senate passed a resolution requiring all freshman students to take a one-hour orientation course cotaught by a professor and an upperclassman. The aim was to help freshmen get their bearings in the radically different atmosphere and culture of life on a college campus and, not incidentally, to help them establish a relationship with a professor in a relaxed setting, something students in a large university often miss.

For decades Kent had had an orientation program, as well as a requirement that a student needed an adviser's signature to register for classes, but both were ditched during the 1960s. In Golding's jaundiced view, administrators of the sixties and early seventies had been mistaken in caving to student pressures against form, structure, and discipline. (In his view, a president should always listen to student requests but not necessarily accede to them.) And, hoping to involve parents in their children's education, he had midterm grades mailed directly to their homes: a key element in his campaign to change the public's thinking about Kent.

As if the reduced state funding, litigation costs, and the damaging publicity engendered by the gym controversy weren't enough, the late-seventies' winter weather refused to cooperate with Golding's well-laid plans to stabilize the school's finances. The winter of 1976, before he came, had battered the entire state with record low temperatures and huge snowfalls. And January 1977 was far worse—the coldest month in Ohio's history. On January 17 several parts of the state registered temperatures ranging from 17 to 25 degrees below zero. And the winter of 1977–78 climaxed with a stupendous blizzard.

For all the kinetic thrills that accompany an experience of nature in high dudgeon, the record-breaking winters of 1976–77 and 1977–78 cost the cash-strapped University dearly. Classes were frequently canceled—once, for a whole week—because parking lots were covered by five-foot-thick blankets of snow and blocked roads kept commuters at home. Heating units broke down and pipes burst and water froze on classroom floors on the Kent campus as well as on some regional campuses. To combat soaring fuel costs, the administration decreed that classroom and office temperatures be set no higher than 55 degrees. One professor wore his doctoral robes over his woolen jacket and trousers when he lectured. To save money, the University decided to convert from gas to coal.

Even as Golding was getting traction on these matters, however, he was forced to deal with the Bermudez scandal, which had rebounded into the headlines in April 1977 when area newspapers reported that at least seventy pages of Bermudez's 262-page dissertation were virtually identical to passages in articles written by tax scholars but were used without attribution. Nothing quite rocks the academic boat like a charge of plagiarism. Golding wanted Kent out of the headlines.

Though he had been briefed earlier on the affair, he had assumed that it had been settled by the findings of the 1976 Faculty Senate investigation. The senate committee, however, was not tasked, nor was it competent, to determine the originality of Bermudez's work. That was the fundamental responsibility of his dissertation committee.

Golding spent much of the first half of 1978 studying documents, reports, transcripts of a July 1977 meeting between Bermudez and KSU administrators, University graduate policies, the report of the senate investigation; interviewing and consulting; and, above all, reading every word of the dissertation itself and its alleged unacknowledged sources. Despite his practiced interest in financial matters and passion for detail, reading a doctoral dissertation in a highly technical field as alien as tax theory must have taxed Golding's modest supply of patience.

At the end of February 1978 the local papers reported rumors of a compromise in the offing: Golding was said to be planning to recommend that the trustees temporarily suspend the dissertation, withdraw it from the Library, and permit Bermudez either to delete or footnote all disputed passages or to rewrite the entire dissertation and resubmit it for adjudication by a panel of outside experts who would make a recommendation to the board. Golding refused either to confirm or deny the reports. On February 28 an editorial in the *Beacon-Journal* reminded him that, if the plagiarism charges were true, he was obliged to the school and all holders of its graduate degrees to uphold the highest standards of academic integrity. No compromise, the paper said, would justify sullying the school's honor, no matter the legal consequences.

The Bermudez affair was another of those crises that seemed to flourish at Kent and that seemed peculiarly ill suited to Golding's disposition and talents. Although it did not involve the unbiddable moral ambiguities that had knocked him off stride temporarily during the gym controversy, it was booby-trapped with intricate legal tangents and slippery terminological nuances. For example, when Bermudez wrote his dissertation, the University had no plagiarism policy, though it did have one on "academic dishonesty." And, of course, the dissertation had passed examination by at least two committees of graduate professors. Doubtless also influencing Golding's attempt to resolve the problem was the University's legal choir of lawyers chanting, "It's cheaper to settle out of court than to go to trial." All this seems to have caused him once again to mislay for a time his superb self-confidence, tempting him to equivocate.

Ultimately, Golding decided against compromise or equivocation. On July 8, 1978, he mailed a long, close-reasoned letter to the board recommending that Bermudez's doctorate be revoked because the dissertation did not "adequately demonstrate" Bermudez's ability "to conduct research in a discriminating and original manner." He also faulted it for what amounted to plagiarism, without mentioning that fraught term. Before the trustees could act on Golding's recommendation, however, Bermudez filed suit in federal court in Cleveland contending that revoking his degree would violate his civil right to due process. When the judge refused to add the case to his already crowded docket, saying it involved jurisdictional questions, it disappeared into legal limbo. And there it languished for the remainder of that year, and the next, until Bermudez died of a heart attack on September 19, 1980.

In the weeks before he assumed office, Golding had studied the University Catalog and its academic calendar. Both were intertwined and, in his judgment, both were wasteful, muddled messes. They had to be set right before the institution could be put on a sound footing. Deciding for tactical reasons to deal with the calendar first, he made known his preference for the semester system and the campus grapevine did the rest. No one was surprised a few months later when an all-University committee of faculty and administrators began studying the desirability and feasibility of changing the school's calendar from quarters to semesters. The atmosphere was auspicious. It was the season of cost cutting, and the sound of snipping scissors filled the air. Anything that promised to save money was worth trying.

The committee's research showed that over time Kent's quarter system had been forced into a dysfunctional marriage between two different systems, quarters and semesters. In a typical quarter system a full study load consists of three courses, each meeting for fifty minutes five days per week for ten weeks. A full study load in the semester system consists of five courses, each meeting two to three hours per week for fifteen weeks. In theory, quarters offer greater breadth or range of learning, while semesters offer greater depth and understanding. The committee discovered that some Kent students were taking as many as a dozen or more one- and two-credit-hour courses per quarter, especially in professional fields, denying them time for study and reflection and making them dance to a frenzied drum. It also determined that a semester calendar would reduce administrative costs and time spent on grade preparation and registration by a third.

The members took into account educational, economic, and other ramifications (not least being student reaction to such a change), but keenly aware that Golding's preference for semesters sat like Banquo's ghost at one end of their meeting table. After due deliberation they unanimously recommended that Kent convert to a semester calendar, and the trustees duly followed suit by approving the switch from three ten-week quarters to two sixteen-week (including an examination week) semesters, beginning in the fall term of 1980. When computer modeling discovered that all final exams could be accomplished in four days, Golding incorporated a midweek, exam-free "study day" to relieve the anxieties and pressures of finals. And later, responding to numerous requests, he shifted the start of the second semester to January, which gave Kent students a head start in the race for summer jobs. Kent's version of the semester system was eventually adopted by its sister schools, though not by OSU.

While the calendar was being studied, Golding went to work on the catalog problem. This ultimately led to a purging of the University's official register of courses, which had grown to massive size during the postwar decades. Departments had been adding new courses as their subject fields changed without cutting courses that were seldom if ever taught. The result was a catalog that misled students and encouraged department recruitment committees to maintain professorial slots no longer justified by professional interest or student demand. But the territorial imperative rules the jungles of academe, and nothing rouses it to rage faster than a move to trim unoffered, unwanted, moribund courses from a school's catalog. Many a department was blood-splattered during the turf wars that attended Golding's mandated revision of the course register. Eventually, however, a new, notably lighter, more descriptively accurate, and economically feasible KSU catalog emerged, and the wounded professors recovered in good time.

An equally significant curricular change—indeed, one of the most important in the school's history—sprang from the calendar and catalog reforms. As the seventies wound down, a number of major universities began scouting for creative ways to cope with the growing fragmentation of the undergraduate curriculum, as evidenced in the professionalizing and consequent narrowing of the curriculum at the cost of the liberal arts. At Kent, though Golding was the impetus, academic vice president Michael Schwartz became herald and spear bearer of the campaign to broaden undergraduate education. He was eloquent in expressing his unhappiness with the burgeoning professional associations, with their tunnel-visioned raising of credit hours required for professional accreditation, which destroyed the humanistic undergirding of higher education. Aiding and abetting the influence of professional organizations, he argued, was the state's system of funding, which allocated funds only for increases in credit hours taught. This meant that each time a professional group raised its hourly requirements, academic departments, moving in lock step, raised theirs, usually at the expense of liberal education requirements. The result was an undergraduate curriculum as incoherent as a Rube Goldberg machine.

In 1981 the long-range planning subcommittee of the EPC, which Schwartz chaired, proposed a set of general education requirements tailored to ensure that students graduating with baccalaureate degrees would "be educated not only to function in a specific field, but also to live intelligently in a civil, complex society."[16] After approval by the EPC, the general education policy went to the Faculty Senate, there to be pounded for three months on the anvil of fierce disputation, not so much over its merits but over its contents: hearing FTEs (state funding jargon for "full-time equivalents") ringing like money in department cash registers, fields of study not usually associated with liberal arts argued earnestly for inclusion on the list of eligible courses. The policy as it emerged from senate deliberations on November 9, 1981, was almost identical to the one proposed by the EPC. However, it did have a new name—Liberal Education Requirements (LERs)—when it went into effect in 1982, thirty years after the first requests. By that time, few of the voices that had argued in the fifties for such a requirement were still around to hear the chimes of its sweet music.

Golding's campaign to change the public's attitude toward KSU by giving it a new image was predicated on his success in making internal reforms. He realized that something constructive had to be done about the annual May 4 commemoration, not only to improve the school's image but also in the interests of justice. In 1978, he established a May 4th Observance Committee composed of on- and off-campus representatives to sponsor the event. He designated May 4 as "Remembrance Day" and put it on the school's calendar. And instead of insisting on "business as usual" on that day, he suspended classes from noon to 2:00 P.M., a much-applauded gesture of sensitivity and sanity that helped defuse the charge that the school was trying to "bury" or "cover up" the shootings.

He also embraced Olds's initiative to make the school accessible to all handicapped people. Kent became a pioneer in mainstreaming university education of the disabled and in making them feel welcome. Golding had several old buildings altered for accessibility, and all new buildings were required to have special bathroom facilities, elevators, ramps, and entrances. He had a University van remodeled for transporting students in wheelchairs, and a model program for training the severely disabled to operate and program computers became part of the business college curriculum.

Like Olds before him, Golding spent much time during his five-year tenure helping plan and develop the Northeastern Ohio Universities College of Medicine (NEOUCOM), which the state legislature had established in 1973. Drawing on the resources of a consortium of area universities—Kent, Akron, Youngstown—the new medical college was intended to prepare doctors for family practice. A charter class of forty-two students of the combined B.S./M.D. curriculum began their studies in 1975, many at KSU, and in 1981 NEOUCOM graduated its first class and received full accreditation.

An important part of Golding's program of changing Kent State's image was redeeming the residence halls, long neglected and abused— or, as he put it, improving "the environmental, the programmatic, and the behavioral conditions in our residence halls."[17] He knew the folly of expecting parents to feel comfortable moving their children into dormitories that looked like hangovers from a three-week binge. He reestablished "old-fashioned visitation hours," imposed common-sense rules for conduct and occupancy, and tightened security to prevent theft and ensure safety, changes that the great majority of students and all their parents welcomed, despite fears to the contrary. Many rooms had been so trashed that they had to be completely refurbished. As a result, empty rooms, long a drag on the budget, were filled nearly to capacity by 1980.[18]

In a sign of the changing face of the campus, Wills Gym for women was condemned and razed in 1979 to make way for more parking space. Kent had ceased being largely a commuter campus in the 1960s. Another aspect of the campus face that needed sprucing up was the grounds. During the seventies one of the sorest sights meeting the eyes of new students and their parents, alumni, and visitors was the bedraggled appearance of the campus, once arguably the state's comeliest. Golding decreed campus beautification to be one of his first priorities, and once again the rolling lawns were mown; shrubbery, trees, and flowers were planted and tended; miles of campus walkways and roads were repaved. The important role he assigned to maintaining the physical plant and cultivating the beauty of the grounds in restoring Kent's image led him to persuade the board to purchase the Battaglia property on the southeast edge of the campus, raising campus acreage to 900. The spacious property included numerous outbuildings and greenhouses; the largest was remodeled to house maintenance shops, and the greenhouses were used as nurseries for growing early flowers to be planted in the wealth of decorative crescents and islands of flowers and grasses that soon graced the campus.

To carry out his principal mandate of returning the University to fiscal health so that it could fulfill its academic mission, he subjected all programs to a cold-eyed, cost-benefit analysis in terms of student need and educational feasibility. As he later told the faculty, his study showed that the school was losing students twice as fast as it was losing teachers, an economically unsustainable rate, and he reminded them that the graduate program was being paid for largely by the undergraduate, often to the detriment of the latter. To many professors, Golding's analysis was a sharp knife dividing undergraduate and graduate programs and their faculties. They maintained that a university education involved factors beyond the reach of a cost-benefit analysis, which ignored important qualitative factors. They were correct, of course, as was Golding, when he reminded them that Kent was living beyond its means in its academic programs. He made the mistake of illustrating his point by publicly naming the individual departments, needlessly offending some distinguished scholars.

By the end of the 1970s Kent had become part of a growing national trend toward shifting undergraduate education from tenured professors to part-time, untenured instructors paid per course but with no benefits or permanent status. Golding did not regard this as a viable solution to the school's long-term problems. To restore a sensible ratio between students and faculty and to increase teaching productivity, he proposed such measures as improving the quality of education by strengthening requirements, giving more "rigorous assignments," and increasing "classroom hours per course" under the coming semester plan. "In good times and bad," he said, "the demanding schools have had waiting lists in their admissions offices. We are good enough, I believe, and proud enough, to be tough."[19] The argument for greater rigor and higher standards, including raising entrance standards, as a way of recruiting and retaining students would be debated often in the future.

No program was spared scrutiny, not even the usually untouchable intercollegiate athletics. He told the faculty in 1979 that he had been able to put more money in academic programs by shifting "a major portion of the expense" of varsity and intramural sports from the educational-general fund to a new, "earmarked fee" on students, by persuading student government to support a new special fee. A year later he reported that he was subjecting varsity sports to the same searching cost-benefit analysis as other programs. Was Kent, he asked, trying to compete at too high a level by belonging to the Mid-American Conference (MAC)? If so, shouldn't it consider moving to one more "appropriate"?[20]

As indicated above, early in his tenure Golding began casting a cold cost-analysis eye on varsity sports. They had grown increasingly expensive ever since 1972, when Title IX outlawed gender discrimination by institutions receiving federal funds. And maintaining membership in the Mid-American Conference exacted ever-higher costs, while state funds were shrinking. Also weighing heavily in his thinking were additional considerations: the mediocre quality of the major programs and the low level of student interest, as measured by their nonattendance (football coach Don James had resigned in part because of weak fan support). At some point Golding in 1980–81 seems to have been on the brink of abolishing varsity sports, either in whole or in part. For whatever reason or reasons, whether pressures from alumni, trustees, or community, he decided to back away from the whirlpool of controversy.

In fact, Title IX's most dramatic and immediate effect was on athletics. After 1972, varsity sports, once largely the preserve of men, opened their creaking doors, slowly, to women, for whom the law mandated the same level of support given male sports. Thereafter *Burr* photos provide a time-lapse progression of women athletes competing, with the same fierce intensity and zest as men, in such sports as field hockey, rugby, soccer, tennis, track and field, and softball. Funding this equal treatment gave administrators and athletic directors mammoth migraines. How, they asked, were they going to fund all these new athletic teams when they scarcely had sufficient money to support men's varsity sports? More than varsity sports programs at most Ohio universities, Kent's has almost from its inception been driven by the imperatives of growth and change as the only way to survive—that is, the only way to get sufficient state funds—in the razor-toothed, steel-elbowed arena of Ohio's politico-educational system. This has forced the university to adopt a rob-Peter-to-pay-Paul strategy for maintaining a variety of sports programs, both in respect to putting them in competition with the academic mission and with each other—women's sports as well as men's—for funds.

As part of this same comprehensive examination of programs, Golding singled out the growth rate of the library's collections. To most of the faculty, the Library was the school's heart and soul, and its growing collections a pledge of the school's commitment to serious study and research. When he received a petition from 200 professors calling for an increase rather than a decrease in library funds, he assured the faculty that he revered the Library as much as they did and then asked disingenuously: "Where shall we find the wherewithal to supplement the Library's present two-and-a-half million dollar budget?"[22] Cost cutting was on his mind when he quizzed head librarian Hyman Kritzer about shelf space. Golding asked if the computerization of library systems then under way would enable the staff to maintain a use-record of each book. Yes, Kritzer assured him, adding that such records were already kept. Golding then asked him with a straight face why the library didn't discard books that had not been used for, say, five or ten years, in order to open up shelf space for new books. Kritzer couldn't decide whether Golding was serious or just pulling his leg.[23]

There is no glamour in budget cutting. And Golding, like all presidents, wanted to leave office with a shiny trophy incised with his name in the school's annals. Trophies often depend on luck, and he got lucky in 1979 when Rachel Redinger, a resident of Dover, Ohio, and friend of KSU, introduced Golding to Shannon Rogers and Jerry Silverman, who were looking for a home for their enormous collection of costumes, dresses, and art objects. Redinger and Rogers, a native of Newcomerstown, Ohio, and one of America's best-known designers, shared an enthusiastic interest in the nearby outdoor theater at Schoenbrun, Ohio. Rogers's business partner, Jerry Silverman, was a fashion magnate and one of the nation's leading manufacturers of women's dresses before he retired. After rejecting a number of institutions, they were delighted by Golding's interest and his ideas for showcasing their collections and putting them to educational use.

The plan Golding had in mind called for the design interests of Rogers and the production/marketing interests of Silverman to dovetail in stages, evolving from a major in fashion design into one of the nation's leading schools of fashion design. Over the next three years, the collections were shipped in stages from various warehouses to temporary storage facilities in Kent, while preparations were under way to store them permanently in the Rockwell annex and to lay the academic groundwork for the fashion program. Bringing to bear his business acumen and experience, Golding persuaded the trustees and the Board of Regents of the collections' educational potential. And with help from Rogers and Silverman, he raised funds from foundations, corporations, and individual donors to support the project independent of state monies. As one observer remarked, while it was true that Golding was lucky to have the Rogers-Silverman gift drop into his lap, he deserved much praise for seeing its full potential and exploiting it.[24]

Not everyone was enchanted, of course. Many professors bridled at the notion of incorporating a trade school program into the curriculum of a university with high academic ambitions. Some saw it as competing for already scarce funds with graduate programs involved in basic research, while some thought it inappropriate for a serious educational institution to be handling women's dresses. The mumblers, kibitzers, doubters, and naysayers only became an organized opposition, however, after Golding disclosed his plan to move the administrative offices to the Library in order to renovate Rockwell for the museum and fashion school program.

Faculty opposition to administrative encroachments on the Library had not abated since Olds's attempt. The Library, they held, was intended solely for study and research, the primary mission of the institution, and not for the convenience and comfort of its managers, those high-paid, blue-suited paper shufflers and bean counters. Golding claimed that the institution would benefit from having the administration at the new center of the campus, to which the faculty responded, "How?" Any usurpation of library space was to be resisted for the same reason a sensible person never lets an insurance agent get his foot in the door: once inside, he never leaves. So the faculty, with great deliberation and solemnity, voted two times against the move. And so the administration remodeled the second floor and moved into the Library. As was its privilege, so Golding reasoned, the faculty had expressed its opinion, and as usual it was wrong. While dutifully bound to listen to faculty as well as to students, he was under no obligation to heed what either said. As he saw it, they were usually wrong because they were not vouchsafed the comprehensive view of an issue available to the president alone from his aerie at the top. He was, however, scrupulously deferential to faculty judgment in curricular matters.

Some faculty members had another objection as well: the wasteful cost of the switch. More than $5 million of state monies was spent on extensive renovations of Rockwell and its 1958 annex, plus large sums on transforming library space into administrative suites. The original Rockwell Hall, the campus's most elegant building, had a few years earlier been renovated to house administration offices, revealing as never before the grace of its ornate cornices, high ceilings, marble stairs and railings, graceful columns, and spacious offices with exquisite woodwork. The frieze of resonant names—Aristotle, Plato, Shakespeare, Montaigne—above the windows on the second floor remained, however, to puzzle and pique freshman students to venture into the enchanted world of humane learning, although the new library was across campus.

A year or so after the move, Golding invited a group of faculty to an afternoon "Meet the President" reception in the new presidential suite in the Library. In the middle of a conversation around the cookies, Golding observed, with a straight face, that he had decided to hold the reception there because it was one way guaranteed to get the faculty into the Library. Professor James Louis, who was present, couldn't tell from Golding's face or vocal inflection whether he was joshing or jabbing.

His relations with faculty were curious. Whereas it made up its mind too quickly about Olds, the faculty never quite agreed about Golding. Oh, everyone conceded that he was a superb administrator, but their assessment of him was flecked with dislike and fear. This could not be explained solely by his difficult personality, which was tough, rebarbative, truculent, and his self-confidence, which shaded into arrogance. Though only of average height, Golding's sense of himself, of his own weight and thrust in the world of affairs, as expressed in his assured bearing, his assertive stride, his solid body, gave him a moral dimension out of all proportion to his physical measurements. He was intensely private, remote, enigmatic. As one longtime Golding observer recalls, "He never encouraged anyone to use his first name. We always called him 'Dr. Golding' or 'Mr. President.' I'm not sure, but I think the practice extended up to the provost."[25] The faculty's reservations seem to have been rooted in Golding's aloofness and sometimes ill-concealed disdain for them, individually (with a few exceptions) and collectively. While it is true that most who worked closely with him in the presidential purlieus liked and admired him, and that his power and easy assurance charmed women, it is also true that he was not above bullying people who irritated him or when it suited his interest or mood.

Well-attested stories of his intimidating persona were legion. In one, a young lawyer, habitually disheveled in appearance, was frozen in his tracks on entering the president's office for a staff meeting by Golding's barking order to get out of the office and *not* return until he was properly dressed. The lawyer stepped back into the vestibule, buttoned his collar, tightened his tie, and returned for the meeting. In another oft-repeated report, in the first days of Golding's presidency, two assistant provosts were having coffee before starting work one morning. Gordon Keller was seated near the door and Tom Moore was in a reverie when Keller broke the spell by suddenly standing up and turning toward the door. Moore looked over and saw Golding filling the doorway. Golding's eyes moved slowly from Moore's face down his torso and along his legs to his feet, which, Moore realized, were resting on his desktop. Before he could react, Golding snapped, "Aren't you in the habit of standing up when the president enters your office?" and walked off.

On another occasion, during a working breakfast for the visiting dean of sciences at the University of Leipzig in East Germany, Golding turned the conversation in the direction of the Kent professor of political science who was squiring the visitor around campus. "My son," Golding said to the visitor, "says he wants to get a Ph.D. in political science, and I told him he should get a degree in physics or chemistry, and then he could be a political scientist by just reading newspapers." Shooting a glance at the political scientist, he smiled at the German, an organic chemist, and asked, "Wouldn't you agree?" The two scientists then threw back their heads and enjoyed a good laugh. The political scientist was more amused than insulted. He later said he felt "like a centurian being told to fall on his sword, so I heartily agreed with him—nothing to it, political science. But I knew he had stuck it to me and I sure wasn't going to argue with him about it and he knew it. He did seem to enjoy putting people in that position. He had a kind of military bearing and I'm sure General Patton had the same deft touch."[26]

Many who attended the series of faculty receptions President and Mrs. Golding held in the presidential suite were puzzled by his chill aloofness, his air of dutifully doing his duty. Golding seemed to regard the faculty as a given, something to be dealt with to keep it from complaining. But its attitudes, its feelings toward him, were a matter of no moment. He measured his performance solely by the pride he derived from knowing that when he left a place, it was better than when he found it. As he told the *Stater*, "My satisfaction is a very inward, personal one. I believe the University is in much better condition than when I took over. The place is not perfect and never will be."[27]

His attitude toward the trustees was of a piece: like students and professors, trustees were a given and had a necessary role, which he defined as choosing a president, setting the school's mission, and then leaving him free to do his job as he saw fit. Above all they must mind their own business. Before he came to Kent, the trustees had, in his view, become too involved in campus affairs, and it was up to him to educate them about their proper place in the scheme of things.[28] As part of his attempt to open up the campus, Olds had involved the trustees as chairs of faculty committees doing long-range planning, budget studies, etc. Golding preferred to have trustees involved as little as possible in campus affairs; he wanted them "on the shelf."[29] And his method set the pattern for the future, serving the interests of presidents very well, affording them more freedom to make decisions, more room in which to operate. But it distanced these trustees from the educational mission of the institution as well from those charged with carrying out that mission, the faculty, and those who were the subjects of that mission, the students. Equally problematic, perhaps, it led to a situation in which the presidents essentially set their own goals and then assessed how well they had met them, which effectively undercuts the board's statutory responsibility for the enterprise.

If the faculty sometimes found Golding forbidding and off-putting—and it did—it also gave him very high marks for his organizational and financial expertise and ultimately concluded, with surprising unanimity, that he was the right man for the job at that ragged moment in Kent's history. For having imposed budgetary and administrative discipline, for his financial planning, and for his decisive leadership, he was widely acknowledged to have turned the school around and put a rudderless ship on an even keel. Decisiveness was a hallmark of his administrative style. He once said that when you're "on the horns of a dilemma," the thing to do is make a decision.[30] He had done this, with conspicuous success, in the gym annex crisis and the Bermudez affair, as well as in resolving the less sensational but equally important problems that regularly cross a presidential desk. As a result of collective bargaining negotiations under Golding, salaries were raised, sabbaticals were restored, and faculty and staff were given fee waivers. His purchase of the Battaglia property greatly expanded the campus.

He increased teaching productivity by one credit hour. He pruned and disciplined the undergraduate and graduate programs' course offerings, and he gave the undergraduate curriculum a liberal foundation. He articulated his educational vision through his deeds.

It mattered not whether he talked about his educational vision. He came to set Kent's house in order, to reorganize its administrative structure and give it fiscal stability—in short, to restore its viability and vitality as an educational enterprise. In those precise terms, he was the most successful president in the school's history. And, by his own exacting standards, he did leave the school far better off than it was when he came. Appearances to the contrary notwithstanding, Golding surely wanted the good opinion of students, trustees, and faculty—but on his own proud terms. The steely disdain and arrogance of his personality were part of the mask of command he acquired during World War II. Behind that personality, however, was a character of extraordinary strength, which, Tom Moore noted, was always far better than his personality.[31] And when he left, no one wished him gone. So, if he did not win the hearts of those he served, he could take great pride in knowing that he earned their respect and gratitude and that he ranks among the very best of Kent State's leaders.

Eleven

THE CHANGING CAMPUS CULTURE

{1970S AND 1980S}

The eye-level vantage point from which we have been looking at the Kent State story to this point must be briefly suspended in favor of a progressive and particular perspective if we are to appreciate an important aspect of campus life that eludes the blandishments of chronological narrative. If the way we present ourselves to the world and the way we conduct ourselves in it, if fashions in dress and fads in behavior reveal our values and inner conditions, then animate the students in *The Chestnut Burr* by riffling pages with your fingers for a kaleidoscopic impression of the manners and mores of the campus during the seventies, the period when exotic styles of dress and behavior seemed sometimes to become what college was all about, and the lower voltage eighties.

When the decade began, women wore their hair long, free, somewhat styled, and their skirts were well above their knees and their boots high and tight. Men's hair was full on top but trimmed close to the ears, and a few "dudes" sported mustaches, excuse-me sideburns, and beards. Gone were the crew cuts of the early sixties. But jeans, regular and bell-bottom, were the order of the day for men and women. Later in the decade, women's hair, though still long, hung lank and unstyled, and most coeds wore elephant pants, both denim and polyester knits, with fringed vests, knit tops, and clunky platform shoes and boots that made locomotion noisy and problematic. Men had contracted a dose of Samsonitis from rock stars, and hair galore was the ideal—curly, straight, and long; mounded on top and ponytailed behind or falling over the shoulders; cropping out of upper cheeks, upper lips, and chins. And shirttails hung down over jeans, which were fashionably distressed, unpressed, and seldom washed. Both women and men's party clothes reflected the hallucinatory colors and designs of the psychedelic culture of the 1960s.

One catches a pungent whiff in these protean styles, of role-playing, of dressing up. Sincerity, the touchstone virtue of the sixties, that encapsulated the yearning for the authentic life of pure feeling, honest self-expression, and spontaneous, uninhibited action apparently found its fullest expression in dress—or, perhaps, in self-mocking dressing up for comfort and self-discovery.

It was during the seventies that the most celebrated and enduring of Kent's many new traditions started, one that epitomizes the rowdy, role-playing spirit of the times: the now-legendary Halloween party that each year drew thousands of young people and spectators from the far reaches of northeastern Ohio to downtown Kent. There, at any given moment, one might encounter a giant toilet ambling on spider legs or Igor and Dracula in a passionate embrace or an entire fraternity in drag, along with the usual grotesquerie of vampires, werewolves, and ghosts. Halloween epitomized then the exuberance, the feeling of being unshackled, unconstrained, the sheer *wheee* that accompanied the throwing off of old, conventional styles of thought and behavior and the search for a new unstructured structure, a new ethic that the sixties' Youth Movement gave rise to.

Along with this emergent style of costume dressing, the *Burr*s of the period also show some of the negative growing pains of that adventure. Photos feature open displays of drug use and binge drinking at downtown bars, of beer cans lining dorm walls and heaped head-high near service entrances, of self-conscious yet uninhibited public embraces sometimes indistinguishable from very intimate couplings. Excess seemed to be the goal of the new ethic.

Yet changes far more significant were going on as well. Identity politics came into its own. The women's movement at Kent expressed itself in myriad and multiform ways: in macro changes, such as the hiring of more women administrators and professors under affirmative action and in establishing a Women's Studies program, women's support groups, and curricular changes to accommodate the dynamic new fields of study and research centered on women's contributions across the whole spectrum of human activity; and in such micro changes as coed honoraries, unisex bathrooms, and androgynous fashions. Many women preferred to "go dutch" on dates and open their own doors, to assert their independence and equality. Gallantry and courtesy were scorned as sexism.

The discovery and affirmation of black identity, which had begun in the 1960s, continued throughout the seventies and into the eighties. No longer was segregation of the old post-Reconstruction type the paramount problem. In 1949, the year Stopher Hall opened for men, the struggle for integration had not even begun, and old prejudices were as virulently alive as ever in Kent and elsewhere in the country: white and black students were not permitted to room together in dorms. Black students were denied service in downtown bars and eateries, and they had to travel to Akron to get their hair cut or dressed. The civil rights movement of the sixties toward equal opportunity and social justice included racial integration in its agenda, but the desire for integration fell victim to the massive, sometimes murderous, reaction of whites against civil rights legislation that culminated with the Voting Rights Act of 1965. This produced a counterreaction, the rise of the militant Black Power movement that sought racial separation, exalting black pride and racial identity. Given the centuries in which African Americans were denied their rights as citizens and human beings, their leaders lynched and murdered, few could question their wish to separate themselves, painful though some of the consequences proved to be.

The principal agent for change at Kent was the Black United Students (BUS), founded on May 21, 1968. During the 1970s, guided by a series of resourceful leaders and speaking through its newspaper voice, BUS proved to be perhaps the single most potent student organization in the school's history. It played significant roles in the founding of the Institute of African American Affairs (1969), the Center of Pan-African Culture (1972), and the Department of Pan-African Studies (1976). It successfully campaigned to have the old Student Union Building renamed in honor of alumnus Dr. Oscar W. Ritchie, the first African American professor in Ohio's university system. (Unable to find suitable housing in Kent City, Ritchie and his family built a home in a rural area of the township.) Among its other achievements, BUS started a dorm security force and an alternate education program to provide Afrocentric educational and cultural services and a free lunch for three neighboring communities. By the end of the seventies

Kent's African American students had their own social fraternities and sororities, clubs, intramural sports teams; they staged and wrote their own plays, studied in their own academic center, and held a weeklong Renaissance Ball and Ebony Achievement Awards, sponsored by BUS. The result was a discernible increase in black pride, ethnicity, identity, and culture. And segregation had a harder time hiding its head.

Another, perhaps older, form of social activism was that practiced for several years during the seventies by Kent's gadfly graduate student Paul Keane. In addition to cosponsoring with activist Greg Rambo a drive to persuade the Justice Department to impanel a federal grand jury to investigate the shootings, he published any number of probing, amusing, and stimulating letters in the *Stater,* helped staff the Center for Peaceful Change in its fledgling stage, and organized a volunteer student group to clear the snow for elderly crossing-guard Louis "Pop" Fischer to get to his post. CBS correspondent Charles Kuralt featured Pop and the "snow squad" on his show *On the Road.*

Traditions are the sinews that give institutions their historical identity and resilient force. The snow squad was only one of the traditions that arose in this period, many of which were longer lived than Pop's. In fact, except in its earliest period, Kent has tended to sow traditions with a profligate hand, on good soil and bad, nurturing some and ignoring others, unable to decide which to keep. Hence the enduring aptness of a joke heard on campus in the 1950s: when there's nothing else to do at Kent, start a new tradition. This changefulness, which shifted into higher gear after World War II, continued into the eighties and beyond.

Kent's founder-president, John Edward McGilvrey, had started the school's first major tradition, Extension Day, to bring students from the off-campus extension centers to the main campus for a homecoming celebration that would give the campus an identity with which they could identify themselves as Kent State students. Sixteen years later, it was renamed Campus Day, and under that name it flowered into a spring idyll celebrated for the next thirty-five years. Its signature events included a parade of festively decorated floats and a songfest, in which vocal groups from nearly every campus organization performed before an audience seated on the lawns of Front Campus.

During the tradition-busting sixties, however, Campus Day as the culminating moment of the academic year withered and went to seed, only to return in 1979 in an exotic new form reflective of the taste of the times, with a free outdoor concert with Guess Who and other folk and rock bands at the Ice Arena; disco music; and performances by the Kent Dance Theatre on the Student Center Plaza. But with no floats and no Songfest on Front Campus.

Campus Day redux had strong competition from a new tradition, one that began a few years earlier when sororities and fraternities made Greek Week the crowning event of the school year for Kent's resurgent panhellenic organizations. Greek Week 1979, for example, featured an inauguration ball (Monday); an all-Greek party (Tuesday); a Greek songfest, with costumes and choreography (Wednesday); a Greek Goddess mock-beauty and beer-chugging contest in the Rathskeller to benefit the King-Kennedy Center (Thursday); a Greek parade, games, pyramid building, and a corn roast (Friday).

To be sure, some venerable traditions stayed afloat among the shifting tides of taste. Coeds still sunbathed on the Engleman deck, and after bountiful snowfalls students and townies tobogganed down the giddy slopes of Front Campus. The bat or bird (it varied) that traditionally haunted University Auditorium still capered overhead during concerts. Students still griped about the quality and quantity and cost of dorm food. The Rock on Front Campus still got several new coats of paint every year, a campus tradition that had begun sometime in the 1930s when Greek organizations started painting their symbols on a large boulder on West Main Street. Before long anyone and everyone with an event worth crowing about took up brushes and buckets, and before long splashing the Rock with flashy colors was so entrenched in custom that in 1972, when Main Street was widened, the Rock was tenderly hefted a safe distance back onto the campus. But by the end of the 1980s the last card was filed in the card catalog, which was fully computerized by 1989. And Pork Barrel, No Time for Classes, and Penny Carnival, events that had bonded the entire student body during the middle years of the twentieth century, vanished without a trace, except in aging memory.

Of the traditions that disappeared in the eighties, none was more tightly knit into the fabric of the University than the annual yearbook, *The Chestnut Burr,* and the University School, both victims of increasing cost and diminishing value. The final edition of the *Burr* appeared in 1985. Even as printing costs were becoming prohibitive and sponsors were disappearing, student interest was waning, and each year large numbers of copies went unclaimed and undistributed. Of course, the

Burr did not really disappear after the 1984 edition; rather, it morphed from a hardbound annual to a handsomely produced magazine issued four times a year that featured some of the same flora and fauna of campus life. Yet for all its high gloss and awards, the new version did not, nor could it, replace the *Burr* as Kent graduates had known it since its first appearance in the spring of 1914. It lacked that elusive quality of tenderness associated with the sheer heft and feel of the old *Burr,* with its aromatic memories of luminous moments and friendships formed when all prospects were full of promise. The old *Burr* was above all an integrated chronicle of a single year in the life of the campus artfully handcrafted by a group of talented and spirited students working against a heartless deadline.

An even more venerable institution vanished in the Golding era when the expense of operating a training school could no longer be justified by its programmatic value. Educational trends had passed it by. On October 14, 1981, Vice President Schwartz formally recommended the closing of the school. As he explained later, Kent "could no longer afford to subsidize a private education for a few children in a situation that did so little to advance the teacher education program."[1] Golding agreed: the lab school was desirable but not essential. Aside from the sedimented affections of generations of the school's alumni, the major obstacle to closing the school was opposition from the parents of current students. But Golding, never loathe to grasp a prickly nettle, met with a large group of hostile parents and students, told them the reasons for his decision, and defended it against their heated protestations. And on January 25, 1982, the Faculty Senate, invoking retrenchment policy, formally recommended that the observation-based teacher-training program be ended, the first termination of a major academic program in the school's history. In 1988, long after the dust of controversy had settled, the building was turned into the Student Services Center (later named the Michael Schwartz Center), collecting several ancillary functions formerly scattered across campus under one convenient, if large, roof: offices of the bursar, financial aid, and registrar, along with disabled student services, parking services, and student conduct.

Not all old traditions disappeared, of course. Homecoming, which began in 1917 as a spring festival associated with baseball and became a fall football event in 1929, survived, but without the romantic nostalgia of former times. Queens continued to be crowned, but with a twinge of self-conscious irony. One year a male student, with one too many beers in his tank, took a dare and competed for Homecoming Queen. His father threatened to disown him. And in 1977 the Kent Women's Action Collective (KWAC) managed to nix the queenship, condemning it as "a sexist thing."[2]

And new traditions continued to appear. In 1981 the black squirrels, which became regarded as pests as they overran campus and town after being imported from Canada thirty years earlier, achieved iconic status. Officials looking for a special event to inject a spirit of playfulness into orientation week made the bold, pesky creature the logo for the Black Squirrel Festival. A daylong event held on the Student Center (later Risman) Plaza, the festival featured live bands, barbeques, campus clubs and organizations, and area artisans showing their wares.

The impulse to help others, successfully embodied in the Peace Corps during the sixties, continued on into the eighties. Sociology, criminal justice, and psychology gradually displaced the arts and humanities as the most popular majors and supplied recruits for one of the most useful and best-known volunteer activities of the period. The Volunteer Ambulance Service (VAS) was a round-the-clock public service. VAS men and women took a rigorous course of training in emergency medical care, leaning how to splint broken limbs, treat open wounds, give CPR, and handle many other emergencies, including delivering a baby. They were fast and dependable, and their esprit de corps was remarkable. Some went on to professional careers in the field.

As the seventies unfolded, campus security became a problem again, but not because of political, social, or civil rights unrest but because of human appetites—theft, drugs, rape, and violence, reports of which became fodder for *Stater* headline writers. In response, and over time, nearly a hundred students, many who also belonged to VAS, enlisted in Night Watch, an escort service. In addition to walking students back to their dorms at night, they checked to see that buildings were secure and kept a watchful eye for anything out of the way. (A cutback of federal funds in 1982 forced the administration to reduce hours in the program.) The sprawling campus, so benign in daylight, could be full of menaces in the late watches of the night. Armed with a heavy ring of keys and a walkie-talkie, each student volunteer patrolled a given area of the campus from 8:00 P.M. to 4 A.M., on the lookout for anyone in need of help and for signs of trouble. Crimes during this period may not have increased in number, but they did increase in kind and violence. For example, in November 1981 a Singing Sam delivery man was shot and killed in front of College Towers, a large private student apartment complex on the eastern border of campus. After the *Stater* carried reports of two acts of violence—a stabbing and a rape—in the fall of 1982, calls for escort service soared. Despite strong efforts by the campus police, drugs were widely available and used in the dorms, a reflection of affairs in the grown-up world outside the campus. And a few dorm users were also petty dealers, which posed a special threat because of money's tendency to excite violent and venal human urges.

Another commendable activity was performed by the cadre of student ambassadors and tour guides who led groups of prospective freshmen, their parents, and visitors around the campus, telling them about places of historic, architectural, and floral interest. They were well schooled in campus lore, their morale was high, they took pride in dispensing reliable information, and they earned extra money doing something they enjoyed. The ambassadors evolved naturally out of that handful of students who, in the first tremulous summer of June 1970, had helped restore campus morale when the school reopened following the tragic shootings.

By 1985, however, morale and volunteerism were being eroded by the resurgence of free-market capitalism and deregulation and the tidal turning-away from communitarianism toward individualism. Unlike the seventies, when there were "10 jobs for every 100 volunteers," said Kent's counseling director, Dr. Richard Rynearson, students "were becoming more concerned with their own careers and making money."[3] Citing a national reduction of humanities programs and a strong trend away from social sciences and toward computer sciences, he told the *Stater* that "it was just not fashionable to be interested in one's fellow man."

Twelve

AMBITION AND ACHIEVEMENT

{1982–1990}

I t is against this dioramic view of campus culture that the search for a new president began after Brage Golding informed the faculty and trustees in December 1981 that he would retire at the end of the academic year, exactly as he had promised when he had agreed to come to Kent five years before. Academic vice president Michael Schwartz had good reason to think he would succeed to the presidency. Hadn't he served as a loyal, vigorous academic leader during the intervening five years? Hadn't he survived a trying apprenticeship under a master administrator whose demanding ways and serrated tongue had sometimes made his life difficult? Hadn't he earned the trustees' respect and Golding's support?

By early February 1982, the search was at full gait. Alumnus Robert Blakemore was once again the chair, heading a thirteen-member committee composed of trustees, professors, an academic dean, and representatives from the community, the alumni association, undergraduate and graduate student government, and administrative staff. The trustees hired professional consultants to facilitate the search. (Later, while conceding that the consultants had been somewhat helpful early in the search, Faculty Senate chair Hugh Munroe said that the candidates they proposed were uniformly unsuited for Kent. Others on the committee said that the trustees wasted $12,000 on the consultants.[1] Still, resorting to professional consultants would become increasingly the fashion, as public universities adopted the corporate business model.)

By May the committee had vetted more than a hundred resumes, agreed on a slate of four candidates, and forwarded it to the trustees. (For reasons never explained, the committee was instructed not to evaluate the finalists, a change from past practice.) The trustees then interviewed the four finalists, each in turn, during a series of lengthy executive sessions held late in May.

Of the four, only two, both young men, seem to have been in close contention, Schwartz and Michael R. Ferrari, interim president of Bowling Green. Each had his supporters: Schwartz was said to be favored by professors and trustees, Ferrari by the younger people on the search committee.[2] In the end it may have been the man who had severely tried Schwartz's patience and pride for five years who tilted the board toward him. Or so Golding thought: "I made Mike president," he told an upper-level administrator.[3] Schwartz would have disagreed.

Schwartz was born in 1938 in Chicago. After two years at Northwestern, he jumped ship to take the exam for his certified public accountant license. But he soon sensed that he had a natural instinct for the academic milieu, so he went downstate to the University of Illinois at Champaign-Urbana, where he took his bachelor's in psychology, his master's in industrial relations, and his doctorate in sociology. Between 1962 to 1976 he scrambled up the academic ladder like a born foretopman, starting as a teacher of psychology and sociology at Wayne State; he then joined the sociology faculty at Indiana University and moved a few years later to Florida Atlantic University, where he was dean of the college of social sciences when Glenn Olds invited him to serve as Kent's vice president for graduate studies and research.

Schwartz, who arrived in Kent in March 1976, was still getting to know the faculty and the campus, its culture and mores, when in June 1977 the trustees made him an offer he couldn't refuse: serve as acting president in the brief interval between Olds's departure and Golding's arrival. That happened, of course, to be the summer of Tent City and the gym annex dispute, certainly one of the most difficult passages in the history of any American university. Schwartz was innocent of any leadership experience that would arm him to do battle with such a hydra-headed monster. But he was a tough Chicago kid with a feisty confidence in his own capacities and an aching ambition to be a university president. He jumped at the offer of the job because it would give his resume a special luster, of course, but also because he wanted to prove his mettle under fire, which he did.

When a *Stater* reporter asked Kent's new president (the second youngest in its history at age forty-four) about likely differences between his presidency and Golding's, Schwartz said that, having been involved in most of Golding's changes, he planned no major ones, but he did hint at a major change of style: "Golding is a very private person who spends a good deal of time on detail. I tend to be more public and outgoing, and while I don't dislike detail work, I won't make a career of it." Golding, for his part, also predicted a change in the style of leadership but, he told the same reporter, Kent's main problem would still be money.

When asked what he thought of Golding's plan to retire to a house without electricity in the woods, Schwartz, on the beat, snapped: "I don't trust air I can't see."[4] That was vintage Schwartz, the wisecrack, the quick riposte. His wit, unsheathed, had flash and point. Time and again, recall those who surfed administrative storms with him, his sense of the ridiculous would ride to his rescue, reducing reality to its proper proportions and relaxing the coiled-spring nerves of a man whose inner tensions were sometimes greater than his outer ones. While Golding's wit shuttled fractionally between the sardonic and the sarcastic, Schwartz's played freely over the entire loom of laughter, warp and weft.

Aside from certain superficial similarities—both were ambitious, hardworking, intellectually keen, and determined to make KSU a better place—Golding and Schwartz were very unlike each other. If Golding made people forget his lack of altitude by the pure power of his attitude, his air of command and brusque aplomb, Schwartz compensated for his with quicksilver smarts, high-voltage intensity, gift of the gab, and a warm personality. Where Golding was taciturn and caustic, reserved and aloof, Schwartz was articulate and voluble, emotional and friendly, and a master of academic seduction. Golding was "very private," Schwartz said, implying that he himself was a people person.[5] And he was, by nature and by profession. Conversation with congenial companions was his meat and drink.

Whereas Golding's leadership style was strictly professional and studiedly impersonal, Schwartz's would prove to be informal, impulsive, affectionate, and highly personal. Schwartz dramatized the difference between their styles by becoming what he called a "walking around" president. Golding typically would listen to student and faculty voices when they reached his office through the hierarchical trellis of governance and appeal. But Schwartz, restless and kinetic, bridled at channels and bucked against the walls of his office. Whenever he could break free of meetings and paperwork, he would walk down the hall to chat with a colleague or light a cigarette and stroll around campus, talking with groundskeepers, food servers, clerks, students, and most especially his faculty colleagues.

Schwartz, eminently approachable in social matters, made no show of pretense. But he expected some recognition that he was the boss, a title he frankly enjoyed. He wore with ill-concealed pride the interchangeable black or blue suit, that sine qua non of presidential prestige and prerogatives, of which he was very jealous. And, though generally tolerant of opposing points of view, he could be prickly about any eye-flick of insubordination or disloyalty, a tendency that increased as the pressures of office mounted. At his best, he was a plainspoken, easy-going, affable, and generous man, tolerant, indulgent, not given to nit-picking or casual cruelties.

Yet, because of his complexly emotional, even histrionic, makeup, his affections could volatilize into cold hard anger and, suddenly, the iron door of presidential disfavor would clang shut, without explanation, against some unwitting offender. Astute subordinates learned to keep a weather eye for the Mike of the moment: was it the well-tempered, easy-going "soft Mike" or the intemperate, ruthless "hard Mike"? The two seldom seemed to coincide. He had a changing roster of pet peeves, professors and trustees the mere mention of whose names would convulse him with rage. It was one of the hazards of a high-voltage personalized presidency.

As an administrator, he was sometimes manipulative, using people as cats-paws or attack dogs to try out an idea or policy he didn't want to be identified with. No micromanager, he would go to extreme lengths to support his staffers, but only as long as they didn't put him at cross-purposes with the board. Then he would dispatch them without a qualm. After all, the university was a hierarchy, not a democracy, he would say, and, as one who served under several presidents remarked, "At the end of the day the only votes that counted were the trustees."[6]

For Schwartz, the essence of a university was the professor-student relationship, and as president it was his job to put "fine professors in touch with good students."[7] Committed to the collegial principle of "shared governance," he treated the students as he treated the faculty, politically, as his constituents, and spent much time getting to know them and letting them know him. He liked the effervescence, the spring-heeled exuberance of young people.

Probably no Kent president rode into office on a higher wave of faculty goodwill than Schwartz. And for that he owed something to Golding, who had left curricular matters and faculty relations largely to Schwartz while he himself set about saving the institution from fiscal and organizational disarray trenching on chaos. Golding's success alleviated faculty members' anxieties about the school's fiscal future, giving them a feeling of stability and safety that had been missing since May 4, 1970. So they were primed for a president like Schwartz, one who would focus on the school's primary mission, education and research, putting it back on track for the long climb up the mountain of Robert White's grand vision of Kent as a first-rate graduate and research institution.

At Schwartz's investiture during the December 1982 graduation ceremonies, trustee chair Norman Jackson, observing that Schwartz would confront such challenges as "dwindling resources" and shrinking numbers of qualified students, emphasized that the trustees had chosen him precisely because he insisted "that the proper response to a decline in numbers is an increase of both entrance and performance expectations of those who teach and those who learn."[8] This was Schwartz's charge from the trustees, and he took it seriously.

One way Schwartz kept in touch with "those who learn"—their perceptions and concerns—was the *Daily Kent Stater*, edited in this period by future Pulitzer Prize winners Connie Schultz and Sam Roe. Between September and December 1982 the paper covered several largely unrelated items which, taken together, enabled one to view campus life by looking over Schwartz's shoulder as he read his morning paper.

On the evening of September 8, 1982, the Williamson House, the presidential residence that he and his family had just moved into, caught fire. Passersby noticed smoke and flames coming from the back porch area, sounded the alarm, and firemen quickly doused the flames. The only occupant at the time was the president's youngest daughter, Rachel, who was alarmed but unharmed, and the house sustained no serious damage. Earlier in the day workmen had been using blow torches to burn off the milk-chocolate-colored paint, applied at Mrs. Golding's request, which proved impossible to cover with farmhouse white, the traditional color to which Mrs. Ettabelle Schwartz wanted to return the house, which was was undergoing its second remodeling in five years. After smoldering for hours, some sparks had burst into flames.[9]

On Sepember 16 another kind of fire broke out at the Student Center Plaza when the fire-and-brimstone evangelist George "Jed" Smock of Terre Haute, Indiana, returned for his annual visit, accompanied by his assistant James Stiles. As the evangelists were haranguing a crowd of students, who were questioning and needling them in a fall ritual both sides seemed to enjoy, Smock began ranting about the "immorality of youth" and pointed to some women in shorts to prove his point. His flagrantly "chauvinist" finger-pointing could not be ignored. Tempers flared, angry hecklers began hooting and hollering, and, during the ensuing hubbub, Smock made an anti-Jewish remark that inflamed student Alan Silverman. He and Jed began shoving each other, and, knowing how scuffles escalate into riots, campus police arrested the evangelists and Silverman.[10] The incident inspired two *Stater* editorials in which the editors reminded students of the indispensable value of differences of opinion and free speech, particularly on a university campus.

A week later a volatile racial incident calling for much tact took place at Koonce Hall when an African American student was arrested and charged with assault for allegedly pushing and striking a security guard. The student and a witness claimed the guard had sparked the scuffle by using a "racial slur." BUS president Kirk Braithwaite vowed to take the matter directly to Schwartz, saying he expected to get justice.[11] And before Braithwaite and Schwartz could meet, the tension increased when the director of campus security and safety said there was "no convincing evidence" that the security guard had caused the trouble.[12] So when Braithwaite walked into Schwartz's office, he was braced for a showdown. But Schwartz disarmed him before he could state his case. Acting quickly to defuse the situation, Schwartz told him that he had already discharged a Tri-Tower desk clerk for writing a "racial epithet" on a student's door and had reprimanded a Rathskeller manager for displaying a "racist" wall hanging in his office. Impressed, Braithwaite told the *Stater* that he gave Schwartz "a plus for this go-round."[13]

On September 29 the Faculty Senate was wrestling once again with the contentious issue of the subjects that would be part of the LERs when the governance chamber was picketed by some 150 black students lobbying for the inclusion of a Pan-African course in the curriculum. At the time, both the administration and the faculty were especially sensitive to the need not only to ease racial tensions but to do so in an enlightened spirit of social justice and respect for the dignity of all students.

Then on October 19 the *Stater* front page carried the headline: "Racial Discord at K.S.U. book says." The book referred to was *The Black Student Guide to College,* which profiled black student "opinion" on 119 college campuses. Among the other incendiary charges against Kent quoted in the article were that "racial disharmony" and "racism run rampant," that "being a black student is a struggle," and that "black students have trouble relating to the white faculty." The *Stater* article was the hot topic of conversation for some time afterward, particularly among bemused, troubled, and irritated professors and administrators, who thought that the book misrepresented the actual state of affairs.

On October 29 the Kent Gay Liberation Foundation (KGLF) was holding its annual Halloween dance in the Student Center when a tear-gas canister burst into the midst of the crowd of 200 dancers, sending them choking and coughing toward exits. Eight were injured in the scramble. Later that month five students were brought up on disciplinary charges for complicity in the affair. The KGLF had been organized in the early 1970s, surviving the initial reflexive prejudice and gaining general acceptance on what was traditionally a tolerant and open campus. The tear-gas episode troubled nearly everyone and seems to have had the reverse effect of increasing understanding of and sensitivity toward gay, lesbian, and transgendered students. *Stater* editor Sam Roe wrote a bold and deliberately provocative editorial that brought down a hail of complaints on his head because of its blunt "street language," chosen to reflect the ironies and ambiguities of prejudice.

That October of 1982 the highly anticipated Kent State University Museum opened in Rockwell Hall, which had been imaginatively reconfigured by Kent alumnus Ted Curtis. The opening was celebrated with a black-tie gala event called Dazzle, which caught something of the glitter and glamour of the dresses and gowns in the Shannon Rogers/Jerry Silverman collection. Celebrities from the worlds of fashion, theater, and film cocktailed in the the museum's atrium before being limousined to the glamorously decorated Student Center, where they dined and danced and watched a fashion show in which Kent students modeled gowns borrowed from the collection. The evening ended with a remarkable light and fireworks show that drew large crowds of townspeople, students, and faculty to the Student Center Plaza. They saw a timed series of laser beams and fireworks explode in fiery hieroglyphics overhead. The organizers might well have called the event "Blast" or "Boom," because the exploding fireworks shattered the nocturnal stillness. "The phone at our home rang with complaints," Schwartz later recalled, "about rattled dishes and window panes and frightened children awakened and crying from the noise. It was my first experience as president with good intentions gone awry. There were to be others."[14]

Then, on November 16, a dispute flared up between the *Stater* and student government: the newspaper reported that the state auditor was investigating Student Senate's allocation of $184 to a religious group called Kent Gospel Rap as a possible violation of the law forbidding use of state funds to support religion. An editorial in the same edition scolded Student Senate for its "loose" practices in allocating student fees to political and religious organizations. Stung, student leaders rejected the charge, claiming they had specifically not funded the proselytizing functions of any groups. They then filed a charge with the All-University Hearing Board (AUHB), claiming the *Stater* was a "detriment to the community."[15]

At this point Schwartz tripped over one of his own quips and fell into the mess. He breezily dismissed the affair as "a dispute between two student groups who want to play hard ball with each other. And all I have to say is, 'Batter up!'"—which prompted a sharp rebuke from the *Stater* editors, who said the senate's filing its complaint with the AUHB was a threat to the paper's independence. It was properly a matter for the Student Publication Policy Council (SPPC) to adjudicate, the *Stater* argued. So student leaders took it to the SPPC, which, after due deliberation, ruled in favor of student government, saying it had dispersed the allocations strictly according to guidelines and scolding the paper for not exercising due diligence in its reporting.[16]

Not content with this victory, however, a student leader published a letter in the *Stater* on December 9, 1982, calling on the paper and its governing board to adopt a "code of ethics" to avoid future journalistic errors. As this call for an ethics code was reverberating in the maze of presidential offices on the second floor of the Library, Schwartz came to understand that an important issue was at stake. A staff member involved in the sometimes-heated negotiations between the warring camps reported hearing a student say, "Those are just ethics; they're not the law." And there the affair rested, for a time.

The fall term ended not with fire, either literal or metaphorical, but with ice. On December 25 four Kent State scientists celebrated Christmas by setting out for Antarctica. Geologist Peter Dahl, who had gone the year before, enlisted colleagues Glenn Frank, Rod Feldman, and graduate student Mark Schmidt to undertake a trek across an unexplored area of the subcontinent in the interests of science and high adventure. This expedition was so successful that in coming years several members of Kent's science faculty succumbed to the frigid charms of Antarctica's white wastes and spent long periods probing its mysteries.

A year later, in October 1983, while Schwartz was drafting his annual report to the faculty, controversial University of California Berkeley psychologist Arthur Jensen lectured on campus. A proponent of genetic determinism, identified especially with its controversial conclusions about the mental inferiority of non-Caucasians, his talks on other campuses had caused much fuss and furor. Kent's administration braced itself for trouble. Jensen drew a large crowd, many of them demonstrators from BUS and their supporters, but he was allowed to speak without interference, although the demonstrators did express their contempt for his obnoxious ideas. Schwartz was delighted and relieved that the students had behaved with "dignity and grace" while permitting Jensen to speak his mind.[17]

Schwartz was acutely sensitive to the problem of racial injustice and was committed to affirmative action and, mindful of Kent's difficult history, determined to preserve freedom of speech and assembly on campus. His concerns about First Amendment rights coalesced around the ethics issue in his "State of the University" speech to the faculty on October 20, 1983. His remarks illustrate the programmatic ply and scope of his mind. Toward the end of the speech, he cited the Jensen incident as exemplifying the kind of values a college education ought to impart to students. Then, referring to the *Stater*-Senate dispute, he said, that the remark devaluing ethics showed that Kent had failed to instill a concern for "ethics, morality and justice" in its students. He then announced that he had appointed a special Presidential Commission on Ethics composed of administrators, staff, faculty, and chaired by former provost John Snyder to study the matter.

After mulling it over for months, the ethics commission proposed several measures aimed at raising the consciousness of students—and of the entire campus community—to the critical importance of ethical and moral concerns in the life of the mind. The main proposal was to use the orientation program to introduce freshmen to the "intricacies of decision-making which involves ethical dilemmas" by using "scenarios" that dramatized ethical quandaries. The other suggestions were of a largely hortatory nature, such as encouraging University agencies to invite outside speakers who deal with ethical and moral problems and establishing a permanent body, with rotating membership, to "challenge administrators and faculty" to actively incorporate "ethical concerns" in all "deliberate" University activities.[18] The commission did as well as can be expected with what was inherently something of an ethical quandary, given the slippery ambiguities and nuances of ethical and moral questions in an era dominated by "situational ethics" and neopragmatist relativity.

All of Schwartz's annual reports were driven in part by his desire to direct the faculty's attention from fiscal matters and call it back to its academic mission. As president, he said, he was not above doing "a bit of cheerleading" in his desire to inspirit the faculty with a fresh sense of dedication and desire to make Kent a major center of academic learning and research.[19] Consequently, his annual addresses, while duly noting problems and concerns, always included a summary of accomplishments and major initiatives.

For example, in his second "State of the University" speech, on October 20, 1983, he referred to such major benchmarks as the LERs; college preparatory programs required of high school graduates for unqualified admission to KSU; a revised and expanded student orientation program; a new mission statement focusing on undergraduate education (followed by another in 1989 stressing graduate education and research in selected areas); a need for faculty rededication to student care and advising; a requirement that foreign teaching assistants speak understandable English in the classroom; two faculty salary hikes and a revised sabbatical leave policy; and a faculty reward system based on individual performance objectives to supplant the current one that rewarded excellent research far more than excellent teaching. The early years of Schwartz's tenure were a tour de force of academic achievement.

In those years, Schwartz's zest for the ambience, the atmosphere of a university campus, its intellectual rigor, the verbal cut and thrust of vigorous discussion, found its proper arena in the Governance Chamber in the Student Center. He relished Faculty Senate sessions in which a disputed phrase or clause in a curricular or governance policy turned the air electric with intellectual energy.

A freeze-frame glimpse of Schwartz in kinetic present-tense action: During a heated debate, he strides in nervous circles around the well of the Governance Chambers, toning up his rhetorical muscles while assimilating the arguments being bandied by the senators seated on the tiered rows above him and marshaling his thoughts under the pressure of the moment. When his turn to talk comes, his adrenaline is in full flow. He mounts the steps to the lectern and, with a droll quip or anecdote, delivers his extemporaneous remarks in vivid vernacular English with no rhetorical frills.[20]

His supple mind, ready wit, and skill as raconteur made Schwartz a virtuosic public speaker, though not an orator in the grand tradition. He was at his best in impromptu talks such as those he gave to new students and their parents. He would put his audience at ease with a quip and then quickly transform them for the moment into members of a campus family about to set forth on a journey fraught with the thrills and derring-do of intellectual discovery. A professor who saw him in action on many such occasions said he was "one of the best off-the-cuff speakers I've ever heard."[21] Many students would remember him as the students' president, undoubtedly because he liked and respected them.

He had a special affection and regard for Kent's faculty, regularly seeking their counsel, both formal and informal, and squeezing the budget to raise their salaries. He believed it was the faculty's extraordinary service that kept the school alive when it was shut down after May 4. He made the school's first buyout, which was designed to grow "cutting-edge" new faculty by trimming the "dead wood," so generous that several departments lost very productive, hard-to-replace senior professors along with those deemed unproductive. Like all presidents in budget crunches, Schwartz's attitude toward faculty and programs tended to be one of survival of the fittest, pragmatic and unsentimental. And he was adept at accentuating the positive (new faculty and programs, promising enrollment numbers, grants and awards) and eliminating or downplaying the negative (unfilled positions, programs trimmed or dropped, the ratcheting cost of favored programs). Academic leaders must master the magician's art of smoke and mirrors.

But they must also deliver real results. In his address to the faculty on November 18, 1985, Schwartz highlighted the success of the selected admissions policy, noting that freshman enrollment was continuing to increase despite demographic trends, while the number of students admitted with conditions was dropping. He also proudly announced that the retention rate, long an intractable problem, was climbing: Kent was recruiting more students and losing fewer than the national norm. Though improved rates of retention were partly a function of the selected admissions policy, he gave most of the credit to the recently introduced Early Advising and Scheduling System, whereby Kent counselors began working with individual students midway through their senior year of high school, bringing them to campus for a day of orientation and advising them on drawing up their initial schedule, all in an effort to ease their transition from high school to college and give them the feeling of being Kent State students.

The general shape and dynamic of Schwartz's academic agenda can be discerned in these initiatives. It was essentially pragmatic and programmatic rather than conceptual or philosophic. He appears to have adopted Robert I. White's dream of making Kent State University into a comprehensive university with outstanding graduate education and research programs, not only because it was already well advanced (if temporarily stalled in the seventies) but equally because it articulated his own maturing understanding of the mission and meaning of public higher education. And it gave free play to his talent for detecting important rising trends in higher education, measuring their strength and value, and then weaving them into the curriculum.

To the task of fulfilling White's dream, Schwartz brought an instinctive academic sensibility and sensitivity to the human and structural stresses and strains, the problems and the costs, of such a complicated undertaking.[22] For, despite all of its complexity—its diversity of interests, agenda, and talents; its individualistic faculty; and its collegial, social, and governmental organization—a university is as supple and sensitive as a vast spiderweb, in which all tangential lines converge on a fixed center: a touch at any thread of the gossamer network can be felt throughout the entire elegant structure. This can be traced, for instance, in the way the state subsidy formula complicates the search for educational and scholarly distinction and how that, in turn, ramifies downward from the graduate into the spreading array of undergraduate programs.

One of Schwartz's abiding concerns was the inordinate drain on the undergraduate program exacted by the exigencies of graduate education and research. Because the state did not fund research projects, and because graduate professors had to be given reduced teaching loads in order to do research, those reductions usually were made in their undergraduate teaching loads. This meant that, as the White plan unfolded over time, undergraduate classes were increasingly taught either by comparatively inexpensive graduate assistants, teaching fellows, or accelerating in the seventies and eighties part-time faculty. Schwartz fretted that even though these classes were often taught well, undergraduate students were still being denied something they had a right to expect: the presence and mentoring of many of the ablest, most distinguished professors. Although he frequently reminded faculty members of their professional responsibility to undergraduates, his exhortations, even when sweetened by his fine-tunings of the reward system, were only partly successful in improving undergraduate teaching.

Much of the difficulty of reform lay in the modern university's culture of specialization, professionalism, and careerism. The National Defense Education Act (1958) accelerated the production of Ph.Ds, but its tight focus on specialization meant that many talented researchers entering the teaching ranks felt unready to teach foundational undergraduate courses which, though falling in their broad fields of study, did not fit comfortably into the narrow plot of their expertise and interest. Over time specialization also strained collegiality by fracturing the common body of knowledge and learning that the community of scholars was called historically to preserve, cultivate, and augment. To a disturbing degree, scholars chambered in their hermetic disciplines and working in buildings far distant from one another talked less and less the same language. As a result, there was perceptible weakening of institutional loyalty, a growing indifference to the vital principle of shared governance, and a marked increase of careerism. This in turn was exacerbated by a reward system geared to individual scholarly achievement. Put in its extreme form: many faculty felt that time given to advising and teaching undergraduates was time taken from their "real work" of research and career cultivation.

In an effort to improve the quality of undergraduate teaching and advising, Schwartz expanded and equalized the reward system, a significant step toward ensuring that excellent teaching and service would get merit awards equal to those for research. This coincided with the nationwide accountability movement in education, which resulted from the convergence of several forces: the belief that lax administrators and irresponsible teachers were to blame for the campus disruptions of the sixties; growing student demand for the right to grade their teachers; and governmental pressures to make public universities and their faculties responsible for the quality of their performances. Starting as early as the 1970s individual professors and departments had begun experimenting with a variety of class evaluation forms with this in view, but most forms ignored the fact that teaching is first of all an art which, though it certainly can be evaluated, cannot really be measured or quantified.

Schwartz, a statistician, knew well the limits of quantifying matters of value and quality, but the pressure of the accountability movement proved hard to resist. A universal form, primarily quantitative, gradually emerged at Kent in which results were reduced to percentages across disciplines and used in judging teaching performance for merit pay. (In some units the form was combined with peer evaluation of classroom performance.) The upside of the universal form was that it was conveniently quantifiable; the downside was that its measurements were so mathematically exact, so finely drawn, that they indicated no meaningful differences between one teaching performance and another. (What exactly did it mean, for instance, if Professor A's average was 0.01 percent higher than Professor B's?) Moreover, teaching evaluation forms fostered in some professors a coercive fear of falling outside the norm by grading too strictly and so being perceived as exacerbating the retention problem. This may well have added to grade inflation, itself a continuing embarrassment for the academic profession. In a university, everything converges—both things that fall as well as things that rise.

The result was that teaching quality went on being evaluated only slightly more meaningfully than it had in the past. Student evaluation forms, combining quantitative and qualitative factors, supplemented by systematic and regular peer evaluation were the most effective way to assess teaching performance. But systematic peer evaluation was difficult to achieve because it was costly of professorial time. And, except for some departments, evaluation of scholarly performance tended to be honored more in the breach than in the observance, because it, too, was very time consuming.

If Schwartz's initiatives to improve undergraduate teaching—especially by equalizing the reward system to encourage faculty to devote the same quality of professional concern and care to undergraduate as to graduate students—were not completely successful, they still stand as admirable efforts in a good cause, and they did materially improve the divisive reward system. There is a telling coda on his concern for undergraduate education that should be noted. He insisted on adding a "caveat" to the employment terms for all new University Professors—that they "teach at least one undergraduate course" each term.

Another facet of the undergraduate program concerned him. Schwartz's conversations with students—three of them his own children—had sensitized him to the inadequacy of Kent's advising system. The problem had multiple causes. One was the physical distances separating students from their professors; students frequently had to make special trips to consult with their professors during established office hours. Another was the size of the student body, particularly the student-faculty ratio in the undergraduate program, in which many basic courses were large lecture sections warehousing hundreds of students. For yet another, as Schwartz knew, junior professors trying to win membership on the graduate faculty were tempted by the reward system to rob time from their advising responsibilities to spend on their research, the only path to higher salaries and the Valhalla of a full professorship and membership on the graduate faculty.

Against that background Schwartz lectured professors attending one of his "State of the University" addresses on their solemn responsibility to care for their students, beginning with keeping regular office hours so that their students could consult them about their classes (the student lament was "My professor's never in his office") and their programs and by counseling them on personal concerns, when appropriate. "The University is not a democracy," he said. "It is a competency-based environment in which those who do know teach and advise those who do not know. It has the characteristics of a master-apprentice relationship and that relationship cannot work if the masters withhold their expertise from the apprentices or if the apprentices feel that they cannot have the time of the masters to advise them in solving problems."[23]

Varsity sports, despite the astonishing success of the Golden Flashes of 1972–73, had become a subject of growing controversy later in the seventies, when funds were shrinking and costs were spiking. Many faculty members began questioning the value and viability of the program at a time when retrenchment was chilling the air and academic programs were under the knife. Olds had tried to reduce costs by sensibly urging the NCAA to limit full athletic scholarships to cases of need, but the NCAA refused. In 1974 the University Budget Committee (UBC) report had included a minority report that called for the phasing out of varsity sports, but the committee had not been able to marshal enough hard data to give their argument ballast.

Golding was so irritated in 1979 by the big bites varsity sports were taking from the general and educational (G&E) budget, allocated for educational purposes, that he created a new earmarked general fee for students in order to remove the majority of the varsity expenses out of the G&E budget. (Incidentally, at the same time he also cut off all funding for the University's marching band, leaving it to the mercy of donor support.[24]) Golding's announcement of this action briefly exposed to full view the heavy cost of varsity sports. Golding knew this was at best a stopgap measure. Expenses kept mounting, money became scarcer, and faculty concern grew apace.

When the search for Golding's successor was at full throttle in the spring of 1982, the *Stater* of April 28 published a report of an unprecedented recommendation by the UBC, one presumably made possible by the collective bargaining movement.[25] UBC chair Thomas Davis (English) persuaded Golding to give the committee access to all documents it required to carry out its charge. Based on its thorough study of the expenses entailed in maintaining a full slate of varsity sports in relation to the school's central mission of education, the UBC concluded that they must become self-sustaining during the next five years or be terminated, recommending that allocations be cut by 20 percent each year for the next five years. According to the report, varsity programs received $32 of each student's full-time fees. But athletic director alumnus Paul Amodio, the *Stater* reported, had testified that the program could not become self-sustaining.

Golding's hat was already on his head and his foot out the door when the UBC report reached the Faculty Senate, and it was President-elect Schwartz who sat in on the senate executive committee meetings when the UBC report was discussed. Several senior professors sharply questioned the wisdom of such a large investment of scarce resources in sports, especially at a time when state subsidies were inadequate to support the school's core educational programs. Schwartz asked that action be deferred until "the new leadership of intercollegiate sports" had a "fair and reasonable chance to perform as professionals." When Sy Baron (psychology) asked what would be a "sufficient amount of time" for him to make such a judgment, Schwartz said he didn't know. Schwartz's plea for time carried the day.

Fiscal troubles persisted and student fees and indebtedness continued to rise, a matter of real concern to Schwartz—and not only because high student fees made it harder for him to defend varsity sports.[26] The UBC recommendation was at odds with his conception of a great state university. Unlike Golding, Schwartz could not examine the matter with the gimlet eye of a cost-benefit analysis. He had a fan's headlong love of sports in general, and he believed in varsity sports. While sports are primarily entertainment rather than education and, in a state as penurious as Ohio, very expensive entertainment, in Schwartz's view they had an ancillary educational component and performed a valuable public relations function in a state university. Besides, other schools of Kent's size had varsity football teams, the most expensive of the sports programs.

So he put the matter off as long as possible, waiting for the right moment to present itself. In the event, it was only after some of his most important academic initiatives were in force or coming on line. Only after some pesky senators and other professors continued barking at him over the burgeoning costs and the mediocre quality of the football team. Only when the state seemed to be floating out of its economic doldrums. Only after the football team in November 1983 had, most fortuitously, ended the nation's longest losing streak of 21 games. Only then did Schwartz publicly address the question.

The occasion was his speech to the faculty on October 25, 1984. Acknowledging that "nagging questions" continued to be asked about "the relevance of varsity athletics to education," he cited recent "studies of the sociological, psychological and cultural role of sports" that clearly affirmed their value to society. Beyond benefiting the athletes themselves, he said, the studies showed that "intercollegiate sports were an important public window on the University," stirring interest in physical education and intramural programs and helping "to satisfy the public appetite for spectator involvement in sports."[27] Rather than subjecting the program to a cost-benefit analysis, he chose to celebrate its benefits, and he changed the subject by beating up on a straw man—an "uninformed Senator" who had questioned the administration's spending scarce funds on a "losing program." Schwartz began by asserting that far from being a losing sports program, Kent's was a successful program, citing the winning records of golf, men's and women's gymnastics, wrestling, and basketball. Then he played his trump card: "The football team," he declared, "is turning around and has begun to show great progress."[28]

The UBC recommendations might have posed a dilemma for Schwartz. If he had decided to support them, he could have, with a stroke of the pen, endeared himself to most of the faculty and students, erased some of the school's fiscal problems and improved its academic programs, and lifted some of the heavy fees off students' backs. And he would have won a place in the modest pantheon of such higher education idealists as Robert Maynard Hutchins. But in doing that he would have betrayed his belief in sports as having a positive role in a public university. Besides, he knew that the trustees would never agree to eliminate intercollegiate athletics—least of all the costliest, football—and if he had tried to do so he probably would have been sacked. Of course, Schwartz was never tempted to follow the UBC recommendation because he was personally and professionally opposed to it. As one observer put it, "Mike kept telling himself every year that the football team would improve and, of course, it never did."[29] Like all true fans he believed in the romantic subjunctive, in the bewitching green light at the end of the dock.

Reasonable people, of course, disagree about the appropriateness of varsity sports, but Schwartz's default decision to continue the program without finding a new and dependable source of funding for it, one separate from student fees, would have both immediate and long-range implications. By the time he spoke to the faculty, the income from Golding's earmarked student fee was already lagging so far behind the galloping expenses of the sports program that, in addition to the funds it consumed from Golding's fee, it was again devouring millions of dollars from the G&E budget. When it became clear in 1984 that donors were not providing sufficient funds for the band, the administration put it back on the G&E budget as well.

About that time Schwartz made several other important decisions regarding athletics. Athletic director Paul Amodio and he decided that the program needed a year-round training facility, a project dating back to Bowman's time. The problem was how to pay for it. The least expensive way was to put it on the capital improvements budget for state funding, but that had a major drawback: the project would be given a very low priority because it was not intended for educational purposes. The alternative was to pay for it through bonds paid out of student fees, the interest of which would add significantly to its total cost. A senior academic officer argued forcefully against using student fees to pay for a facility that would be used by no more than 500 students a year, when there was far greater need for a new A&S building, which the state would fund and which would serve the educational needs of thousands of students each year. Schwartz decided to build a field house.

Billed as the "Field House," it was marketed as "a general purpose athletic facility for use by the various intercollegiate athletic teams as well as the student body," but the order of users indicates the building's primary purpose.[30] (Another of its uses frequently mentioned at the time was that it would provide a place where the marching band could practice during inclement weather.) Though certain times of day were reserved for general student use, the Field House was never meant to be a recreational facility, and the students knew that.

High student fees raised their head a year later in Schwartz's annual report, in which he felt compelled to explain a budget embarrassment: he had raised student fees two different times in one academic year. In recent months, he said, the state had enacted another of its funding psychodramas by passing its appropriations budget after state schools had been required to submit their projected budgets for the coming biennium. That first projected budget had contained what he described as a "modest" hike in student fees. But when the legislature got around to passing its final biennial appropriations budget, it contained a shocking $30 million reduction in the higher education subsidy, leaving Kent with a shortfall of $750,000 for the current academic year and Schwartz no recourse but to raise student fees a second time.

With the Field House project now moving toward construction, Schwartz decided to solve another athletic problem by converting Memorial Gym into a proper basketball arena, giving the school its long-needed convocation center while transferring all indoor training functions to the Field House. The result was the Memorial Athletic and Convocation Center and Annex (the MAC Center), completed in 1992. The Field House opened in 1989. Still, even after it had been used for several years, football success continued to be as promising, and elusive, as a runaway bride.

Enrollment climbed throughout the eighties. By the fall of 1988, the combined figure for all eight campuses approached 30,000 when Schwartz told the faculty he had decided to raise admission standards once again. A grade point average of 2.3 would be required for admission to the next Kent freshman class. This would not only help control enrollment, he said, it would also help ensure that students admitted to Kent would be better prepared to do the work required of them. A smaller freshman class than the previous two would be likely, he conceded, but the attrition rate would drop, which meant that Kent's retention rate would rise, a key factor in the school's budget, because the state subsidy per student progressed toward graduation.[31]

In October 1990 enrollments on the Kent campus reached 24,099. But costs grew too, which the state and the administration passed on to students in the form of higher fees. In 1979, for example, fees were $503 per semester; in 1990 they jumped to $1,503.

Beginning in the sixties long-range planning studies had projected research centers and institutes focused on particular aspects of a discipline as one of the most promising ways of achieving excellence within a comprehensive university like Kent, which could not realistically foresee having the financial wherewithal to offer a universal, or "supermarket," curriculum. By the end of the seventies an array of centers of excellence had arisen, including: Regents Professor Glenn H. Brown's Liquid Crystal Institute; education professor Gerald H. Read's Center for the Study of Socialist Education; University Professor Lawrence S. Kaplan's Lyman L. Lemnitzer Center for NATO Studies; University Professor Richard Varga's Institute for Computational Mathematics; University Professor August Meier's library collection of African American historical materials; and the Child Development Center for teaching and research in early childhood education.

Several new centers also opened during Schwarz's tenure, including the Center for the Study of World Music and the Institute for Bibliography and Editing, which established definitive scholarly editions of the collected works of such novelists as Charles Brockton Brown and Joseph Conrad. Already-functioning centers continued to expand, especially the Institute for Computational Mathematics after the arrival of Per Enflo, a new University Professor who was an accomplished musician as well as mathematician. And the Liquid Crystal Institute, under physicist William J. Doane, grew enormously in size and reputation as the leader of its field, garnering extramural funding, producing numerous patents, and adding staff regularly. Schwartz appointed three other new University Professors: famous Egyptian-born composer Halim El-Dabh, physicist Richard Madey, and physical anthropologist Owen Lovejoy.

The Child Development Center, which now claimed a national reputation, moved into a new building (1991) on Loop Road, a result of Schwartz's efforts to marshal a legislative cohort favorable to Kent. New doctoral programs in computer science, applied geology, music, and biomedical sciences were just a few of the research programs to develop during his tenure. A new master's program in Liberal Studies, going against the trend toward specialization, offered a comprehensive program of study, designed by the student, along interdisciplinary lines.

The centers of excellence movement was not, however, limited to research programs. The Center for International Programs and Comparative Studies, to cite the most prominent example, was devoted to giving a global reach to the University's educational and academic mission. The core idea was first broached in 1925 by John McGilvrey. In dismissing him, the trustees had thwarted Kent's first attempt to establish an international student-exchange program.

After World War II President Bowman appointed English professor Leslie Garnett adviser to KSU's international students. In 1972, as a touchstone of his program to open Kent to the outside world, Glenn Olds imported Dr. Raga Elim from the State University of New York system to grow a major international center. Elim, a man more given to motion than to movement, remained just three years, but long enough to build the framework for a study-abroad program in Geneva, Switzerland. His successor, political scientist Robert Clawson, immediately saw the Geneva program's potential and with imagination and shrewd advertising, quickly transformed it into one of the nation's most successful study-abroad programs, attracting students from colleges across the country. Headquartered in the John Knox Center, where students lived and studied, the Geneva program became the flagship of a fleet of foreign study and faculty-student exchange programs that spanned the globe.

Schwartz supported international and comparative programs. He understood their workings and their value to the school's academic mission. He was generous with his moral support and presidential blessings, if not with his money. By the end of his term, he counted the agreements he signed with "sister universities in Europe and Japan" among his proudest moments.[32] These arrangements involved exchanges of students and professors. Some, like the one with the University of Vilnius in Lithuania, were initiated in the seventies and completed in the eighties. Those signed during Schwartz's tenure included exchanges with Volgograd University (Russia), Shimane University (Japan), the Aristotelian University (Thessaloniki, Greece), the University of Kraków (Poland), and Karl Marx University (Leipzig, Germany). The arrangement with Aristotelian, for example, proved especially valuable for the Schools of Music and Library Science and the English department, while the Institute for Applied Linguistics and Translation Studies got expert advice at its inception from Professor Dr. Albrecht Neubert from Karl Marx University, who spent a year in Kent helping establish what became a nationally known degree-granting program.

The eighties were also halcyon days for honors at Kent State. The honors concept, which had embodied the ideal of academic achievement since the Middle Ages, took root at Kent when the liberal arts college began. In 1934 a few courses carrying honors credit were offered in the liberal arts, and a few students were permitted to present an honors thesis for graduation credit. (Three of them returned from WWII and became esteemed members of the faculty: Marvin Koller [sociology], Edgar McCormick [English], and Gerald Read [education].) After the war, Dean James Olson (political science) started a movement that culminated in the founding of the Honors College in 1965, which, along with having its own student body, offered courses at all undergraduate levels and an honors thesis or creative project. Three years later, under the leadership of Michael Lunine, the college was actively recruiting its own students and offering merit scholarships and, what became the bedrock of the program, the freshman Honors Colloquium.

Honors at Kent achieved the highest possible recognition on December 6, 1976, when the school was notified that its application for a chapter of Phi Beta Kappa was one of eleven new chapters to be honored that academic year. Over a generation of planning and hard work culminated in this moment. In the days before most of the students on campus in 1976 were born, Kent professors who were members of Phi Beta Kappa chapters had begun a program aimed at raising the quality of undergraduate education to meet the high standard required for membership in the nation's oldest and most prestigious academic fraternity. Like all new chapters, Kent's was awarded in recognition of the scholastic excellence of its liberal arts program, library holdings, faculty, and its twenty-five distinguished graduates. President Glenn Olds, followed by a score of Phi Beta Kappa members, proudly led the academic procession at which the chapter was invested.

During the eighties, the Honors College expanded rapidly under the direction of deans Mel Feinberg, Ottavio M. Casale (English), and Ben Bassham (art history), increasing its cultural offerings, introducing an optional semester-abroad in Florence, Italy, and attracting gifted students with short-term, get-acquainted summer scholarships to outstanding students poised to begin their senior year in high school. By the end of the decade Kent's Honors College was among the nation's largest and most respected programs, with 820 students, 597 on scholarships, its own offices and dormitory in Van Campen Hall.

A significant scion of the Honors College sprouted in 1982 when English professor Dan Fuller enlisted a team of knowledgeable honors students, drilled and prepped them, and entered them in the national College Bowl competition. In the format of a quiz show panel, College Bowl tested the breadth of contestants' knowledge under pressure. Kent's teams were soon more than holding their own with representatives of some of the most eminent universities in the country. In 1988, 1989, and 1990 Kent won the regionals and placed in the nationals, defeating teams from OSU, the University of Michigan, Brandeis, and the University of Chicago. Moreover, Kent's team captain in those years, Victor Rosenberg, was the unanimous choice as captain of the All-Star Team, the equivalent of being judged by his peers to be the outstanding College Bowl player in the country.

After he had been in office for several years, Schwartz and his family had begun feeling "cribbed, cabined, and confined" in the century-old, white clapboard farmhouse on the corner of East Main and Midway Drive. The house had been remodeled for the Oldses and, more extensively, for the Goldings, but Schwartz found that it lacked adequate parking space and room for entertainment—and privacy. Too often, he said, boisterous students returning from a night on the town would disturb his family. He requested a new presidential home on a three-plus-acre plot in Twin Lakes. The trustees rejected the proposal but agreed to purchase an existing home on Overlook Drive in University Heights, about a half mile from campus. The house on Overlook required considerable renovation, for which the University Foundation footed the bill. At that time the board was informally committed to building a proper presidential residence on campus but lacked sufficient funds. In the end neither Schwartz nor the board—nor the next president—was happy with the Overlook property. The episode strained his relations with some trustees.

When Schwartz assumed the presidency in 1982, the May 4th Task Force petitioned him to build a permanent memorial to those killed and wounded on May 4, 1970. He was, of course, conscious that all previous efforts to find a symbolic resolution for the tragedy had been met with hot opposition or cold indifference. His own first testing under fire, after all, had come during Tent City. Earlier, both White and Olds had hoped that an academic program, the Center for Peaceful Change, would satisfy the inchoate but powerful need for a fitting symbol. And Golding, in turn, had made several attempts, including printing an account of May 4, 1970, in student schedule books, posting a May 4 information box at the entrance of the Prentice Hall parking lot, and placing benches where people could meditate on the event—all of which failed to satisfy the May 4th Task Force and the former students involved with it. Golding had even considered erecting an arch near the entrance to the Prentice lot, an idea that died aborning when the *Stater* compared it to a Roman triumphal arch.

And there was the fiasco of the Abraham and Isaac sculpture. Early in 1978 the Mildred Andrews Fund offered to commission a bronze memorial sculpture by noted artist George Segal. Golding accepted, but only after establishing certain stipulations with Segal and the donor. But instead of sending, in order, a written description of the piece, a pencil sketch, and a clay model for approval before he began making plaster casts, Segal surprised Golding with a package containing the plans and three large blowups of the full-sized plaster casts of the sculpture, called *Abraham's Sacrifice of Isaac.*

Segal's title alone may have jinxed the sculpture on the spot. For one thing, it was inaccurate, Golding thought; in Genesis the Lord intervened and Abraham sacrificed a lamb, not Isaac. (At that time Segal's grouping included a lamb in a bush.) There was another problem with the piece. In Golding's opinion, an image of imminent violence was simply too provocative to stand as a permanent memorial on a campus as violence haunted as Kent's. The May 4th Observance Committee discussed the matter and, as Golding wrote, "reached a consensus, shared by me and other officers of the University, that a memorial featuring a middle-aged man apparently about to kill a stripped and bound youth was 'inappropriate.'"[33] Golding's tactful attempts to persuade Segal to change the subject of the sculpture smashed against the artist's vision and pride. Segal refused to change his conception.

Of course, the entire affair got major media play. It once again divided opinion about Kent—this time over its judgment and aesthetic taste. And as a result the memorial made for Kent's campus ended up on the campus of Princeton University, between its library and its chapel. Unless one holds that artistic value trumps all other claims, it is hard to fault the conduct of either party in the affair. Obedient to his own creative impulses, Segal produced a powerful and moving work of art, one any campus would be proud to harbor, especially now that Segal has established himself as one of the era's leading sculptors. Still, given the place and the relative proximity in time to the actual shootings, Golding's reluctance to memorialize the victims with a sculpture fraught with threatened violence should not be brushed off as political timidity or craven philistinism.

By the time Schwartz received the petition for a memorial, it had become what one observer calls "the third rail" for Kent's presidents,[34] fatal to the touch. Still, Schwartz overrode objections from his cabinet and persuaded the trustees to appoint a committee of alumni, townspeople, students, faculty, and administrators, chaired by F&PA dean Harry Ausprich. After long months of meetings and consultations, the committee unanimously approved a carefully nuanced recommendation, which the trustees accepted. The committee urged the construction of a memorial, to be paid for by private funds. The theme would be educational. It would encourage visitors to "inquire, learn, and reflect" on the events of May 4, 1970, in order to understand what had happened, how it might have been avoided, and what might be done in the future to avert such tragedies. The commission designated a site on the wooded flank of Taylor Hall near the Prentice parking lot where the students were struck down.

Great care was taken to avoid any misstep. A national design competition—funded in part by a grant from the National Endowment of the Arts and guided by a competition expert—harvested the second-largest number of entries in the nation's history for such a competition. An impressive panel of recognized experts in art, art history, architecture, ecology, and landscape architecture studied each entry, discussed its merits, and finally selected a winner and two runners-up. But, confirming the validity of the third-rail theory, the winning entry turned out to be by a Canadian who, no sooner declared the winner, was discovered to have violated a residential stipulation of the rules by his place of birth.

The first runner-up, Bruno Ast, was then declared the winner and given the contract. But when fund-raising efforts lagged, the administration was forced to ask Ast to "scale back his original" design to make the memorial affordable.[35] Ast agreed. The scaling back of Ast's original design, coming on the heels of the disqualification of the original winning entry, outraged the diehards of the May 4th Task Force, and, as Schwartz described it, they tried "to make mighty their objections through the media." He was not intimidated. He had never wasted patience on the most vociferous Task Force veterans, and their behavior now confirmed his suspicions that they really didn't want a memorial for fear it "would put them out of business."[36]

The memorial was dedicated on May 4, 1990, a cold, rainy, uncomfortable day of somber skies, umbrellas, raincoats, and slippery walkways. No one would have chosen such weather for the occasion. Still, bleak though it was, it had a rightness of symmetry that made it profoundly appropriate for a memorial dedicated to the tragedy enacted two decades earlier on a day so very different, a warm, clear, comfortable day under the bright gaze of noon. Now, two decades later, 4,000 spectators huddled around the north porch of Taylor Hall and heard Governor Richard Celeste offer, at last, official apologies from the State of Ohio to Allison Krause, Jeffrey Miller, Sandra Scheuer, William Schroeder and their families, words that even the judicial process had been unable to extort. Senator George McGovern, hero of World War II and the anti–Vietnam War movement, and Kent professors Richard Bredemeier, Henry Hallem, and Jerry Lewis also spoke.[37] And the May 4th Task Force picketed the event. That, too, was part of the symmetry.

A few years later Schwartz recalled that he slept unusually well that night, his overwound nerves loosened by "a sense of closure to an event that might have destroyed universities with faculty and staff of lesser will and determination." That same night also marked the beginning of his valedictory "understanding" that the time was coming for him to "step away from the presidency." A "new perspective," he realized, would be needed for the new decade at hand. These reflections indicate that he wanted to end his term on a high note sustained by his feeling that he would be leaving Kent "a better place for all of us."[38]

Left: In 1977 Brage Golding became Kent's eighth president. He was a veteran of World War II and brought to the position administrative experience in both business and higher education. President Golding is photographed here with his wife, Hinda.

Below: Alumni trustees Robert Blakemore (left) and George Janik played important roles between 1973–1987.

Outside the Memorial Gym, protesters attack the fence around the construction site. The hazards faced by Faculty Observers are dramatized in this shot showing English professors Dolores Noll (facing camera, in back in stocking cap), and Thomas Davis (at right, in a Greek fisherman's cap). Seconds after this photograph was snapped, police began teargassing the protesters and the Observers.

Above: The Rock has long provided an informal canvas for student expression. Following the terrorist attacks of September 11, 2001, an unknown artist painted this American flag, a visual testament that lasted for several days.

Left and below: There was a new look in the appearance of students and their dormitory rooms on into the 1980s. These photos show students in 1973 and a Stopher Hall dorm room in the early 1980s.

Right: Kent's ninth President, Michael Schwartz, pictured here with a group of students, came to Kent in 1976 as vice president for graduate studies and research, served as acting president in the summer of 1977, and was named president in 1982.

Below left: First fruits of the Kent–Aristotle University program were harvested in December 1986 when the first four Greek exchange students received M.A. degrees.

Below right: With support from the Early Childhood Education Department, in 1972 the University established the Child Development Center, an all-day program for children from ages two-and-a-half to five.

President Golding oversaw the donation of a major collection of costumes, dresses, and art objects to the University by fashion designer Shannon Rogers (right) and his business partner Jerry Silverman. Rockwell Hall was converted to house a fashion museum, and the Rockwell annex became the Shannon Rogers/Jerry Silverman School of Fashion Design and Merchandising. In the fall of 1981 the museum opened with a gala event called "Dazzle." Every year the fashion school puts on a New York–style fashion show to showcase student work.

The Black United Students (BUS) organization played a vital role in establishing the Institute of African American Affairs (1969), the Center of Pan-African Culture (1972), and the Department of Pan-African Studies (1976), and it campaigned to have the old Student Union building named after Oscar W. Ritchie, the first African American professor in Ohio's university system, shown here with Marvin R. Koller, his colleague and coauthor of their book *Sociology of Childhood*.

Below: The building, renovated in 2008, houses the Department of Pan-African Studies.

Above: A forty-year tradition at Kent State is the Halloween celebration in downtown Kent, where thousands dress up in costumes or simply come to marvel at the spectacle.

Women's athletics, always prominent at Kent, really came into their own in the 1990s with Title IX. Clockwise from top left: The 1990 women's softball team posted a 43–9 record and went to the Women's College World Series. The women's gymnastics team, winners of the 1988 MAC crown. Basketball star Mary Bukovac, MAC Player of the Year in 1989, won first team all-conference honors two years in a row.

Top: In 1961 Larry Woodell, Kent's long-serving super-intendent of grounds, imported a rare species of black squirrels from Canada to Kent. They have become a campus icon and spawned the annual Black Squirrel Festival.

Left: *The Chestnut Burr*, Kent's annual, was published from 1914 to 1985.

Below: In 1989 the sprawling Field House next to Dix Stadium opened as a practicing space for athletic teams and as a venue for track-and-field events.

President Schwartz appointed three new University Professors, Owen
Lovejoy (anthropology, top left), Richard Madey (physics, top right)
and Halim El-Dabh (music, above), an internationally known composer,
shown here in native costume playing a drum.

Kent's Honors College was established in the early 1930s and grew to be a large and distinguished academic unit. Top left: Here is the staff in 1989: (left to right) Assistant Dean (and later Dean) Ben Bassham, Anita Bixenstine, Helga Kaplan, Wilma Crawford, Dean Ottavio M. Casale, and Patricia Gerber. Honors is now located in the new Stopher-Johnson Hall (above) where students in 2006 listened to a small lecture (top right).

Thirteen

NEW PERSPECTIVES, NEW MODELS

{1990–2006}

On March 21, 1990, Michael Schwartz announced his decision to resign, and the news struck the campus like a thunderbolt from a clear sky. Maybe it should not have come as a surprise, but few people had gauged the toll his intensely personal style of leadership in the rough-and-tumble of academic administration—with an increasingly restive and fractious board pushing on one hand and a critical and demanding faculty pulling on the other—had taken on his nervous system. Nor had they reckoned with his itch to return—to use the academic cliché—to his first love, research and teaching (though he had taught an occasional statistics course during his presidency). Although Schwartz was, at fifty-four, still a young man, contemporary photographs show him looking older than his years, tense and worn. And, as he hinted later, he may have been daunted by intimations that the world of higher education, with its humanistic commitment to the life of the mind, would be changed beyond all recognition by the economic, sociopolitical, and, above all, technological crosscurrents hurrying it toward the enigmatic new millennium.[1] Whatever his reasons, his decision to resign was an almost universally unpopular one.

In April the trustees hired professional consultants to assist the search committee, which it formally commissioned in May. Chaired by trustee Alicia Miller, it included four professors (two from the Kent and two from the regional campuses); four trustees; one academic administrator; two student senators, an undergraduate and a graduate; the Alumni Association president; and two staff members, a departure from previous search committees. Their charge was to draft a profile of "desired presidential qualifications"; conduct a national search along affirmative action guidelines, with in-progress reports; and set a timeline "so that the names of not less than three, but not more than five," unranked finalists would reach the trustees by November 1990. All meetings would be executive sessions in order to "observe complete confidentiality to protect the candidates."[2]

During the next four months, committee members processed 110 nominations and reviewed eighty applications submitted by candidates from around the country, gradually sifting out all but ten prospects, who were interviewed in Cleveland rather than vetted on campus, a major curtailment of the tradition of open searches. Four survived the final cut and one withdrew "reluctantly," as Alicia Miller explained later, "after lengthy discussions with the candidate's trustees, colleagues, and family."[3] The trustees identified the finalists at its meeting on October 26: Kendall Baker, provost and vice president for academic affairs at Northern Illinois University; Carol Cartwright, vice chancellor for academic affairs and professor of human development at the University of California at Davis; and Terry Roark, president of the University of Wyoming. Baker was recommended by "someone outside the university," board secretary alumna Anita Herington said, while Cartwright was a late entrant, having been recruited by the consulting firm at the trustees' request for a minority candidate in the pool after a black male candidate, who had made the final cut, had withdrawn. Roark was nominated by "several individuals affiliated with KSU," as well as by people from other universities.[4]

Prior to his move to Northern Illinois, Baker had chaired the political science department at the University of Wyoming and headed Bowling Green's arts and sciences college. Before her stint at UC Davis, Cartwright had been vice provost and dean of undergraduate programs at Penn State and, earlier, associate dean for academic affairs and professor in its education college. Roark had held a professorship in astronomy as well as several administrative posts at OSU before coming to Kent as its chief academic officer (1983–87). All three candidates fit the presidential profile; all had the requisite academic and administrative resumes. Only Roark had actual presidential experience, though, which, together with a large fund of goodwill acquired during his years at Kent, made him odds-on favorite for the job. After all, the two previous presidents had come with presidential experience. In November the three finalists and their spouses came to Kent for meetings and interviews. Baker dropped out soon after, however, leaving the trustees with two sharply contrasting candidates: the tall, owlish, low-key scholar Roark, with his unassuming good manners and reflective nature; and fifty-year-old Carol Cartwright, petite, precise, prepared, assured, with signature white hair, Irish blue eyes, and concentrated energy. The contest promised to be very intense.

Yet when the trustees met on December 7, the only candidate still standing was Carol Cartwright, and they named her the institution's tenth president—its first woman president and the first woman to head an Ohio public university or college. A smiling Michael Schwartz was on hand to welcome her with the keys to the president's house on Overlook, which she would never occupy. Cartwright's selection had been assured three days earlier when Roark, pleading a renewed demand for his services at Wyoming, discreetly withdrew from contention. Thus, each featured performer danced into the wings to make way for the star to take stage center, observing the long-established choreography of presidential searches, which is designed to save the losers' faces and give the appearance of inevitability to the winner. When everything—firsthand knowledge of the campus, much residual goodwill, and hands-on presidential experience—seemed to point to early-favorite Roark, why had latecomer Cartwright been chosen?

The apparent ease of her victory is deceptive. It was, in fact, a close-run contest, a "tight two-person" race, according to faculty representative Myra West (physics). Roark had dropped out, Alicia Miller guessed, because he felt the lengthy Kent search was undermining Wyoming's confidence in him. But trustee Thaddeus Garrett, a local African American pastor-politician, and alumnus of Akron University, was more forthright. By choosing Cartwright, Garrett said, the trustees had shown that a "woman or a minority" was capable of heading a large university system. He had been impressed by Cartwright's diversity agenda at UC Davis, a subject over which he said he had tangled with "the outgoing president." Cartwright, however, downplayed the notion that her gender was a significant factor in her selection, saying that "being female" was just "one of the many characteristics I bring" and would be soon forgotten. As president, she promised to consult widely and push diversity.[5]

Given the candidates' stark differences and the closeness of the race, it is doubtful that the trustees started the search with a clear notion either of the kind of president they wanted or of the direction they wanted KSU to take. They do seem, however, to have been disposed toward finding a qualified minority candidate. And the evidence argues that Cartwright made up their minds that the minority candidate would be a woman and that her name would be Carol Cartwright. Other than her resume, the search committee and trustees knew little about her until shortly before she arrived in Kent. But at her interview, said another faculty member of the search committee, "she just blew us away."[6] What they wanted and needed, Cartwright convinced them, was a new departure, a can-do optimist who would bring an extra dimension to the presidency and give the institution a dynamic and attractive new public image. Tellingly, the trustees were rumored to have given Cartwright just three broad mandates: to cultivate corporate donors, to communicate Kent's story to the public, and to appoint a new cadre of upper-level administrators.

One conspicuous result of the outsourcing of governmental services that attended the Reagan Revolution was the increasing privatization of public education in general and of higher education in particular. By the end of the eighties, university presidents were being harried to direct most of their energy to nonacademic, extramural activities: courting and cosseting private donors and corporations, joining corporate boards, networking, marketing the institution, shaking the money tree wherever it grew. Dying were the days when universities could survive on the low-hanging fruit of state subsidies. The era of the CEO as hero was ascendant, and boards of trustees tended to be dominated by businessmen who thought of universities as multimillion-dollar businesses that should be led by CEOs.

Schwartz, with his traditional view that universities were fundamentally different in kind from businesses, had seldom had more than three trustees in his corner. One ongoing source of friction was his perceived unwillingness or inability to tap the Cleveland business community for contributions to build up a large endowment as counterweight to cutbacks in state support for higher education. He had commissioned a study to determine how "potential donors" would react to a major capital campaign, and "the answer came back loud and clearly," he said: "It would not have been received well, and our chances of success were nil." The long shadows of May 4 and Tent City still dimmed Kent's public image.[7] People who worked closely with him agree that he hated fund-raising, perhaps because his ironic self-awareness made it hard for him to treat it purely instrumentally, as Cartwright, with her strongly practical nature, was able to do with apparent ease.

Carol Cartwright took office on March 16, 1991, determined to make important changes, especially in administrative as well as campus culture. As an administrator, she showed a strong preference for innovation—for new structures, methods, and approaches to problem solving. Golding and Schwartz tended to respect established processes. But Cartwright preferred to establish new standing committees, with expansive charters, to study administrative and curricular proposals and operations.

She moved on several fronts. She began making plans to change the institutional planning and budget review processes. She appointed a special University-wide committee to develop ways to spread diversity across the campus, and, perhaps her signature initiative, she persuaded the Faculty Senate to appoint a special committee to study the idea she had made the centerpiece of her inaugural address. Dissatisfied with the long-standing merit categories of research, teaching, and service, she wanted to expand the concept of scholarship to cover the full range of professorial activities that should qualify as genuine scholarship—in particular the scholarship of teaching, which she hoped would eliminate the prevailing invidious dichotomy between teaching and research. This concept originated in a Carnegie study commission on which she had served prior to coming to Kent.

Even before taking office, she had designed and launched what would become one of her signal contributions: a major student scholarship fund aimed at enhancing the quality of the undergraduate experience and making a first-rate education available to hundreds of young scholars who otherwise could not afford one. She gave the Founders Scholars Program, as it was called, such momentum that it was already accreting large contributions—including one of $10,000 from her and her husband, Phil—even before its official commencement that fall with a glamorous black-tie inaugural ball. The initial target of $250,000 was quickly met, and a year later the fund had grown to nearly $1 million. In subsequent years it grew at the same steady pace, drawing academically qualified students, most from Ohio, to the University each year.

Another hallmark of her leadership style was extensive consultation; she was determined to have a full-throated medley of voices and viewpoints expressed in policy development. Giving everyone an opportunity to shape a policy, she reasoned, would help ensure its acceptance. Administration from the top down alone was ineffectual; it lacked the creative tension provided by administration from the bottom up. This became one of the themes in her annual "State of the University" addresses, as her understanding of presidential administration waxed. To deal with the unexpected problems that arise willy-nilly on a large campus, she would appoint ad hoc study groups and committees.

In her first year she was challenged by two events no one could have anticipated. She was diagnosed with breast cancer and required almost immediate surgery. She recovered rapidly from her surgery and resumed her full-time duties five days later, as if she had suffered no more than a minor indisposition, save that she was thereafter a forceful public advocate for breast cancer prevention and research.

The second challenge was of a professional and very public nature. On the night of December 12, 1991, a student, sensing something odd about a man sleeping in a chair in the Kiva, touched his shoulder to check on him and he crumpled onto the floor. He was dead on arrival at Robinson Memorial Hospital in Ravenna. Campus police determined that he had been shot in the back with a .38 caliber pistol. They identified him as a campus maintenance worker and part-time student. Before fear could infect the campus, the Christmas holidays supervened and the students went home. When school reconvened a month later, the *Stater* of January 21, 1992, reported that the victim had worked the 10:30 P.M.–7:00 A.M. shift in the Business Building and quoted his mother as speculating that he had probably been shot because he had "seen something he shouldn't have."

Then at 7:33 P.M. on January 30, a man about to exit White Hall through a ground-floor door suddenly wheeled around, aimed a pistol at student Sarah R. Smith, standing just four feet from him, shot her in the chest, and walked out. Smith survived. She described her shooter as a white male, about six feet one inch tall, between twenty-five and thirty years old, wearing "a tan waistcoat and knit cap."

By all accounts, Cartwright's response to this challenge was exemplary. She set up a special investigative task force, showing the public that Kent took these matters seriously. To ease the anxieties and fears of students and their parents, she arranged a twenty-four-hour information hotline, expanded University information and internal communication services, and doubled security in all dorms. Campus uniformed officers worked extended shifts, with no days off, while city police patrolled the many miles of campus roads.

Ballistics results released a week later showed that the same .38 caliber gun was used in both shootings. Police said they were "looking for the same person,"[8] and that "same person" was soon back in the news. At 9:00 P.M. on February 11, a dozen windows in Glenmorris Apartments adjacent to the Michael Schwartz Center (formerly the University School) began shattering, and soon afterward police spotted a suspect near the Business Building and gave chase. After a running gunfight down Summit, the chase ended when the police killed the suspect in a backyard on South Willow. A pistol found near the body proved to be the gun that killed Frazier and wounded Smith. The shooter was later identified as a Kent alumnus named Mark Cunningham.

Cartwright soon revealed herself to be a very quick study who took pains to learn the rudiments of the subjects and materials that came within her official purview; whether it was some arcane rule or device of intercollegiate sports or the nature of liquid crystals, she wanted to be able to refer to it knowledgeably. She gave diligence a new, more exalted meaning, never failing to be present, punctual, and prepared for every appointment, whether it was with a select group of wealthy prospective donors or a large audience of regional campus faculty (of the sort she addressed five days after undergoing surgery for cancer) or a Friends of the Library dinner or a departmental awards ceremony. She drove herself so hard at the beginning that she had a couple of minor traffic accidents on the roads circling campus—much to the amusement of students.

She seemed constitutionally incapable of remaining in a prolonged state of repose. There are a few unconfirmed reports that she actually slept, on occasion, but if so it was doubtless while she was multitasking on her exercise bike or talking on her cell phone. Despite her punishing schedule, however, she was a gracious and attentive conversationalist, entering readily into the spirit of any gathering. And, despite her sometimes hyperefficient professional demeanor, she had a ready sense of humor and an unforced laugh. Then there was her artesian well of energy, a source of genuine wonder. Not only was she never tired. Not only was she never less than impeccably and appropriately dressed. Not only was her hair never seen to be less than coiffed and styled each-hair-perfect, but, according to one bemused observer, never in her fourteen years at Kent did she even catch a cold.[9]

Cartwright was also quick off the mark in establishing the pattern of her presidency. After extensive consultations, she planned an elaborate and successful campaign for increasing alumni growth and giving and its participation in campus life. She worked hard to take the Kent State story to the corporate world of northeastern Ohio and, via an expanding network of local alumni chapters, to the nation. And as part of her charter to represent the institution to the public, as well as her personal belief that a university must serve the public good, she joined the Akron Regional Development Board, the Akron Round-table, and the Greater Cleveland Roundtable, lending Kent's support to their efforts to promote regional development. She also accepted invitations to serve on three corporate boards, discharging her duties in her spare time. For each of these positions she received compensa-tion, along with some grumbling criticism, though she was clearly fol-lowing a demarche from the trustees.

In addition to continuing her longtime involvement in national educa-tion associations, she was named a trustee of the prestigious Woodrow Wilson Foundation, which promotes scholarship and dialogue in inter-national relations, and she rose to the governing circles of the National Collegiate Athletic Association. Like Schwartz, she was a sports fan and had an informed spectator's interest in most sports, fueled by a fan's enthusiasm. She especially enjoyed basketball and football games and had a fund of anecdotes about famed football coach Joe Paterno acquired during her years at Penn State.

Her enthusiasm for football, and her adventurous streak, led her to tinker with one of Kent's most hallowed traditions, Homecom-ing. She was scheduled to lead the 1994 Homecoming parade in her husband's sports car, but Roy Sibit, a director of the Alumni Asso-ciation's national board and a motorcycle enthusiast, urged her to ride behind him on his Harley-Davidson. She did both. Her lead car, finishing its route ahead of the floats, circled back to the Williamson Alumni Center, where Sibit awaited her with proper gear. Suited up in helmet, gloves, and leather jacket, she then climbed into the saddle behind Sibit and entered the parade with a dramatic roar, to the sur-prise and delight of onlookers lining Main Street. Cartwright and "the Hog" remained part of the Homecoming tradition until 2003, when she decided to drop the parade. But in 2004 and 2005, astride a Harley now driven by Sibit's son, Cartwright thundered onto Dix Stadium to deliver the game ball. Of course gender matters. If any of her male predecessors had tried such a stunt, it would have lacked the woman's touch, the frisson that makes a moment memorable.

The increasingly winning ways of Kent's basketball teams during her tenure delighted her, and not only because it diverted attention from the misfortunes of the football program, which continued to provoke more jeers than cheers and had partially obscured Kent's remarkable intercollegiate achievements.

While it's beyond the ambition of the present book to undertake anything like a full accounting of Kent's varsity sports, a few highlights merit mention.[10] Kent's wrestling tradition is arguably unsurpassed in the annals of intercollegiate athletics, nurtured in recent decades by Joe Begala's successors, Ron Gray and alum Jim Andrassy; and its golf teams have also consistently ranked among the nation's best for nearly as long, most recently under the tutelage of alumnus Herb Page, one of whose pupils, alumnus Ben Curtis, won the 2003 British Open. Throughout the eighties and nineties, men's baseball and women's softball, as well as men and women's track and field, soccer, field hockey, and gymnastics, all compiled admirable records. And beginning in the nineties, under coaches Jim MacDonald, Gary Waters, Stan Heath, and Jim Christian, the men's basketball squads came to dominate the MAC and became a national powerhouse, making the NCAA playoffs four times (1999, 2001, 2002, 2006) and even the Elite Eight in 2002. The women's basketball teams have been equally stellar, winning a series of MAC championships and four trips to the NCAA championships. And despite the fumblings of the football program, it has produced as many individual professional stars (e.g., Don Nottingham, Joshua Cribbs, James Harrison, and Antonio Gates, the great Kent basketball star who became an all-pro tight end for the San Diego Chargers despite never playing a day of college football) as has the highly successful baseball program (e.g., Steve Stone, Gene Michael, Thurman Munson). And this is only a few of the stars who have graced Kent's intercollegiate rosters.

One of Cartwright's first administrative initiatives was the all-university Diversity Planning Committee (1992), chaired by geologist Don Palmer, which devised ways and means of increasing understanding and acceptance of the range of racial, ethnic, gender, political, and religious differences among members of the campus community. In a few years the work of this committee sharply increased the number of faculty and staff positions held by minorities and women. Cartwright made it a personal point to put qualified women in important administrative posts. As an aspiring science student, she had bruised her head on the academic glass ceiling, leading her to change her major to education. She was determined to shatter it at Kent.

Another important early move was to merge, and expand, the functions of the University Budget and Long Range Planning committees, with both of which she was reportedly frustrated, to create a new campuswide University Priorities and Budget Advisory Committee, cochaired by the provost and the treasurer instead of faculty members. It fell to this committee to propose strategies for responding creatively to a drumbeat of legislative mandates, mediated by the Board of Regents, intended to make state universities more accountable, more cost-effective, and, above all, more focused on undergraduate education and teaching.

The committee's first strategic plan, in 1994, set new coordinates for ensuring that the highest administrative officers would be involved in student issues: reducing graduation requirements to 121 hours, enabling students to graduate in timely fashion; integrating Kent's eight campuses into one system (this helped block a move to turn the state's regional campuses into independent colleges); supporting the scholarship of teaching and stressing teaching development; expanding existing and forging new collaborative efforts and partnerships with sister institutions; reinforcing Kent's "leadership in research and creativity at state and national levels," even beyond the Carnegie Research II classification awarded in 1993; and utilizing all state-of-the-art technologies for teaching and communication.[11]

Cartwright learned with a jolt that money would be the leading concern of her tenure on her first day on the job, March 16, 1991, the day the governor sent the legislature a budget wrapped in blood-stained butcher's paper. Inside were the shambles of the higher education subsidy that had survived his cleaver. This would be just the first of a series of budgets that portended major changes in higher education—and major headaches. Two months later Cartwright was so worried about reducing expenses that she invited employees to consider volunteering to have their work hours shortened; there is no record of any volunteers. In July the administration laid off a number of administrative and civil service staff because $9.6 million had been lopped off Kent's biennial budget. Money was so tight that fall that the University Marching Band could not perform at football games, which it had been doing since its inception in 1919, prompting the Alumni Association to start an endowment drive that had raised $250,000 by May, enough to put the band back on the football field in 1993, plus another $50,000 for new uniforms.

Over an eighteen-month span Kent's eight campuses eliminated 151 positions, including thirty-two unfilled faculty slots and civil service positions cut after retirements, resignations, and nonrenewals. Another thirty-six contract cleaning jobs also vanished. Neither continued increases in enrollment nor the $3.5 million saved by shifting to a computerized system of energy management could significantly mitigate the baleful effects of so severe a drop in state support. Not until 1999 did Ohio even return to the low funding levels of 1990. And from then on state subsidies were flatlined.

It was in this dismal climate that Cartwright delivered her first "State of the University" address on October 27, 1992. She began by telling her colleagues that all her former assumptions about the dependable bedrock of support for higher education, despite periods of economic instability, had gone with the winds of change. Her somber tone suggests that those winds had also swept away her initial assumptions about the nature of the job she had accepted with such zest and that she was formulating new ones. "We are at a watershed point for higher education in Ohio, and indeed, in the nation," she said. "And it will not be business as usual for us when the economy improves." She cited a *Chronicle of Higher Education* study showing that state appropriations nationwide for 1992–93 were lower than they had been two years ago, the first two-year drop in the country's history. Nothing like it had happened before, even during the Great Depression. Even more disturbing than the economic downturn and the drag of post-boomer demographics, Cartwright said, were the signs of a vast change already under way in the American public's attitude toward higher education, a change of values and expectations.

To survive and prosper, she said, universities must fashion a new model of higher education, a new idea of the University, one more sensitive to its various constituencies even as it helped to shape their expectations and needs—in order to "enable their dreams." Then, digging into what she called her "pocketful of optimism," she challenged her audience to see this as an opportunity rather than an occasion for despair.[12] The new model of the future university was still evolving, and she urged the faculty to take an active role in its shaping instead of being left behind in the years of "experimentation and refinement" that lay ahead. She then listed a few of the coming issues: further emphasis on international programs, reform of intercollegiate athletics, increased accountability, diversity, new roles for faculty and faculty shortages, continued budget problems, more emphasis on undergraduate teaching, and more technology programs.[13] Mark that she made these comments before the legislature mandated initiatives that would shape her administrative agenda for the remainder of her tenure and make it impossible for her to carry through on all of them. It would be interesting to know what reforms she had in mind for certain items on her list.

While the public recognized the value of a college education, a great many people doubted that they would be able to afford it in the future, given that its expenses were being shifted onto the backs of students and parents. There was also a growing demand among voters and legislators for colleges to educate people to enter the workforce and rebuild the state's economy. This, however, portended a reprise of the historic debate over the meaning and purpose of a college education—Was it to educate or to train?—that traced back into the early nineteenth century with the founding of the Rensselaer Technical Institute, followed by the appointment of a professorship of agriculture at Yale and a program in business at Harvard.[14] In retrospect, those early departures from the classical curriculum by America's great private universities decided the issue of public education once and for all. All that remained was to find ways to do both—to strike a productive balance between educating and training.

This is far harder to do than to say, especially in Ohio, partly because of the conceptual, purposive, and historic differences between education and training, and partly because of the hidden hand of the state's enrollment-driven funding formula, which pays money for enrollment growth and effectively deducts it from institutions that have stablized enrollments by setting high admission standards designed to ensure that their students are capable of doing college-level work. Some faculty discontentment with Cartwright that surfaced later would spring from the push-pull between state pressures on trustees and presidents to heed the public's desire for education-for-employment and the faculty's traditional understanding of college education as providing a systematic grounding in the ideas, events, and cultural creations that produced some of humanity's supreme achievements. For many professors, education was qualitatively different from learning a trade or getting technical training.

After 1995 a variety of state mandates centered on student concerns. With freshman enrollment still growing each year, along with drop-out rates, Cartwright took several measures. She simplified the graduation requirements by recommending a new standard of 121 credit hours, enabling students to get degrees in four years. She established an administrative unit called Student Success (later the Undergraduate College) to improve student advising and retention, and she commissioned a long-term comprehensive enrollment plan. Meanwhile, she continued holding forums with students to stay in touch with their attitudes, perceptions, interests, and felt needs. The student image of her as "Queen Carol" that started with her elaborate inaugural festivities lost its negative resonance as she demonstrated to them her "hands-on" style of unqueenly diligence and energy.

From the late-1980s on, colleges and universities were forced to compete fiercely, if discreetly, for qualified students by making campus life more convenient, comfortable, and homelike, all of which cost money. This competition included amenities that would flabbergast students of former eras, when a bunk, a desk, and a chair were the standard furnishings. Now dorm rooms were being wired not only for telephones, television, cable, and sound systems but for computers and Internet access as well. During the nineties the original eighty computer "stations" in the Library spawned 800 more terminals in nearly every campus building, and that was but a down payment on what was to come. Students could research library holdings, correspond with professors and each other, download music, and explore the ever-expanding cyber universe beyond—all while seated in front of the terminals in their dorm rooms, which they were given a free hand to furnish and decorate. And a dozen dorms were designated for students of similar career and creative interests, an idea that started under Olds.

All these innovations paled before the rise of the college-as-spa fashion of the mid-1990s. The preeminent example of this on the Kent campus was the fabulous Student Wellness Center (1999) across Summit from the science complex, with its workout rooms gleaming with state-of-the-art exercise equipment, swimming and wading pools, whirlpools, saunas, massage and therapy facilities and staff, spinning room, hand- and racquetball courts, tracks, and climbing wall. Because it was not primarily educational in nature, the facility, when first publicly discussed in the early nineties, had little likelihood of getting state capital funding. Those pushing for it in the administration and faculty knew, of course, that it would have to be paid for by hiking student fees, just like the Field House. But lingering student disgruntlement over the Field House made that problematic.

Though a few prominent students eventually headed the campaign for the facility, they had significant behind-the-scenes help and material support from professional consultants and University administrators in marshaling student support. The issue was debated periodically in *Stater* editorials, news columns, and letters. Meanwhile, student fee hikes kept getting bigger as the state outsourced the costs of a college education to individual students and their families. After several years, a proposal to pay for a fitness center with a special student fee won a skin-of-the-teeth victory in a vote in which only a few thousand students bothered to cast ballots. Still, it was judged to have involved a statistically representative percentage of eligible voters and therefore constituted a legitimate election. The Wellness Center, as it is called, quickly became enormously popular and no doubt attracted many students to Kent. The International Recreation Sports Association later ranked it among the nine top facilities in the country.

The Wellness Center is an example of the way enrollment growth depends in significant part on an institution's willingness and readiness to respond to student expectations. Cartwright's admissions and enrollment staffs reinforced what she learned in part from her student forums about the key role of marketing and communications, for which she hired experts. When she learned that these developments were causing muttering among the faculty, she decided to confront the issue. In addressing the faculty on October 19, 1995, she acknowledged that words like "marketing" and "customers" grate on academic nerves. But, she said, "they are not educational expletives unless one is trying to make something out of nothing." But the grumbling got louder, so she revisited the matter a year later while discussing the radically altered condition of higher education. "The reality of external events is that now, we must think of students as 'customers' and education as a 'commodity.'" Assuring her colleagues that she, too, recognized the difference between business and "educating students and generating knowledge," she challenged them: "Why can't we be fervent about protecting academic freedom and still be kind when answering the telephone?" Then she added: "And can't we adhere to rigorous academic standards while also adhering to scheduled office hours?"[15] It was a fair point to make, if not tactful. Her necessarily instrumental view of the University's condition seemed radically at odds with the existential view that many faculty members felt was the only way to preserve the integrity of their profession. While her overriding task was to keep the ship afloat and move it ahead by tacking through stormy seas, theirs was to ensure that its cargo was intact, its rigging trimmed, and its course true.

In discussing Kent's progress during the first decade of her presidency in her "State of the University" speech on October 5, 2000, Cartwright singled out the school's redefinition of scholarship, its adaptation to information-age technology, and its strong commitment to serving its constituents—both its students and the general public. In the past decade, she reported, some 47,000 students earned degrees; 65,000 international students studied at KSU; the faculty attracted $200 million in grants and contracts; financial aid almost tripled; scholarship funds jumped by 400 percent; and twenty-one varsity teams won MAC championships. Between 1995 and 2000 the freshman class grew by 45 percent, while the average high school GPA of freshman had reached 3.0, prompting another hike in minimum admission standards.

For Cartwright, the secret of leadership was a clear vision and well-planned goals. She attributed some of the most significant advances to her emphasis on all-university budget and long-range planning processes. On the academic front, the Faculty Senate adopted new promotion and tenure policies along lines laid down in the Boyer report calling for the redefinition of scholarship to encompass the broad spectrum of professorial activities. The new categories of scholarship were discovery (adding new knowledge), integration (integrating basic research into still-larger patterns), application (applying knowledge to consequential problems), and teaching (transmitting received knowledge and thereby extending and transfiguring it). In addition, she created the University Teaching Council to encourage "excellence in teaching," and in 2002 bookended it with a "select group" of Distinguished Professors to celebrate outstanding scholarly contributions.

Cartwright had revealed her metric of success in her inaugural address: is a particular policy or procedure consistent with our determination to lead the nation in scholarship and research, and does it fulfill our obligation to repay the public trust by serving the public good? This reveals the importance of diligence and dutifulness in Cartwright's moral economy and explains what one observer has described as her "24/7 presidency."[16] By that yardstick alone, she was justified in regarding her stewardship as successful.

At a university, construction projects, unlike curricular developments, tend to overlap presidencies. At Kent, plans begun a decade earlier for restoring President McGilvrey's crescent of classic buildings on Front

Campus started bearing fruit in 1984 with the renovation of McGilvrey Hall (geography and geology). Moulton Hall, long abandoned to the ghosts of thousands of women residents, was completely renovated into the Learning and Technologies Center (1997). The school's first classroom building, Merrill Hall, was gutted and transformed into classrooms and offices for sociology (1994), while Lowry Hall, the first women's dorm, was rejuvenated for anthropology, the University Press, and administrative offices (1995). And before Cartwright left office, the other original buildings, neglected so long, would be restored, or on their way toward restoration: Kent Hall for sociology (2005) and Franklin Hall for journalism and mass communications (2007).

In 1993 the mathematics and computer sciences programs moved out of Merrill Hall into a new building on Summit Street, an arresting structure of diverse architectural notions. And in 2001 a $9.5 million wing was added to Cunningham Hall. At decade's end, plans were drawn up for completing Kent's evolution from a largely commuter school, as it had been for several decades, to an extensively residential one. And within a few years a handsome complex of six state-of-the-art residence halls, called Centennial Court, went up between Dunbar and Tri-Towers.

Among the many other architectural changes on Kent's dynamic campus in the eighties and nineties, the University Auditorium—where former generations of students had heard so many famous political figures, actors, singers, musicians, and writers and sat through large lectures of Intro to Psych—was handsomely renovated (2002) and named in honor of Cartwright on her retirement. But as with sports stars, groundbreaking research projects, and individual achievements and performances by Kent's creative students and faculty, there are too many new facilities, renovations, and additions to existing structures to pay each its proper due.

One organizational structure that Cartwright decided early on needed to be changed was the decade-long coupling of both academic and student affairs in the same administrative unit. She thought it cumbersome and inefficient to force the two units to compete for the attention of one vice president. After appropriate consultations, she severed student affairs from academic affairs, making two independent units, each with vice presidential rank. To facilitate and enrich students' educational experiences, she established the Division of Enrollment Management and Student Affairs in 1994, which was responsible for enrollment, retention, and advising.

This freed the provost to give total attention to academic programs and personnel. In October 1992 she brought in a new treasurer, as vice president for business and finance, a post left vacant by the retirement of long-serving Richard Dunn. And six months later, following an extensive search, she recruited an experienced provost, Myron Henry, to replace the interim provost appointed by Schwartz following an administrative convulsion near the end of his tenure. Being able to work comfortably with her provost was important to Cartwright. Their relationship, she said in an early interview, must "be one of trust and responsibility," because, working so closely together, they should be able to finish "each other sentences."[17] Coming into the office without presidential experience and with a commission to spend most of her time on external affairs, Cartwright presumably hoped to delegate day-to-day operations to her chief academic officer, the provost. This would enable her to get a gradual feel for the operation without having to plunge immediately into the crosscurrents of such academic matters as due process; faculty salaries, tenure, and promotion protocols; curricular development, liaising with the trustees, the college deans, and the Faculty Senate; overseeing undergraduate and graduate programs; and the myriad personal and professional disputes to which professors are prone. For that degree of empathy to develop, however, not only must the personalities and dispositions of the president and provost mesh, but the provost and the treasurer also must be compatible. If such was her hope, it soon shipwrecked on the vagaries of human nature.

Cartwright could find little rapport with either the interim provost, a legacy from Schwartz, or the provost she chose to replace him. Both men were independent-minded, seasoned hands with their own ideas about their roles and responsibilities, and they seemed to question most of her proposals. Neither of them, in turn, could work with the new treasurer, who was suspicious of them. Worse yet, the treasurer felt threatened by the provost's chief budget officer, Cheryl Casper, a professor of economics. Because of this dysfunctional administrative ménage à quatre, Cartwright found herself having to step in and settle testy disagreements and disputes. The experience seasoned her as a presidential administrator, giving her confidence in her ability to make executive decisions. But, by reinforcing her strongly practical instincts and her need to get things done, it made her impatient with the tradition of academic discourse, of decisions made after a thorough airing of differing points of view, of that free exchange of ideas that is fundamental to shared governance in which she believed—all of which takes time and can seem, to a decisive, task-driven individual, to be little better than wheel spinning or bloviating.

Other events also helped to bend the arc of her presidency. In January 1993 the trustees approved the collective bargaining agreement her team had worked out with representatives of the American Federation of State, County, and Municipal Employees Local 152, which had 153 members. This, however, only cleared her desk for a more incendiary labor issue. Earlier, on September 16, 1992, attempts to renegotiate the contract with the faculty union had broken off. Over the next five months bargaining positions, along with emotions, hardened on both sides, each viewing the other as intransigent and duplicitous. It happened that in this impasse the UFPA leadership, which was unusually militant, decided to mount a hard-hitting public campaign to present its case to the public.

Barbs edged with personal venom were aimed directly at Cartwright, the leader and very public face of the university. Though they doubtless smarted, she forbore, refusing to show her bruised feelings or let her nerve fail. Talks resumed in time and the negotiating teams agreed on terms for a new three-year contract between UFPA and the university, which the trustees duly ratified in April. This passage of arms may have soured Cartwright's feelings somewhat toward the faculty at large, making her uncertain of its respect and support. The fact that she remained cool and unruffled throughout, however, was mistaken for emotional detachment and indifference. That was a warped perception of her manner, however, and not an accurate reading of her nature or feelings or character. She may have been, as a foreign visitor once remarked after meeting her, "tiny [but] tough," but there is no reason to doubt that she very much wanted the faculty's respect and good wishes. She knew that she was working day and night for the university, which for her meant the faculty as well as the students and the staff. The courage and dignity she displayed during this period greatly increased the respect at least one observer felt for her.[18]

It was during another protracted collective bargaining disagreement in 1999 that Cartwright's relations with the faculty became most volatile and acrimonious. The dispute centered on the terms dealing with such issues as salaries and intellectual property to be included in the new (or renewed) master contract between UFPA and the administration. But bargaining negotiations were probably not so much the cause as the determinative context in which some professors decided to raise the issue of faculty confidence in the administration. They circulated copies of a petition, unsigned and absent a bill of particulars, calling for the Faculty Senate to hold a formal vote of no confidence in President Cartwright. After determining that the petition had acquired the requisite number of valid faculty signatures, the senate executive committee agreed to hold a special session for an open discussion of the matter on March 22, 1999. The chair of the trustees denounced the no-confidence vote and informed the senate by letter that the board was dead set against any administrative review.

A variety of complaints were voiced during the tense, emotional meeting in the Governance Chambers of the Student Center. The stakes could hardly have been higher. Few academic leaders, no matter how strongly their boards have backed them, have survived a faculty vote of no confidence. One of the first complaints to be expressed concerned Cartwright's and the trustees' refusal to agree to a review of administrative officers of the sort conducted periodically of academic units, a much-gnawed bone of disagreement between the senate and the president. When another speaker charged Cartwright with neglecting academic affairs, others picked up the theme. One claimed that KSU ranked twenty-fourth out of twenty-five in percentage of full-time faculty; others mentioned low faculty moral, unequal pay for some female faculty, and the president's "corporate thinking" that led her to refer to students as "consumers." Several said that many faculty members feared retaliation if they expressed their unhappiness or signed the petition. One senator faulted Cartwright for her "selective application" of the strategic plan and for spending Foundation funds on facilities such as the Wellness Center and new administrative offices.[19]

Opponents of the no-confidence vote (including former president Schwartz) tended to advocate resolving disagreements by discussion and petition rather than by calling the president before the bar of public disgrace: a vote of no confidence would do KSU more harm than good. Several were troubled by the anonymous nature of the petition as well as the absence of a list of grievances supporting a no-confidence vote. Cartwright, who was in India at the time, had acting provost Gordon Keller provide whatever materials were relevant to the issue and wrote a letter offering her performance in office as her defense and expressing her confidence in the faculty.[20]

The ballots were distributed to all eight campuses on April 6, with a return date of April 16. On that day, at the administration's request, senate and administration representatives observed the tally through a one-way mirror, to ensure its accuracy. Results appeared in the April 20 *Stater* under the headline: "Faculty Votes for Confidence." The count was 396 for and 254 against. The spray of complaints voiced in the public meeting indicates an underlying general sense of uneasiness and discontent, a feeling that the institution was being forced by Cartwright's "realities of external circumstances" to change itself without benefit of due reflection and consideration. This may account for the large number of faculty who didn't trouble themselves to vote. One senator summed it up: "The faculty, by and large, has a very difficult job and wants to be supportive but has serious concerns." In the end, the majority was not persuaded that Cartwright was the problem.

One significant change in the University's mission that shifted into high gear under Cartwright was directly related to one of those "realities of external circumstances"—the growing public demand, expressed through the legislature, for programs geared to prepare people for jobs, training for the "real world." Many school-to-job programs sprang up on the Kent campus during this period—hospitality management and a B.A. in paralegal studies, to name just two. The Regents also pressed state schools to adopt "performance-based funding," which distributed state monies according to productivity in the following priority areas: timely completion of degrees, economic development and workforce training, and research and technology transfer.

The regional campuses experienced their greatest expansion during the Cartwright years, partly because of the increasing emphasis on workforce training. In the new millennium Kent's network of seven regional campuses covering all of northeast Ohio, among the state's largest, accounted for about a third of the institution's total enrollment. The regional campuses, which flourished throughout the seventies under William Stephans, developed in academic range and quality during the next fifteen years under the leadership of Gordon Keller. Some campuses grew far beyond original expectations by seizing the opportunity presented by "performance-based funding," which, among other things, enabled them to enrich their campuses with a host of new facilities to support new work-related fields of study, including justice studies, applied communication, business management, nursing, technology education, workforce development, radiologic technology, computer technology, physical therapy, occupational therapy, and horticulture.

In 2000 Cartwright's efforts to elevate the University's standing in graduate research paid off when the Carnegie Foundation retooled its classification system and put Kent in the "Doctoral/Research University—Extensive" category, ranking it among the nation's ninety leading institutions and putting it in such heady company as Harvard, Yale, Case Western Reserve, and OSU. And the next year the chair of Kent's first full-force fund-raising campaign, Linda Allard, alumna and head designer for Ellen Tracy, announced that it was three-quarters of the way to meeting the $100 million goal. In 2003 the Campaign for KSU surpassed that figure by $30 million. The funds were dedicated to scholarships, faculty chairs, and technical achievements.

On May 4, 2000, alums and thousands of students gathered on the Commons for the thirtieth commemoration ceremony. Among many highlights of that event was the inaugural Symposium on Democracy, featuring some of the nation's leading historians, political scientists, and journalists. The symposium became an established part of the May 4 ceremony. In 1998 word had spread virally over campus that plans were afoot to change the parking lot adjacent to Taylor and Prentice halls. Some 250 students had marched up to Cartwright's office on the second floor of the library to protest any changes to the general area where four students had been gunned down more than a generation earlier. Determined to forestall a return of the shades of the gym annex and Tent City controversy, Cartwright ordered four metal markers set up on the parking lot commemorating the exact spots where the four students had fallen. The markers swiftly became important focal points for future commemorations of May 4 and for remembering the human beings slain there that day.

On October 5, 2005, Cartwright announced her decision to retire, saying, "It has been an enormous privilege" to have led Kent State for fourteen years, adding, "I do believe passionately in the special role of public universities to serve the public and have tried to live that belief." Rumors had been hatching for some time—that she was looking for another position, that she was going to retire—so the news brought no shock of surprise. She had worked as hard as any president in living memory, trying, in volatile circumstances and with diminishing state support, to find the right path across a terrain in which familiar landmarks seemed to change or vanish with every step. Trustee chair R. Douglas Cowan said he could think of nothing "she tried to do" that she hadn't achieved, adding that the board was "very, very pleased" with her service.[21]

The board's approval must have pleased her. As a consequence of her feeling that the faculty did not appreciate her efforts, Cartwright seems to have gradually come to regard the trustees as her stay and prop, the group she most wanted to please. Her relations with the trustees were, to all appearances, remarkably warm. Every president must achieve a modus vivendi with the group that has the power to hire and fire, and the character of that relationship is determined by the chemical interaction between the personalities of the two parties as much as by the expectations of the one and the performance of the other.

Olds, with his prime agenda of opening up the campus after its closure and letting fresh breezes sweep it clean of suspicion and ill will, encouraged the trustees to become involved in key faculty committees, hoping that would let them see the faculty more sympathetically, as professionals trying to do their job in tough circumstances rather than stereotypically, as irresponsible instigators of mayhem and riot. That didn't work as he hoped partly because the faculty, the campus, and the trustees were simply too dislocated by the shootings and the shutdown of the campus. Golding came to office and ordered the trustees back into their cage, and in a wink they were lions perched obediently on their stools, such were his powers of moral suasion.

Schwartz, with his personal charm and strenuously academic ply of mind, was unable to tame more than a few of the lions at a time, and those he cultivated assiduously while keeping a nervous eye on the others. Cartwright, with her professionalism, her efficiency, and her personal charm, simply turned the lions into pussy cats, achieving a degree of control almost as great as Golding's. But her antennae quivered at the slightest sign of trouble. One trustee, who joined the board eager to serve his alma mater, sent her what he thought was a helpful letter suggesting consideration of certain matters. But, as he reported, he soon realized that doing so had put him on "her list."[22] Dismayed at being isolated, he resigned. If she had one major weakness as an academic leader, it was that familiar blend of insecurity and touchiness that caused her to confuse dissent with disloyalty.

Cartwright had set some of the landmarks she intended to achieve during her tenure in her inaugural address, delivered before members of her family and a large audience consisting mainly of ceremonially robed professors, administrators, and presidents seated in a large white tent near Manchester Hall on October 11, 1991. To read this speech with the memory of having heard it at the time is to be struck by a sense of her unabashed enthusiasm, effervescent optimism, and uncomplicated delight at the prospect of being entrusted with the leadership of Kent State University. She spoke of "the fire that burns within me," a legacy of her father's gift of "perpetual optimism," that inevitably brings to mind her extraordinary energy. And while she became far more guarded and less self-revealing as she weathered the storms of office, that fire of energy never dimmed. One administrator who worked with her throughout her tenure said she was "a good person, who worked very hard and did not get the support she deserved."[23] She was also an excellent administrator and effective president who will undoubtedly look better and better when seen through the tempering lens of historical perspective.

Carol Cartwright's retirement announcement on October 5, 2005, confronted the trustees with a dilemma: how was Kent State to survive and grow given the grim realities of diminishing state support, rising student fees, and the changing nature and mission of higher education in general in the new millennium? Decisions they made over the next few months suggest that, while keeping in view Kent State's long-standing aspiration to become a major research institution, they agreed to change the strategy for reaching that goal. With their corporate mind-set, this meant that the next president, in addition to being a prodigious fund-raiser and promoter of the University, should be essentially a CEO with a free hand to act decisively and unilaterally in making painful decisions about people and programs.

They appointed a seventeen-member search committee of trustees, professors, administrators, students, staff, alumni, and community representatives, chaired by trustee alumna Sandra Harbrecht and advised by a professional consultant. The consultant's argument that top candidates avoid searches without assurance of strict confidentiality overrode the objections of some members that abridging the custom of wide consultation would sour the presidential honeymoon.

From a field of 150 applicants contacted initially by the consultant, the committee eliminated all but six and brought them to campus under strict confidentiality. After reducing the list to three candidates, the committee sent their resumes to the trustees. All three finalists had experience as provosts but not as presidents; one experienced public university president had been eliminated earlier in the process. From the finalists the trustees chose Lester A. Lefton, senior vice president for academic affairs and provost at Tulane University, a prestigious private research institution. Although all three looked equally strong on paper, Lefton's performance at the interview and his reputation for fund-raising carried the day. Departing from practice, the board then reconvened the search committee and secured a unanimous recommendation. Following negotiations, the trustees gave Lefton a contract with a salary, housing and expense allowances for him and his wife, and backloaded with incentive bonuses commensurate with his CEO status, immediately putting him among the best-compensated presidents in the state system.

Thus, on the morning of May 6, 2006, the trustees surprised the campus with a fait accompli. After introducing the new president to faculty leaders at an early morning meeting, they formally appointed Lefton. In brief remarks accepting the appointment, Lefton promised to make academic freedom the heart of "research and scholarship" and "academic excellence" the goal of students, faculty, and staff. He would tackle the "great problem" of making KSU accessible economically and that he would nourish a "culture of philanthropy" in order to build an endowment base that would compensate for shrinking state support and enable the University to pursue its aspiration to become a world-class research institution.[24] After the trustees' meeting, Lefton went to a reception on Risman Plaza, where he circulated among a gathering of administrators, faculty, and students. Cheryl Casper (economics) told the *Akron Beacon Journal* that Lefton had "excellent credentials and good administrative experience," but, she added, "I can tell you the reaction among faculty has been shock and surprise."[25]

Lefton, a robust, fifty-eight-year-old man of brisk energy and brusque manner, brought thirty-four years of academic and administrative experience to the job. Author of many scholarly articles and a widely used introductory psychology textbook, he took his B.A. in psychology at Northeastern University in Boston (1969) and his Ph.D. at the University of Rochester (1974). At the University of South Carolina he rose from assistant professor (1972) to full professor (1982), serving as chair of psychology (1986–94) and as liberal arts dean (1992–94). Between 1997 and 2001 he was arts and sciences dean at the Columbian College of George Washington University, before moving to Tulane in 2001.

Lefton's reputation for making "tough decisions" had been stamped and sealed by one of his earliest actions at Tulane—eliminating the entire engineering college. "If you have $50 to spend," he said, "you don't want to give 50 programs each ten cents." A colleague at South Carolina described him as "quick to determine the direction in which an institution should go."[26] He revealed his tough-mindedness and his idea of Kent's "direction" a few weeks later in explaining how he could put Kent among the country's top universities in ten years: by improving graduation rates, retaining more freshmen for their second year, and putting money into "good programs," while letting others shrink by attrition. So far Kent, he said, had not made "the difficult decisions" necessary for it to become "a strategic player in a few disciplines," as he intended to make it.[27]

At his first meeting with the Faculty Senate, on September 11, 2006, he announced that retention was "Job One." The trustees had made "academic excellence" and "student success" (as measured by graduation rates) its top priority for the year, he said, urging the faculty to do the same. Studies showed that "faculty engagement" and the impression students get "in their first six weeks on campus are likely to determine" if they return as sophomores.[28] In an interview for the alumni magazine, he talked of making the campus technologically smart, with every class and dorm room wired, with students and faculty having "access to first-tier" labs and teaching areas, and of increasing the size and quality of the faculty to meet the needs of the school and the state. (Student-teacher ratio is an important factor in Kent State's national ranking, rumored widely to have been a key concern of the board in the search for Cartwright's successor.) His answer to the ongoing challenge of competing successfully in the diminishing pool of college-bound high school graduates was mounting a major campaign to recruit and retain more in- and out-of-state students and enabling them to graduate in timely fashion. He would also add professional and job-related programs to "meet the needs of Ohio's employers" and "enhance our reputation."[29]

These statements paint in broad strokes Lefton's intentions for Kent State as it approached its one-hundredth birthday. In 2006, when he took office, the attention of both the political and press estates was focused on kids, college, and jobs—all in the context of a dwindling population and prolonged economic malaise. A consensus had developed that colleges and universities held the key to unlocking the state's industrial and technological energies and to growing its population. for only they were able to discover new knowledge and invent new machinery and technologies, which would create new jobs, and to educate and train the workforce needed for those jobs and to keep Ohio-educated citizens from leaving the state.

In his "State of the University" address on September 9, 2008, Lefton announced the appointment of a Presidential Task Force to make the campus environmentally sustainable and pledged to make the University more inclusive. He also added several initiatives to his goals. To help students graduate in timely fashion, he proposed "simplifying Liberal Education Requirements," raising some faculty hackles of suspicion. He called for more recruiting of out-of-state and international students. It's "no longer enough to offer a few study-abroad and exchange programs," he said; students must be able to "interact with people beyond the borders of geography and ideology." As for Kent's Regional Campus system, he supported expanding baccalaureate degree offerings and adding more "two plus two degrees"—i.e., two years at a community college plus two years at a regional campus. Plans for a School of Public Health would be completed by the end of the academic year, he said. He also set goals for doubling research funding in five years.[30]

Three years into Lefton's term he found himself—partly by design, partly by circumstances—with a new cadre of vice presidents and academic deans (most from other institutions) whose loyalties would be primarily to him in carrying out his agenda. While their newness inoculated them against the virus of sentiment in making tough decisions, it also meant that they didn't know the campus ethos, the faculty, the staff, each other—or even Lefton. This deprived them, and him, of the incalculable knowledge to be drawn from the rich banks of institutional memory. It also denied them those bonds of affection and trust that undergird morale and esprit de corps, critical elements in enlisting faculty and staff to raise retention rates by devoting extra time and care to mentoring.

He had expanded the upper administration. When Golding left in 1981 there were three vice presidents, and six when Schwartz (1991) and Cartwright (2006) left. while the student body had stabilized at roughly 20,000 at the Kent campus (plus 10,000 at Regional Campuses) since the eighties, the Kent campus tenure-track faculty had shrunk; in 2009 the tenure-track faculty was 850, with 350 nontenure-track teachers. In 2009 there were nine vice presidents, with staffs of associates, and the Vice President for Academic Affairs/Provost position had been reconfigured into that of Senior Vice President for Academic Affairs/Provost, and the new position of Senior Associate Provost had been created.

At the end of 2008, following a historic national presidential election, the economic picture in Ohio and the nation darkened dramatically. Within weeks the financial system collapsed, stocks plunged, shrinking institutional and individual retirement funds; hundreds of thousands of people lost their jobs. It occurred at a time when the state was in its thirteenth straight year of below-average job growth; falling revenues had forced the governor to cut spending every few months; and the Regents had frozen fee increases at state schools in exchange for increased support in state funding.

In March 2009, after Kent State had suffered its first operating loss in history ($2.2 million), Lefton informed the trustees of his strategy for dealing with an even greater projected loss in the next fiscal year. To trim labor costs he planned to offer faculty, staff, and administrators with fifteen or more years of service a voluntary buyout. Some ninety faculty and 100 administrators and staff were projected to participate, enabling Lefton to hire replacements at lower salaries, while redeploying or not filling others. He characterized the plan as giving him an "opportunity to reassess our student needs" and "to create an opportunity to trim."[31]

While the economic collapse increased the difficulties facing Kent State by an order of magnitude, it did not change its mission or sense of purpose. Its immediate plans for confronting the Rubik's Cube of challenges confronting higher education in the new millennium might have to be put in layaway against the day when prosperity returned. But one thing was certain: Kent State would remain true to its historic mission as a university—to serve the public interest through "the advancement of learning."

Professors would go on opening doors and windows upon the transformative worlds of science and the arts, laying bare the mysteries of nature and human behavior. They would go on teaching and mentoring their students, cultivating their powers of reason and imagination, enabling them to fulfill themselves as individuals and equipping them to become responsible and productive citizens of their communities and nation. And student-scholars in their laboratories and classrooms would go on being surprised by the new and unexpected, being swept up in the adventure of discovery, and learning how to ask the right question and how to puzzle out the right answer so that they can make their own contributions to the world's storehouse of knowledge and wisdom.

And as the windows and doors opened, ideas would continue to be debated and developed, old assumptions challenged, sensibilities cultivated and refined, understandings expanded and deepened, and students' professional and personal lives would be enriched beyond measure—just as they have been from that springtide of promise and aspiration a century ago when the silhouettes of the first buildings began to take shape against the sky over Normal Hill, high above the town and the river.

Top: On May 4, 1990, after much planning and many difficulties, a memorial to the tragic events of May 4, 1970, was dedicated. Designed by Bruno Ast and located east of Taylor Hall, near the site of the shootings, the hillside near the memorial was planted with 58,175 daffodils to represent the number of Americans killed in the Vietnam War.

Above: Aerial view of the complete memorial.

Right: An Ohio Historical Marker describing the events of May 1970 was placed on the site in 2006 and dedicated in 2007.

In 1991 Carol Cartwright became KSU's tenth president. She appears here with three of her predecessors, (from left) Michael Schwartz, Brage Golding, and Glenn Olds.

Left: Charles L. Green, vice president for Human Resources (1987–2000), was a seasoned administrator and trusted advisor to several Kent State presidents.

Above: Even before taking office, Cartwright established a scholarship fund for students called the Founders Scholars Program, which features an annual black-tie dinner. The 2008 scholarship winners are assembled on the steps of the Student Center.

Clockwise from top left: In 1998 wrestler Nick Magistrelli attempts a takedown against Buffalo. Magistrelli went on to win the Mid-American Conference championship in his weight class that year. President Cartwright was a hit at the 1994 Homecoming parade when she appeared on the back of a motorcycle, a ride she repeated at future Homecomings. In 2002 the men's basketball squad won the MAC title and made it to the Elite Eight in the NCAA playoffs. Antonio Gates (2004), a great Kent State basketball star, became an All-Pro football star for the San Diego Chargers. Pictured here in 1999, alumnus and golf team standout Ben Curtis won the British Open in 2003. Seniors Andrew Mitchell, Trevor Huffman, Eric Thomas, and Demetric Shaw pose on the court at Cleveland's Gund Arena with their MAC trophy.

Left: Beginning in the 1990s, Kent became a wired campus. In this 2004 photo, assistant professor Melanie Carrico, left, works with a student in the CAD lab in Rockwell Hall.

Below: The impressive Student Recreation and Wellness Center opened in 1999.

Since its very beginning Kent State has reached out to the area through a regional campus system, establishing campuses at Ashtabula (shown here at right), Burton, East Liverpool, New Philadelphia, North Canton, Salem, and Warren.

Above left: Dean Gordon Keller led the regional campus system for nearly fifteen years.

Above right: Mark Sherratt (center) teaches horticulture to students during a class in the greenhouse on the Geauga Campus in Burton.

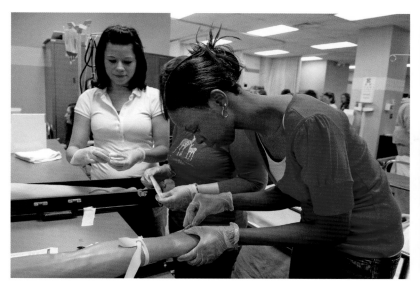

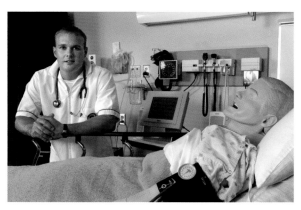

Clockwise from top left: Nursing students at work on the East Liverpool Campus. As students observe, Mildred Johnson inserts an IV. On the Salem Campus a student works on a painting. A student practices TIG welding in the College Tech Prep program at the Trumbull Campus in Warren. A nursing student poses with "Simm Man," a medical simulator, in the Science and Advanced Technology Center on the Tuscarawas Campus in New Philadelphia. An employee spends his lunchtime at the gazebo by the pond on the Stark Campus in North Canton.

Above left: The Aeronautics Division of the College of Technology offers degrees in aeronautics, aeronautical engineering, air traffic control, aviation management, and flight technology. Flight technology major Adam Bezilla flies over the Kent State Airport in Stow in 2004.

Above right: Professor Philip Bos holds a prototype of a liquid crystal-based beam steering device at the Liquid Crystal Institute.

Right: Created in 2001 by artist Brinsley Tyrrell, Behind the Brain Plaza, occupying what was formerly the Ellipse, offers a quiet sanctuary near Merrill Hall in the heart of Kent State's North Campus.

Below: For more than forty years the annual Kent State Folk Festival has featured local, national, and international performers. At the 2007 festival (left to right) Joel Mabus, Tom Paxton, Odetta, and Loudon Wainwright III gathered for a group performance.

Above left: WKSU grew to be an award-winning public radio powerhouse during the Cartwright administration. *Morning Edition* host Jeff St. Clair prepares for his broadcast.

Above right: Poet Toi Derricotte gives a reading in the Kiva in 2008 during the twenty-fifth-anniversary celebration of the Wick Poetry Program, a scholarship and outreach program endowed by Robert and Walter Wick in memory of their sons, Stanley and Tom.

Left: Members of the Kent Dance Ensemble of the School of Theatre and Dance perform *Dance! 2006*, part of the spring program that year at the E. Turner Stump Theatre in the Music and Speech Center.

Below: Kent State's gospel choir prepares prior to a 2002 performance in the Ballroom.

Above left: Associate Professor of Music Donna Lee advises a Piano Institute student at the School of Music.

Above right: The old Administration, then Auditorium, Building was extensively renovated in 2006 and renamed Cartwright Hall.

Right: In 2007 the School of Art's Downtown Gallery moved to East Main Street in the heart of Kent, giving students the chance to display and sell their art alongside that of regional and national artists.

Above: Following 2005's devastating Hurricane Katrina more than 400 Kent State volunteers helped with reconstruction in Mississippi. Here freshmen Sarah Weekly, left, and Danielle Diener clear debris in Biloxi, while sophomore Lauren Henin and others put on a roof in Pass Christian during spring break 2006.

Left: The Cartwright years saw a growth in the numbers of international students on campus. Here, members of the Indian Students Association plan the celebration of Diwali, the annual festival of lights, which includes dance, music, a fashion show, and an authentic Indian dinner.

Below: In 2007 the Kent State University Press published the fourth and final volume of *The Papers of Robert A. Taft,* edited by Clarence Wunderlin (history). Pictured (left to right) are Wunderlin; S. W. Reid, director of the Institute for Bibliography and Editing; Hope Taft; former Ohio governor Robert Taft; Press director Will Underwood; Press director emeritus John T. Hubbell; and Provost Robert G. Frank.

Right: The early 2000s saw the construction of new state-of-the-art residence halls, Centennial Court, and the updating of the Eastway complex.

Below: A student relaxes at the Eastway complex, one of Kent State's twenty-first-century residence halls.

Facing page: By the time of Kent State's centennial anniversary, an attractive pedestrian esplanade extended from the Liquid Crystal Institute on the campus's southern edge, through the Student Center, past the University's oldest buildings to South Lincoln Street.

Right: After fourteen years as KSU's president, Carol Cartwright announced that she would retire on October 5, 2005.

Below: Dix Stadium underwent a major renovation that was completed in time for the opening of the 2008 football season.

Left: Lester Lefton, shown here with his wife, Linda, celebrating before the 2007 Homecoming game, became KSU's eleventh president in 2006.

Below: A happy grad and her dad embrace following commencement at the Memorial Athletic and Convocation Center.

Overleaf: Students watch a fireworks display during the 2006 Orientation Blastoff at the track behind the DeWeese Health Center.

EPILOGUE

Dark as the economic picture was, however, and problematic as the future loomed for higher education and Kent State at the end of its tenth decade, its history teaches us a lesson embedded in the warm memories and the words revealed to us here: that we have been part of "a most noble enterprise."[1] The words are from an address by Henry Steele Commager, then dean of American Historians and former visiting professor at Kent State, at the dedication of the new Library on April 10, 1971. That moment was almost a year after the May 4 tragedy and Kent State was still in the eye of history, "beleaguered and besieged," in Commager's words, by a host of forces seeking to close the school or, that failing, to divert it from its ancient mission—the advancement of leaning—by strangling its animating spirit of academic freedom.

Commager's drift was clear: Because of May 4, Kent State was privileged to bear more than the usual burden of history that devolves on institutions of higher learning. Having become the standard-bearer of the university "as a citadel of reason," Kent State had the high historical responsibility not only to endure the forces of ignorance, malice, and fear but to triumph over them by remaining true to itself and its mission as a university—to be the "powerhouse and clearing house of ideas." For at the heart of the mission of higher education and scholarly excellence beats the freedom that belongs not only to the scholar but that is vital to the society that sustains the scholar and the institution. "For here, as elsewhere," he said, "freedom is not only the tribute which an irrational society pays to reason, it is the price which an imperiled society pays to survival."

Kent State did survive that decade-long crisis, somehow. President Schwartz said it would not have survived even the aftermath, when the campus was closed and students scattered, "without the kind of faculty it had." With students to be taught and graduated, professors "took them into their homes." And because they housed, fed, and taught them, he said, Kent State was never closed: "If it hadn't been for that, I believe that the University would not have survived the decade. So if anybody asks you, how do you account for the survival of Kent State, tell them it's the faculty."[2] His praise also embraced the contributions of Faculty Marshals, peacekeepers, and the unheralded Senate Executive Committee.

But that is only part of the truth. What would all that exemplary activity have amounted to without the students? What if they hadn't returned when the campus reopened? What if they had heeded the advice of parents and friends and transferred to another school? Or if they hadn't identified so intimately with *their* campus in its crisis, cared so deeply about it and what it stood for that they questioned its takeover by the National Guard? What if so many hadn't chosen to uphold the ideal of the campus as a sanctuary for critical thinking, for free speech and free assembly, for the free play of reason, imagination, and creativity?

Ultimately, the University survived because of its students, the well-springs of its character and bearers of its spirit. From the students have always come the moral sinews that have enabled the school to endure the buffetings of a hundred years without compromising its integrity or commitment to a purpose that transcends the blind passions of fear and unreason. Traditionally Kent's students have been mostly second- and third-generation children from hardworking third- and fourth-generation factory and farm families of mixed ethnic and racial backgrounds. They have come in part because of their parents' dreams and in part because of their own strong if inchoate need for a college education. And here they have discovered a capacity to grow to the measure of the worlds opened to them. A great many have been taught by Kent alumni, some of whom were the children and grandchildren of Kent graduates. Others have increasingly come from other states and corners of the world.

All have helped write the story of Kent State; all have benefited from and contributed to its tap-root tradition articulated by John Edward McGilvrey in his valedictory message to students after his dismissal — the tradition that education produces a "moral and intellectual quickening of the human spirit." Summoning them to that tradition, he concluded: "A fight for the better thing is always worth while, even though the battle be lost . . . and the spirit of the struggle lives on in the lives of thousands of Kent State students."[3]

And nearly a hundred years later that selfsame spirit lives on in the hundreds of thousands of Kent students whose lives have been quickened and enriched by Kent State University.

ACKNOWLEDGMENTS

Many hands went into the making of this book.

When I undertook writing a history of Kent State University's first hundred years, I knew that I could rely on the help of numerous old Kent hands. Almost the first one I turned to was Dean Keller, one of my collaborators on an earlier book about KSU, whose rare good sense and knowledge of the school's complicated history are matched by his mastery of the vast resources and labyrinthine ways of a research library. He helped me get my bearings, and his good counsel kept me on track during some difficult twists and turns.

I'm indebted as well to Kathy Stafford and Dean Mark Weber (Library and Media Services). Kathy's enthusiasm for the project helped launch it, and Mark's gift of moral and material support helped secure its safe passage.

I also had invaluable assistance in my research from Cara Gilgenbach, Head of Special Collections and Archives, and her staff—archivist Steve Paschen and librarian Greg Simpson. They wasted no time and spared no effort in answering my countless questions and hurry-up appeals for help, and they were unfailingly courteous. A work of this sort, of course, would be a season in Siberia without such support. Thanks are also in order to Gary Harwood and Robert W. Christy of the Office of University Relations and Marketing for their help.

One of the most pleasant surprises of this project was rediscovering, after a decade in retirement, the graces of collegiality and friendship. So, with a deep bow, I thank the four interviewees who spent many hours patiently answering questions and giving me their firsthand knowledge, insights, and understandings of many individuals and issues, all the while helping me make sense of Kent State's past forty years: George Janik, Gordon Keller, Jim Louis, and Tom Moore. Warm thanks go as well to Ben Bassham, Ed Bixenstine, Ken Calkins, Dennis Carey, Bob Clawson, Denny Cooke, Ray Heisey, Sally Kandel, Bob McCoy, Susan Rogers, Denise Seachrist, and Pam Speck for their invaluable help in giving me access to documents, publications, personalities, processes, and helping me find answers to puzzling questions.

Thanks also to all those who responded to appeals for help or enlightened me unawares, especially: Walt Adams, Dick Bredemeier, Cheryl Casper, Alan Coe, Ray Craig, Wilma Crawford, Flo Cunningham, Pete Dahl, Laura Davis, Tom Davis, George Gaiser, Margaret Garmon, H. Roger Grant, John Hubbell, Jasmine Jefferson, Jerry Lewis, Pat Nash, Charlene Reed, Norm Sandvoss, Tom Schmidlin, Edith Serkownek, Elizabeth Slanina, Sheryl Smith, Kathy Stafford, Charlie Taylor, Gene Wenninger, and Dick Worthing. I am especially grateful to those most clubbable members of the Old Boys Book Club for sharing their collective wisdom, rich fund of memories, and their rare bonhomie.

Any documentary search encounters difficulties—and mine was no exception. Through no fault of the Library or its staff, the Archives' rich holdings, save for those of the Board of Trustees, vary in kind and quality because of KSU's general disregard for its own history. To illustrate: provosts as a rule do not send their papers to the Archives, denying students of the institution an invaluable source of information on an array of important programmatic and personnel initiatives and decisions. (It's anyone's guess what becomes of collegial records.) And, while some presidents have left extensive documentary evidence of their activities, providing clear footprints for the researcher to follow, others have tended to leave a paltry trail of crumbs, forcing him or her to depend heavily on official news releases, newspaper reports (especially the excellent *Daily Kent Stater*), and interviews. Another caveat: my account of the Cartwright presidency suffers from the foreshortened historical perspective from which I had to view her tenure and the fact that her large collection of papers was still being processed, which effectively rendered them unavailable. The latter limitation kept me, for example, from pursuing certain themes, such as the May 4 memorials and student protests during the Iraq War. Lester Lefton's papers were not, of course, available.

A Most Noble Enterprise would not have seen the light of day were it not for the Kent State University Press: thanks to Managing Editor Mary Young and Design and Production Manager Christine Brooks, whose skills are much appreciated.

My editor, Joanna Hildebrand Craig, did what the legendary American editors have done: challenged every aspect of the manuscript, from the most harmless of commas, facts, and non sequiturs to the most penetrating interpretations and triumphant turns of phrase, not to mention my signature similes—all in aid of making the book as good as it could be. But for her tough love, intelligence, and devotion to it—and me—this book would be a sorry thing indeed. I owe her a soda and a hotdog at Kresge's lunch counter.

Finally, there was always Ann, whose love, grit, and candor buoyed and saved me from many crosscurrents of doubt and writer's remorse during the three-year voyage. Her excellent research and critical skills were indispensable. And the play of her mind—her insights, ideas, knowledge, wit, and wisdom—is, to the noticing eye, everywhere apparent in the text. I promise her a poem.

NOTES

PREFACE

1. Henry Steele Commager, "The University and the Community of Learning," speech given at Kent State University Libraries, 1971, KSU Archives.
2. *Akron Beacon Journal,* Dec. 30, 2008.

1. WISHES AND FISHES

1. "An Ordinance for the Government of the Territory of the United States North West of the River Ohio, 1787," in *Journals of the Continental Congress, 1774–1789,* ed. Worthington C. Ford et al. (Washington, D.C.: Library of Congress, 1904–37), 32:340.
2. Phillip R. Shriver, *The Years of Youth: Kent State University, 1910–1960* (Kent, Ohio: Kent State Univ. Press, 1960), 9, 7.
3. *Kent Courier,* Sept. 16, 1910.
4. Karl H. Grismer, *The History of Kent* (Kent, Ohio: Courier-Tribune, 1932), 18–19.
5. Shriver, *Years of Youth,* 20.
6. Ibid., 26.

7. *Biennial Report of the Board of Trustees of the Kent State Normal School . . . for 1911–1913,* Feb. 15, 1913, p. 9, KSU Archives, Kent State University Library.
8. *Kent Courier,* June 21, 1912.
9. *Quarterly* 1 (Oct. 1912).
10. Shriver, *Years of Youth,* 39–40.
11. Ibid., 36.
12. Ibid., 45–46.
13. *Kent Stater,* May 30, 1933.
14. *Kent Courier,* July 11, 1913.
15. Ibid., July 31, 1914.

2. THE STORMY PETREL

1. See "Per Capita Appropriation for Instruction . . . for the Fourth Quarter," John E. McGilvrey Papers, KSU Archives.
2. Shriver, *Years of Youth,* 92.
3. *Kent Tribune,* July 22, 1920.
4. Phillip R. Shriver Papers, KSU Archives.
5. *Searchlight,* Feb. 25, 1926.
6. Shriver, *Years of Youth,* 87.
7. Ibid., 91–95.

8. Ibid., 94.
9. Ibid., 91.
10. *Cleveland Plain Dealer*, Oct. 30, 1938.
11. Trustees' Minutes, Jan. 16, 1926, KSU Archives.
12. Trustees' Minutes, Jan. 16, 1926.
13. Trustees' Minutes, Jan. 22, 1926.
14. Shriver, *Years of Youth*, 68.
15. *Ravenna Tribune*, Feb. 18 and Jan. 21, 1926.

3. Turbulence and Frustration

1. Shriver, *Years of Youth*, 102.
2. *Kentonian*, Oct. 1926, KSU Archives.
3. *Akron Beacon Journal*, Mar. 14, 25, 1926.
4. Ibid.
5. Ibid., Mar. 24, 25, 1926.
6. Trustees' Minutes, Aug. 2, 1927.
7. *Akron Times-Press*, June 4, 8, 9, 1927.
8. Shriver, *Years of Youth*, 109.
9. *Cleveland Press*, June 7, 8, 1927; Shriver, *Years of Youth*, 110.
10. Shriver, *Years of Youth*, 109.
11. Trustees' Minutes, Sept. 19, 1927, Jan. 16 and Sept. 19, 1928.
12. Trustees' Minutes, Jan. 25, 1929.
13. Shriver, *Years of Youth*, 120.
14. *Ravenna Evening Record*, Apr. 29 and May 3, 5, 1933.
15. Shriver, *Years of Youth*, 132.
16. Ibid., 132–33.
17. Trustees' Minutes, June 29, 1933.
18. Shriver, *Years of Youth*, 134.
19. *Ravenna Evening Record*, June 29, 30, 1933.
20. *Kent Stater*, Jan. 17, 1935.
21. Ibid., Nov. 28, 1934.
22. Shriver, *Years of Youth*, 142–43.
23. Ibid., 143.
24. *Kent Stater*, Mar. 14, 1935.
25. Shriver, *Years of Youth*, 152.
26. Ibid., 153.
27. *Plain Dealer*, Aug. 27, 28, 1935.
28. *KSU Bulletin*, Sept. 4, 1936, KSU Archives.
29. *Akron Times-Press*, Mar. 22, 1935.

4. The Leebrick Revolution

1. *Akron Times-Press*, Nov. 2, 3, 1935.
2. Ibid., 157.

3. Ibid., 158.
4. *Kent Courier-Tribune*, Oct. 21, 1938.
5. *Kent Stater*, Dec. 16, 1938, Feb. 17, 1939.
6. Trustees' Minutes, Jan. 21, 1939.
7. Shriver, *Years of Youth*, 171–72.
8. Ibid., 175–76.

5. The Bowman Years

1. *Akron Beacon Journal*, May 24, 1955.
2. Loris C. Troyer, *Portage Pathways* (Kent, Ohio: Kent State Univ. Press, 1998), 231.
3. *Kent Stater*, Nov. 21, 1944.
4. Shriver, *Years of Youth*, 192–93.
5. *Bulletin, Annual Catalog*, 1946–47, KSU Archives.
6. *Bulletin, Annual Catalog*, 1950–51, KSU Archives.
7. Shriver, *Years of Youth*, 195.
8. Cara Gilgenbach and Theresa Walton, *Kent State University Athletics: Images of Sports* (Charleston, S.C.: Arcadia, 2008), 49.
9. Ibid., 42.
10. Ronald Q. Lewton, letter to author, Aug. 15, 2007.
11. Troyer, *Portage Pathways*, 229.
12. Minutes of the faculty meeting, Sept. 23, 1949, KSU Archives.
13. Shriver, *Years of Youth*, 228.
14. Ibid., 224.
15. Ibid., 238.

6. Big Dreams

1. Trustees' Minutes, Jan. 16, 1962.
2. Hyman Kritzer, interview with Dean H. Keller and author, Apr. 15, 1996.
3. *Kent Stater*, Apr. 15, 1965.
4. Ibid., Apr. 20, 1965.
5. Kent Chapter, American Association of University Professors, "Report of the Special Committee of Inquiry" (1959), KSU Archives; Kenneth Calkins, "The Frustrations of a Former Activist," in *Kent State/May 4: Echoes through a Decade*, ed. Scott L. Bills (Kent, Ohio: Kent State University Press, 1982), 102.
6. Ibid.
7. *Record Courier*, Apr. 17, 1969.
8. Ibid., Apr. 23, 1969.

7. Four Days in May

1. *Akron Beacon Journal*, May 24, 1970.
2. *The Report of the President's Commission on Campus Unrest* (Washington, D.C.: Government Printing Office, 1970), 241 (hereafter cited as *Scranton Commission Report*).
3. Ibid., 242.
4. Ibid.
5. James A. Michener, *Kent State: What Happened and Why* (New York: Random House, 1971), 119–22.
6. "Town in Crisis," interview with Lucius Lyman Jr., in Bills, ed., *Kent State/May 4*, 69.
7. *Scranton Commission Report*, 246.
8. Ibid.
9. Ibid., 247, 174.
10. Michener, *Kent State*, 176.
11. G. Dennis Cooke, email to author, Nov. 12, 2007.
12. Donald Schwarzmiller testimony found in Commission on KSU Violence, "Minority Report," p. 61, Barclay McMillen Papers, KSU Archives.
13. *Scranton Commission Report*, 253; "Minority Report," 80.
14. *Scranton Commission Report*, 253–54.
15. *Akron Beacon Journal*, May 24, 1970.
16. *Scranton Commission Report*, 255.
17. "Chain Reaction," interview with Leigh Herington, in Bills, ed., *Kent State/May 4*, 78; Lloyd Agte to author, Aug. 1980.
18. "Minority Report," 94.
19. *Scranton Commission Report*, 259.
20. Ibid., 257; also in Michener, *Kent State*, 246.
21. James J. Best, "Kent State: Answers and Questions," in *Kent State and May 4th: A Social Science Perspective*, ed., Thomas R. Hensley and Jerry M. Lewis (New York: Kendall/Hunt, 1978), 17.
22. Ibid., 18.
23. Ibid.
24. Michener, *Kent State*, 328, 330.
25. Ibid., 329.
26. Ibid.
27. Ibid., 337.
28. *Scranton Commission Report*, 266.
29. Ibid., 267; Michener, *Kent State*, 338.
30. *Scranton Commission Report*, 268; Best, "Answers and Questions," 21.
31. *Scranton Commission Report*, 268.
32. Ibid., 275.
33. *Akron Beacon Journal*, May 24, 1970.
34. Ibid.
35. Ibid.
36. Ibid.
37. Ibid.
38. Glenn Frank, "Anatomy of a Tragedy," pp. 60–61, unpublished manuscript in possession of Nellie Lou Williams Janik; see alumnus Howard P. Ruffner's photo in Michener, *Kent State*, 382.
39. Frank, "Anatomy of a Tragedy," 61.
40. *Akron Beacon Journal*, July 25, 1971.
41. Ibid.
42. Frank, "Anatomy of a Tragedy," 61–62.

8. The Aftermath

1. Michener, *Kent State*, 425–26.
2. Trustees' Minutes, May 10, 1970.
3. Meeting of the Faculty Senate, May 22, 1970, Faculty Senate Minutes, KSU Archives.
4. "Introduction: The Past and the Present," Bills, ed., *Kent State/May 4*, 22.
5. Informal Review, Board of Trustees, July 7, 1970, May 4th Collection, Kent State University Library.
6. Martin K. Nurmi, "The Years of Growth: 1955 to 1970," in *A Book of Memories: Kent State University, 1910–1992*, ed. William H. Hildebrand, Dean H. Keller, and Anita Dixon Herington (Kent, Ohio: Kent State Univ. Press, 1993), 112.
7. Robert I. White Papers, KSU Archives.
8. *Scranton Commission Report*, 90.
9. "Report of the Special State Grand Jury," in Ottavio M. Casale and Louis Paskoff, *The Kent Affair: Documents and Interpretations* (New York: Houghton Mifflin, 1971), 192–93.
10. "The Ones They Missed with Bullets," interview with Bill Arthrell, in Bills, ed., *Kent State/May 4*, 93.
11. *Inside*, Nov. 1970, White Papers.
12. Thomas Moore, interview with author, Mar. 28, 2008; "The Presidents," in Hildebrand, Keller, and Herington, eds., *Book of Memories*, 1.
13. "The Candlelight Vigil: A Way of Participating," interview with Jerry M. Lewis, in Bills, ed., *Kent State/May 4*, 173.
14. Speech draft, n.d., White Papers.
15. Anonymous report to White, n.d., White Papers.

9. TROUBLED TIMES

1. Gordon Keller, interview with author, June 6, 2007.
2. *Chestnut Burr*, 1977.
3. D. Ray Heisey, email to author, Feb. 28, 2008.
4. Thomas Moore, interview with author, Mar. 22, 2008.
5. Frank, "Anatomy of a Tragedy," 180.
6. Ibid., 180–83.
7. Edwin Arlington Robinson, "Richard Corey."
8. *Chestnut Burr*, 1976, 122–23.
9. Harris L. Wofford, *Of Kennedys and Kings: Making Sense of the Sixties* (Pittsburgh: Univ. of Pittsburgh Press, 1992), 208.
10. Ernest J. Boyer to George Urban, May 10, 1971, D. Ray Heisey Papers (private collection).
11. Martin K. Nurmi to author, June 10, 1971.
12. Letter to the faculty, Sept. 15, 1971, box 8, folder 2, Glenn H. Olds Papers, KSU Archives.
13. Olds to Faculty Senate, Oct. 23, 1972, box 25, folder 99, Olds Papers.
14. Letter from Provost Hall, Jan. 17, 1972, box 8, folder 10, Olds Papers.
15. Order to disperse, May 31, 1972, box 10, folder 41, Olds Papers.
16. Report to Faculty Senate, June 5, 1972, box 8, folder 10, Olds Papers.
17. Olds to Faculty Senate, June 5, 1972, Olds Papers.
18. Eugene P. Wenninger, email to author, Mar. 17, 2008.
19. Olds to Faculty Senate, June 5, 1972, Olds Papers.
20. Gordon Keller, interview with author, Feb. 5, 2008.
21. Faculty Senate Minutes, Oct. 23, 1972, Olds Papers.
22. *Akron Beacon Journal,* Nov. 10, 1972.
23. Newspaper clipping, Nov. 10, 1972, Olds Papers.
24. Provost Hall to Olds, Nov. 13, 1972, box 25, folder 28, Olds Papers.
25. Memo from Harold Kitner to Olds, Nov. 14, 1972, Olds Papers.
26. Harold Kitner to Gordon Keller, Nov. 30, 1972, Faculty Senate Collection, KSU Archives.
27. Olds to Harold Kitner, Nov. 19, 1972, Olds Papers.
28. *Chestnut Burr*, 1973.
29. *Chestnut Burr*, 1977, 281.
30. Ibid., 298.
31. UFPA resolution, Apr. 16, 1976, V. Edwin Bixenstine Collection (private collection).
32. UFPA resolution, Apr. 16, 1976.
33. *Chestnut Burr*, 1977, 51.
34. George Janik, interview with author, Feb. 10, 2008.
35. *Chestnut Burr*, 1977.
36. Ibid., 141.
37. George Janik, interview with author, Feb. 10, 2008.
38. *Akron Beacon Journal*, Sept. 11, 1980.
39. Guy Russo to Walter Bruska, June 13, 1975, University News Service Factfile, KSU Archives.
40. Thomas R. Hensley, "Kent State 1977: The Struggle to Move the Gym," in Hensley and Lewis, eds., *Kent State and May 4th*, 126.
41. George Janik, interview with the author, Feb. 10, 2008.
42. George Janik, interview with the author, Feb. 10, 2008; Gordon Keller, interview with the author, June 17, 2008; "Sensitivity to an Image," interview with D. Ray Heisey, in Bills, ed., *Kent State/May 4*, 192.
43. *Akron Beacon Journal*, May 4, 1977.
44. "Meet the Demands," unsigned leaflet, Olds Papers.
45. "Tent City: A Real Community," interview with Nancy Grim, in Bills, ed., *Kent State/May 4*, 224.
46. "Introduction," Bills, ed., *Kent State/May 4*, 43, 46.
47. Hensley, "Kent State 1977," 133.
48. *Record Courier*, July 7, 1977.
49. Trustees' Minutes, Nov. 11, 1976; *Record Courier*, July 7, 1977.
50. Dennis P. Carey, email to author, Apr. 14, 2008.

10. THE GOLDING RESTORATION

1. *Kent Magazine*, Apr. 7, 1977.
2. George Janik, interview with author, Oct. 14, 2007.
3. George Janik, interview with author, Oct. 14, 2007.
4. "The Gym Controversy: A Massive Assault on This Institution," interview with Michael Schwartz, in Bills, ed, *Kent State/May 4*, 212.

5. George Janik, interview with author, June 20, 2007.

6. George Janik, interview with author, June 20, 2007.

7. *Akron Beacon Journal,* Aug. 8, 1977.

8. Ibid., Aug. 6, 1977.

9. George Janik, interview with author, June 20, 1977.

10. *Record Courier,* Aug. 13, 1977.

11. *Chestnut Burr,* 1978, 3.

12. "State of the University" speech, Jan. 19, 1979, Brage Golding Papers, KSU Archives.

13. "State of the University" speech, Jan. 20, 1978, Golding Papers.

14. Letter to parents, Mar. 16, 1981, Golding Papers.

15. Robert Clawson, email to author, May 13, 2008.

16. Hugh Munroe to Golding, Nov. 23, 1981, Golding Papers.

17. "Initiatives Taken, September 1977–June 1982: A Select List, June 10, 1982," Golding Papers.

18. "The President: Follower or Leader?" speech delivered at the American Association of State Colleges and Universities, Williamsburg, Va., Nov. 17, 1980, Golding Papers.

19. "Address to the Faculty," Jan. 19, 1979; "State of the University" speech, Feb. 24, 1980, p. 18, both in Golding Papers.

20. "State of the University" speech, Jan. 19, 1979, Golding Papers.

21. George Janik, interview with the author, June 20, 2007.

22. "State of the University" speech, Feb. 24, 1980, Golding Papers.

23. Hyman Kritzer, interview with author, May 10, 1998.

24. George Janik, interview with author, June 20, 2007.

25. Robert Clawson, email to author, May 13, 2008.

26. Robert Clawson, email to author, May 13, 2008.

27. *Kent Stater,* Sept. 9, 1982.

28. *Kent Magazine,* Apr. 17, 1977, 3–4.

29. George Janik, interview with author, June 20, 2007.

30. "The President: Follower or Leader?" speech.

31. Thomas D. Moore, interview with author, Aug. 24, 2008.

11. THE CHANGING CAMPUS CULTURE

1. Michael Schwartz, "Change and Reconciliation, 1980 to 1992," in Hildebrand, Keller, and Herington, eds., *Book of Memories,* 235.

2. *Chestnut Burr,* 1977.

3. *Kent Stater,* Oct. 26, 1985.

12. AMBITION AND ACHIEVEMENT

1. *Kent Stater,* Sept. 17, 1982.

2. Ibid.

3. Gordon Keller, interview with author, Aug. 8, 2008.

4. *Kent Stater,* Aug. 31, 1982.

5. Ibid.

6. Gordon Keller, interview with author, Aug. 8, 2008.

7. "State of the University" speech, Oct. 20, 1983, Michael Schwartz Papers, KSU Archives.

8. *Inside,* Dec. 22, 1982.

9. *Kent Stater,* Sept. 9, 1982.

10. Ibid., Sept. 10, 1982.

11. Ibid., Sept. 24, 1982.

12. Ibid., Sept. 28, 1982.

13. Ibid., Nov. 20, 1982.

14. Schwartz, "Change and Reconciliation," 233–34.

15. *Kent Stater,* Nov. 18 and Dec. 9, 1982.

16. Ibid., Nov. 20, 1982.

17. "State of the University" speech, Oct. 20, 1983, Schwartz Papers.

18. "Draft Statement," Presidential Commission on Ethics, Apr. 17, 1985, Schwartz Papers.

19. "State of the University" speech, Oct 25, 1984, Schwartz Papers.

20. Gordon Keller, interview with author, Aug. 8, 2008.

21. Ben Bassham, email to author, May 29, 2008.

22. Thomas D. Moore, interview with author, Mar. 5, 2008.

23. "State of the University" speech, Oct. 25, 1984, Schwartz Papers.

24. "Address to the Faculty," Jan. 19, 1979, Golding Papers.

25. Robert Clawson, email to author, May 13, 2008.

26. "State of the University" speech, Oct. 20, 1983, Schwartz Papers.

27. "State of the University" speech, Oct. 20, 1983, Schwartz Papers.

28. "State of the University" speech, Oct. 20, 1983, Schwartz Papers.
29. Gordon Keller, interview with author, Aug. 8, 2008.
30. "Facilities Development for the Kent Campus: Possible Elements and Options," Office of Facilities Planning and Design, Dec. 22, 1986, KSU Archives.
31. "State of the University" speech, Nov. 14, 1988, Schwartz Papers.
32. Schwartz, "Change and Reconciliation," 234.
33. "Address to the Faculty," Jan. 19, 1979, Golding Papers.
34. Gordon Keller, interview with author, Aug. 8, 2008.
35. Schwartz, "Change and Reconciliation," 238.
36. Ibid.
37. Ibid.
38. Ibid., 239.

13. New Perspectives, New Models

1. Schwartz, "Change and Reconciliation," 239.
2. Trustees' Minutes, May 23, 1990.
3. *Record Courier*, Oct. 28, 1990.
4. Ibid.
5. *Kent Stater*, Dec. 9, 1990.
6. Virginia Carroll to author, Nov. 1990.
7. "Statement at Special Meeting of the Faculty Senate," Mar. 22, 1999, KSU Archives.
8. *Kent Stater*, Jan. 31 and Feb. 6, 1992.
9. Gordon Keller, interview with author, Aug. 8, 2008.
10. For a full account, see Gilgenbach and Walton, *Kent State University Athletics: Images of Sports*.
11. "State of the University" speech, Oct. 25, 1994, *Collected Addresses: Dr. Carol A. Cartwright, Tenth President of Kent State University* (Kent, Ohio: KSU Board of Trustees, 2006).
12. "Inaugural Address," Oct. 11, 1991, ibid.
13. "State of the University" speech, Oct. 27, 1992, ibid.
14. "Inaugural Address," Oct. 11, 1991, ibid.
15. "State of the University" speech, Oct. 19, 1995, ibid.; "State of the University" speech, Oct. 3, 1996, ibid.
16. Allan Coe, interview with author, Aug. 13, 2008.
17. *Inside*, Jan. 14, 1991.
18. Robert Clawson, email to author, May 13, 2008; James Louis, interview with author, July 31, 2008.
19. *Inside*, Jan. 14, 1991.
20. Faculty Senate Special Meeting Minutes, Mar. 22, 1999, KSU Archives.
21. *Akron Beacon Journal*, Oct. 6, 2005.
22. Norman Sandvoss to author, Feb. 5, 2008.
23. James Louis, interview with author, May 21, 2008.
24. Trustees' Minutes, May 6, 2006.
25. *Akron Beacon Journal*, May 9, 2006.
26. Ibid., July 22, 2006.
27. Ibid.
28. Faculty Senate Minutes, Sept. 11, 2006.
29. Susan Rogers, "Getting to Know You, Getting to Know All About You . . . ," *Kent State Magazine* 6, no. 2 (Winter 2006): 4–7.
30. Ben Wolford, "Lefton: Kent State 'on the right path': Address Outlines Goals," Sept. 26, 2008, accessed Dec. 19, 2008, from www.kentnewsnet.com.
31. *Akron Beacon Journal*, March 19, 2002.

Epilogue

1. Commager, "The University and the Community of Learning."
2. "The Gym Controversy," in Bills, ed., *Kent State/May 4*, 219.
3. *Searchlight*, Feb. 25, 1926.

INDEX

Abraham's Sacrifice of Isaac (sculpture), 266–67

Academic freedom: curtailment of, 111, 141, 167–69; free speech and, 248, 251; in Kent State's mission, 321–23; presidents' protection of, 95, 302

Accreditation, Kent's, 50

Accreditation, Northeastern Ohio Universities College of Medicine's, 226

Accreditation, professional, 225

Ad Hoc Committee on Innovative Curricular Change, 164

Adams, John, 215

Administration, 164; Bowman's, 82–83; buildings named after, 96–97, 104; Cartwright's, 282–83, 294–97; Cartwright's style of, 283–84, 295–96; changes in, 87, 96–97; closed campus and, 155, 160, 166; collective bargaining with faculty and, 194–95, 198–99; conduct codes and, 107, 110; due

process and, 102–3, 110; effects of business college scandals on, 196–98; faculty and, 45–46, 102, 157, 158, 189, 194; Golding's, 216, 231–32, 243, 283; increasing number of women in, 236, 287; Lefton's, 304; May 4th Coalition *vs.*, 172, 203; Olds's, 184, 200; on presidential search committees, 243–44, 280; protesters and, 136, 142–43, 172, 255; responses to demonstrations, 109–10; Schwartz's, 295; sensitivity to black students' concerns, 248–49; shootings and, 158, 159, 162, 166, 167–69; size of, 181, 186–88, 219, 304–5; space for, 14, 231; space in Library, 187–88, 230–31; space in Lowry Hall, 294, 297; structural changes in, 97, 181, 294–95; students and, 42, 111–12, 142, 190, 221; studying calendar change,

223–24; teaching by, 77, 164, 183; White's inaccessibility, 110–11

Administration Building, 14, 55, 65, 89, 109, 168; construction of, 23–25; inadequacy of, 187–88; renovations of, 51, 314

Admission standards: raising, 97, 227, 261, 293; relation to enrollment, 253, 290

Advising: Early Advising and Scheduling System, 254; efforts to improve, 220, 257, 291; under Enrollment Management and Student Affairs, 294–95; of international students, 263

Advisory committees, 76–77, 161, 288

Aeronautics Division, of College of Technology, *312*

African Americans, 159, 162, 248. *See also* Black United Students (BUS); collection of historical materials of, 262; identity politics of, 237–38;

pressure for Pan-African courses, 248–49; walking off campus, 109–10

Agitators, outside: governor as, 140–42; mixing with students, 134, 136–38, 217; National Guard searching cars for, 155

Agriculture, 19; elimination of program, 41, 51, 75; farmers backing Lowry Bill, 4–5

Agte, Lloyd, 141

Airport, at Stow, 77, 84, *312*

Akron, 161, 193, 237

Akron-Fulton Aiport, 77

Akron Regional Development Board, 282

Akron Roundtable, 282

Akron, 218, 226

Allard, Linda, 299

Allen, Howard, 101, *126*

Allyn, Arden L., 59, 88–89, 104

Alumni, 104, 163, 299; Cartwright's skill at involving, 285–86; as faculty and parents of students, 322–23; goals for KSU, 52, 57; McGilvrey and, 19, 40,

Faculty, 42, 78. *See also* Teaching, at Kent; administration and, 102, 157, 172, 194, 230–31; after shootings, 157, 159–60, 167–68, 194; alumni as, 322–23; Anderson and, 44–46; on Antarctic expeditions, 251; blamed for disorders, 161–62, 255; Bowman and, 83; buildings named after, 96–97, 104; Cartwright and, 289–90, 296–99; for Center for Peaceful Change, 170; changing roles for, 289–90; collective bargaining by, 194–95, 198–99, 296–97; in College of Education, 76; "culture of aspiration" and, 264; in curriculum changes, 164, 183–84, 224; demographics of, 72; dislike of marketing focus, 292, 297; dissent and, 107, 158–59, 167–68, 172; education of, 50, 72, 86, 94–95, 101; effects of budget crises on, 178–79, 181–82, 184, 186–88, 194; effects of establishing doctoral program on, 97–98, 101, 185, 264; Engleman and, 54; evaluations of teaching by, 255–56; for Experimental wing of Honors College, 164; for extension programs, 29, 85; first members of, 16, 64; in foreign-exchange programs, 263; in Free University Movement, 109; Golding and, 218, 227, 231–33; importance of Library to, 229, 230–31; importance of students' relationship with, 94, 220–21, 246–47, 303; increasing interest in research, 94–95; increasing number of, 19, 72, 76, 86, 94, 101; increasing number of women as, 236, 287; in investigations of shootings, 162, 166–68; involvement in budget issues, 184–85, 187, 227,

252, 293; involvement in decision making, 76–77, 97, 102, 181–82; on KSU mission, 95, 185, 290, 298; Leebrick and, 76–77, 81; Lefton and, 302–3, 305; liberal arts college and, 48–49; McGilvrey and, 16–17, 28, 39; morale, 103, 169, 187–88, 297; National Guard and, 144; number of, 79, 83, 289, 304; obligations to undergraduates, 252, 255–57; Olds and, 178, 181–82, 184, 186–89, 199–200, 231; ombudsman for, 102–3, 185; on presidential search committees, 173–74, 243–44, 280, 301; public relations by, 161–62, 220; publication by, 94–95; questioning Kent Econometric Association, 197–98; questioning value of athletics, 257–60; relations among, 83, 255; reopening campus after shootings, 166; resisting conversion of normal school to mental asylum, 52; reward system for, 51, 98, 103, 178–79, 186–89, 194, 233, 252–53, 256, 293; saving university after shootings, 158–59, 322; Schwartz and, 247, 251–53, 257; sensitivity to black students' concerns, 248–49; shortages of, 86, 289; students and, 94, 107, 194, 220–21; studying calendar change, 223–24; teaching loads of, 95; teaching *vs.* research by, 103, 185, 252, 254–57; tenured *vs.* "instructors," 227, 304; trying to get students credit and graduation after shootings, 157, 159–60; veterans as, 102; White and, 101, 170
Faculty chairs, Campaign for KSU funding, 299
Faculty Marshals/Observers, 137, *270;* fear of pending National Guard confrontation with students, 136,

142; mediating between National Guard and students, 152–54; trying to keep peace, 136, 171
Faculty Senate, *208;* administration and, 189, 195; after shootings, 159, 162; on budget issues, 190, 258–59; Cartwright and, 283, 297–98; curriculum and, 164, 220–21, 225; ending teacher-training program, 240; establishment of, 97, 103–4; on integrity of presidential search process, 174–76; new promotion and tenure policies by, 293; no confidence votes, 195–96, 297–98; Olds and, 181, 184, 185–86, 195–96; Schwartz and, 252–53; on student recruitment and retention, 220–21
Farrari, Michael R., 243
Fashion design program, 229–30, 273
Federal agents: on campus, 107, 168; investigations of shootings by, 163, 167
Fees. *See* Tuition and fees
Feinberg, Mel, 264
Feldman, Rod, 251
Field hockey, 283
Field House, 260–61, 276, 291
Filo, John, 150
Filthy Speech Movement, 111
Fine and practical arts departments, 75
Fine and Professional Arts, College, 94, 183
Firefighters, at ROTC building fire, 138–39
Fischer, Louis "Pop," 238
Fisher, William, *208*
Fletcher, dorm named after, 104
Fonda, Jane, 190
Football, 30, *211;* Cartwright as fan of, 282; coaches for, 56, 57, 90; continuing losses in, 261; cost of, 259; Schwartz's optimism about, 259–60; victories in, 192
Foreign-exchange programs, 33, 263, 272. *See also* Study-abroad programs

France, Elmer E., 5, 6
Frank, Glenn, 251; as Faculty Marshal, 136, 155; mediating between National Guard and students, 152–54, *207;* on presidential search process, 174–76; response to shootings, 157
Frank, Robert G., *315*
Franklin, Doris, 162
Franklin Hall, 96, 294
Fraternities. *See* "Greek" life
Frazier, murder victim, 284–85
Free University Movement, 109
Freemont, competing for normal school, 12
Friedbolin, Carl D., 55
Front Campus, 90, 92, *119,* 293–94
Fry, J. A. B., *113*
Fuller, Dan, 265
Fuller, R. Buckminster, 190, *210*
Fund-raising, 293; campaigns in, 197, 299; Cartwright's skill at, 283, 285–86; corporate, 282; Lefton's skill at, 301–2; president expected to engage in, 282, 301; Schwartz's unwillingness to do, 282–83
Funding, 197. *See also* Budgets; Education, Ohio funding; for Center for Peaceful Change, 170, 184; for construction, 72–73, 104; Engelman's reluctance for PWA grants, 73, 113; extension program lacking, 85; for fashion design program, 230; fear of Kent losing after shootings, 158, 164; for Field House, 260–61; for Founders Scholars Program, 283; Kent Econometric Model to provide, 196–98; for Liquid Crystal Institute, 262; for marching band, 258, 260, 288; for May 4 memorial, 266–67; to move Memorial Gym annex, 204, 215; for new presidential residence,